# SAFEGU ... ER
# PEOPLI E

## Critical contexts to policy and practice

Angie Ash

*rices*

*t*

First published in Great Britain in 2015 by

Policy Press
University of Bristol
1-9 Old Park Hill
Bristol BS2 8BB
UK
+44 (0)117 954 5940
pp-info@bristol.ac.uk
www.policypress.co.uk

North America office:
Policy Press
c/o The University of Chicago Press
1427 East 60th Street
Chicago, IL 60637, USA
t: +1 773 702 7700
f: +1 773 702 9756
sales@press.uchicago.edu
www.press.uchicago.edu

British Library Cataloguing in Publication Data
A catalogue record for this book is available from the British Library

Library of Congress Cataloging-in-Publication Data
A catalog record for this book has been requested

ISBN 978-1-4473-0567-5 paperback

Cover design by Qube Design Associates, Bristol
Printed and bound in Great Britain by CMP, Poole
Policy Press uses environmentally responsible print partners

In memory of my mother,

Elizabeth Margery

# Contents

# Acronyms

| | |
|---|---|
| 2007 ASP(S) Act | Adult Support and Protection (Scotland) Act 2007 |
| A&E | Accident and emergency department (emergency treatment in NHS hospitals in the UK) |
| DH | Department of Health |
| DP | Direct payment |
| GP | General practitioner |
| HCC | Healthcare Commission |
| IB | Individual budget |
| NHS | National Health Service |
| PB | Personal budget |
| POVA | Protection of vulnerable adults |
| SDS | Self-directed support |
| WHO | World Health Organization |

# About the author

Angie Ash is director of the UK health and social care research consultancy, *Angela Ash Associates* (www.ashassociates.co.uk), and is a registered social worker. Angie's career has spanned university-based social research, social work practice, charity sector management, research and management consultancy to government, charities and businesses. She is a past winner of the Jo Campling Memorial Prize awarded by the journal *Ethics & Social Welfare* for her paper on ethics in adult safeguarding. Since completing the research described in this book, Angie has held research fellowships at the University of Bristol and Swansea University alongside her research consultancy.

# Acknowledgements

An unpayable debt is owed to the older people whose experiences of care and mistreatment have driven the completion of this book, which was a labour of love.

I am grateful to the many people working in health, social care and adult protection services with whom I have worked, and who have talked with me about their work with older people and in adult safeguarding. My particular thanks and appreciation go to the staff and their managers who took part in the research described in this book.

I acknowledge with gratitude the award of the UK's Economic and Social Research Council post-doctoral fellowship PTA-026-27-2617. The primary research reported in Chapters Six and Seven of this book was funded by the UK-based research and development consultancy *Angela Ash Associates.*

My thanks and appreciation go to Dr Liz Lloyd, University of Bristol, for going out of her way to provide me with material, as well as to: Dr Tova Band-Winterstein of the University of Haifa; Professor Marie Beaulieu, Université de Sherbrooke; Professor Simon Biggs, University of Melbourne; Professor Derek Birrell, University of Ulster; Dr Claudia Cooper, University College London; Dr Briony Dow, National Ageing Research Institute, Melbourne; Professor Keith Grint, University of Warwick; Professor Jill Manthorpe, King's College London; and Professor Lynn McDonald, University of Toronto. Also, conversation over dinner in a rain-soaked Oxford summer in 2012 with Dr Herwig Reiter of the German Youth Institute was fortuitous.

Professor Randall Smith of the University of Bristol kindly gave considered and perceptive comments on early drafts of some chapters. All of these were helpful; none is the reason for any shortcomings that may remain. Isobel Bainton, Emily Watt and the staff at Policy Press were always considerate and helpful. The accommodating, resourceful and ever-pleasant staff of Monmouthshire County Council library and information services in Wales never let me down. I am grateful to the anonymous reviewer for feedback.

Finally, warm thanks and gratitude are due to David Mayer for our long comradeship and for digging me out of so many cyber-holes; to Carolyn Sally Jones for a writer's solidarity; and for pretty much everything else, to Ruth Cook.

# ONE

# Contexts to safeguarding older people from abuse

Mrs R's family were concerned that she would not receive food and drink while in Southampton University Hospitals NHS Trust unless they helped her to eat and drink.

When Mrs H was transferred from Heart of England NHS Foundation Trust to a care home, she arrived bruised, soaked in urine, dishevelled and wearing someone else's clothes.

The care and treatment that Surrey and Borders Partnership NHS Foundation Trust gave Mr L contributed to a loss of his dignity and compromised his ability to survive pneumonia. (Parliamentary and Health Service Ombudsman, 2011, p 3)

These are three of the ten cases reported by the Parliamentary and Health Service Ombudsman for England on 14 February 2011. Nine of the ten people discussed in the Ombudsman's report – titled *Care and Compassion?* – died during, or shortly after, the events considered occurred. The Ombudsman observed that 'the circumstances of their deaths have added to the distress of their families and friends, many of whom continue to live with anger and regret' (Parliamentary and Health Service Ombudsman, 2011, p 8).

This book is about safeguarding older people from abuse. Notwithstanding reference to the Parliamentary and Health Service Ombudsman cases referred to above, it is not intended as a hand-wringing, head-shaking 'where did we go wrong' account of care and support to older people, nor as a hatchet job on social care or publicly funded, free-at-the-point-of-delivery, healthcare or on those who deliver it to citizens irrespective of their means. Older people may be abused and mistreated in community-based, domestic settings by people they know and would otherwise trust, for example, paid carers, family members, friends and neighbours.

A core intention of the book is to identify and critically appraise the influence of contextual factors on decision-making by those involved in adult safeguarding, including social workers, and their NHS (National Health Service) and police partners. The book's purpose is three-fold. First, it sets out to understand, at a deeper, theoretical level than the transient reporting of scandals of mistreatment, with their attendant action plans and the familiar 'learning of lessons' suggests, why otherwise decent, initially well-motivated, highly trained professionals, such as nurses, social workers and doctors, and other practitioners or paid carers, can appear blind to poor and abusive care of older people or, worse, why they may apparently perpetrate egregiously bad 'care'.

Second, the book aims to examine contexts of care and support to older people who are abused. That abuse and mistreatment happens in families and domestic dwellings, as well as in private, public or not-for-profit institutional care. If there is one message this book wants to convey, it is that we ignore the nature and the impact of those contexts of care at our peril. Except that 'peril' will not generally be visited on the 'aging enterprise' (Estes, 1979) that constitutes adult safeguarding systems and processes particularly, or the care and support to older people more generally. Rather it is the older people at risk of abuse who suffer the threat, danger and risk that this 'blindness to context' poses. If action plans and 'lesson-learning' were enough to stem the abuse and poor care of older people, they might have prevented systemic failures (with devastating outcomes for younger as well as older patients) such as those reported in Mid Staffordshire NHS Foundation Trust, England (Francis Report, 2013a), or they might have better succeeded in raising public awareness about elder abuse.

Third, this book is a call for 'right action' in safeguarding older people from mistreatment. 'Right action' is used here to mean the construction and maintenance of theory-hungry, ethically, compassionately and competently delivered care and support to older people who have been, or are at risk of being, abused. It is a call for a clear-headed, compassionate and dispassionate politics, policy and practice in safeguarding older people from abuse. It is an appeal, not for vacuous policy sloganising about 'putting people first' or 'caring for our future', the customary chanting of which can become an end in itself, but for committed professional and political intention, with systems to support it that can critically interrogate contexts of health and care, generally, and safeguard older people from abuse, in particular. That call is not for more standards, targets, or witch-hunts of often hapless front-line health and social care staff, accompanied by their ritual sheep-dipping through hastily constructed re-training programmes if things have gone wrong, but for a policy, practice and political awakening to the sound-surround system, as it were, of elder abuse. That surround includes ageism, a socially and culturally created and sustained fear and loathing of dependency, frailty and 'oldness', a public, political policy obsession with targets, service-system fragmentation and profit in the UK generally, and in England particularly. A key message of the book is that more numerical targets in health and social care will result in more box-ticking bureaucracy that may or may not hit the hallowed targets, but may well miss the point. The point is the older citizen at risk of abuse. The point is the priority their health and well-being is afforded.

Although this is not primarily a theoretical book, nor one directed at one particular profession or discipline, it makes the case for a rigorous, lucid and critical use of theoretical concepts, theory-informed research and learning in adult safeguarding policy and practice development. Social work and social policy, for example, have not shared the closest of relationships at the ground level of social services agencies. Still less, understanding the realities, the constraints and dilemmas of policy implementation by human services workers has too often been carried out in the breach – think of 8-year-old Victoria Climbié (who died in London in 2000 at the hands of her great aunt and her boyfriend, and who was known to two police child-protection teams, two housing authorities, the NHS, four social services departments and a leading child protection charity) – not in the routine, the mundane, the everyday stuff of front-line healthcare, social care, social work, or safeguarding practice more widely.

This book argues that any professional or practitioner distaste for 'theory' as an ivory-tower activity endured for the sake of meeting qualification and subsequent continuing professional development (CPD) requirements, would be as ill-considered as any academic view of 'practice' solely as a source of data, 'partnerships' or 'networks' necessary for research grant capture. Both are instrumental views of the 'other'. Both are means to an end but that end may not be the abused older person. The case for bringing findings of research into practice and policy-making, and for driving research endeavour, policy development and health and social care practice by the reality of elder abuse, and the centrality of the experience of the older person, is argued here to be an end in itself. Here, the process is the goal. In Buddhist practice, for example, 'right action' forms part of a practical guideline for ethical behaviour and development of compassion and kindness. In this frame, 'right action' involves honesty, kind and compassionate behaviour, and an abstinence from causing harm to sentient beings. Used thus, 'right action' – ethically driven policy and practice – is a goal this book seeks to present, for policy-makers, academics and practitioners.

## Origins of the book

This book derived directly from research, policy and practice in safeguarding older people from abuse, and particularly from case reviews this author had undertaken over a number of years, commissioned by various UK statutory bodies, where adults at risk, including many older people, came to harm. As is usual, the findings and recommendations of these reviews remain confidential to the agencies and organisations that commissioned them. Nonetheless, these cases and the circumstances they uniquely and collectively presented, raised three particularly recurrent themes (Ash, 2011a).

First, in cases where the adult at risk (who may have been a person with learning disabilities or mental ill-health problems, or an older person) had come to harm, the potential for harm, or 'risk factors' to use the ubiquitous professional vernacular, were known about before the events under investigation occurred. In other words, these cases had a hinterland which, with increasing predictability, the retrospective reviews of what went wrong cast light on. The professionals and paid workers involved in health and care delivery of one type or another usually had available to them information that could have alerted them to harm, had they followed the 'trail', for example, joining up their information with others' information and raising a safeguarding alert. But this did not always happen. Professionals were reluctant to raise concerns about the quality and the care offered by other paid professionals to the adult at risk. They would tick their own box, for example, make a phone call (and record it – they understood the professional risk if the next recording audit found they had not) to pass on information, but either did not follow it up, or showed a reluctance to put the information in words that conveyed *concern* or challenge of other professionals. The anodyne passing of information was stripped of its core purpose, and devoid of any challenge to poor or failing support to the adult at risk. But that box ticked, the paid worker or professional had to turn to deal with the myriad other demands they faced that day.

Second, in some of these cases that had gone wrong, there had been a professional reluctance to use adult safeguarding policy. If used, adult protection (or safeguarding) procedures provide a multi-agency framework to bring together social services, the police, NHS and other partners. But in some cases under review, often those where mental health and NHS staff were the key professionals involved, this had not always happened.

A third theme from these reviews was a professional reluctance explicitly to draw on, or else an ignorance of, well-established findings of research on, say, family violence or elder abuse, or any critical interrogation of the validity of common-sense understandings of those risk factors. Professional understandings of the stresses of care-giving and care-receiving, of the nature, exercise and abuse of paternal, parental or filial power in conflicted family relationships, are part of the bread-and-butter basics of professional health, medical and social care practice. They are omnipresent, empirically supported social phenomena. Nonetheless, in some cases these understandings were sidelined to adult protection exigencies of holding meetings within a set number of hours or days. Professional skills of intervention in the conflicted, abusive dynamics of some family situations seemed not to be drawn upon, if indeed any longer practised, in the multi-agency world of adult safeguarding.

Further, the outcomes of inquiries, case reviews, routine or exceptional inspection reports on health and social care services would, inevitably, generate one or more action plans, allowing items to be ticked off, training days to be delivered, reports made back to a regulator and elected local politicians, and for the box-ticking show to go on. It is, obviously, entirely proper that those charged with statutory responsibilities have sound data that tell them, for example, how many social services or NHS staff have completed awareness training of the signs of elder abuse. But these cases that were reviewed often highlighted behaviours, practices and ways of thinking, from senior managers down to front-line staff that, for instance, viewed delivery of thousands of hours of awareness training as an end in itself. There was less critical questioning about 'so what?' Were older people or other adults at risk safer? What research-informed content was delivered to these people? What happens to paid staff when they go back to work? How do the systems, structures and processes of their work, their day-to-day practice, drive their understanding and recognition of elder abuse, and what should they do if they are concerned? Does that context itself support right action and sound practice in the messy, predictably unpredictable worlds of human beings using human services?

These three themes were the impetus behind research that set out to examine that context of care, and the influences on professional decision-making in safeguarding older people from abuse. That research is reported in Chapters Six and Seven; aspects of it have been reported in Ash (2010) and Ash (2013). Its findings, if nothing else, highlighted some outcomes of a policy and practice blindness to the *influences* on professional decision-making that lie at the heart of adult safeguarding decisions. This book attempts to set out elements of that context. This context includes ageism, and a social and cultural aversion to getting and being old; fragmented, under-resourced health and care services and systems that some older people have to rely on; a policy-making, public and political overestimation of what regulation and compliance-driven activity can achieve in adult safeguarding, and an ignorance of what it cannot; an uncritical policy obsession, particularly in England, with chasing of numerical targets and cost-shunting between health and social care; and a naïve worship of the gods of 'choice', 'control' and 'independence', devoid of any deeper interrogation as to their meaning and implication in the care and safeguarding of older people. The findings of the research reported in Chapters Six and Seven highlight some of the unintended consequences of 'doing things right' – for example, uncritically embracing an older person's 'right to make bad choices' as upholding their self-determination – rather than 'doing the right thing', for example, working with the older person to understand options, risk and protection, and providing support and protection while they are doing this. Abused, battered, denigrated beings may be in need of a bit of help and support to remember what choice and control are. They may need a while, safe and free from harm, and in loving and compassionate circumstances, to get to grips with empowerment.

## Structure of the book

The book as a whole is a challenge to policy-makers, academics, teachers, managers, professionals and practitioners to engage in critical, theory-informed work in safeguarding older people from mistreatment. Chapter Two makes the case for this in policy and practice to safeguard older people from abuse. Chapter Three considers the process and outcomes of 'naming of elder abuse' in the UK and internationally. Research on the prevalence and nature of elder abuse is discussed and, in particular, the incidence and response to domestic violence in older age. That discussion is set within a context of ageism and reference to the fundamental and irreducible human rights of older people.

Chapter Four discusses the development of policy and practice in adult protection and the safeguarding of older people from abuse against the backdrop of personalisation and individualisation of care. This chapter considers legal and policy development in adult safeguarding across the UK, and the differential foci of the development of personalisation across the UK's four nations. It discusses potential impacts of this policy trajectory on safeguarding older people, and other adults at risk, from abuse.

Chapter Five situates discussion about action to protect an older person from abuse within a theoretical frame. In particular, this chapter considers Michael Lipsky's (1980) work on street-level bureaucracy, and discusses the nature and extent of the exercise of discretion by public servants using policy to safeguard older people from abuse. Chapter Five considers the significance of *context* in understanding both the action adult safeguarding professionals may take when dealing with potential abuse of an older person, and the constraints and realities they grapple with when weighing up what to do. In essence, the chapter sets out the conceptual scaffolding for the research reported in the following two chapters.

Chapters Six and Seven describe the findings of research carried out in a social services department in Wales that aimed to identify the constraints and dilemmas social workers and their managers faced when using adult safeguarding policy to protect an older person from abuse. Among the findings of this research was the reticence of social workers and other professionals to challenge known poor care to older people. This leads, in Chapter Eight, to a wider discussion about cultures and contexts of *complicity*, and the features and factors implicated in this apparent silence and tacit tolerance. Chapter Nine returns to the theme running throughout the book, that of the significance of contexts, whether social, political or cultural, on the quality of care and support older people might receive and on safeguarding elders from abuse particularly. A case is made for the development of ethically driven systems, structures and contexts that support work to safeguard older people from abuse. Without ethically driven public policy and a supportive state that embraces, rather than commodifies or out-sources ethical action, system failures in adult safeguarding will continue to be met with increased regulation, standards and restructuring that may hit targets but, again, are likely to miss the point – the older person at risk of abuse.

## A note on the terms used in this book

The book mostly, but not exclusively, considers safeguarding older people from abuse in the UK. Health and social care have been devolved areas of government and administration in the UK since 1999, so legislation, policy and terminology have increasingly diverged in the four nations.

**'Social services'**: Adult and children's services are not separate entities in Wales or Scotland as they are in England. 'Social services' is a term used in Wales and Scotland. 'Social care' has come to replace it in England to describe provision to adults rather than children, and 'adult services' arrange delivery of this. In Scotland, 'social service workers' includes people working in social work and social care, such as care homes, community-based services to adults and children and nurseries or after-school clubs.

This book uses the term 'social services' in the context of safeguarding older people from abuse. 'Social services' is also used to denote local authority (local council) engagement in safeguarding older people from abuse; social services have a lead role in co-ordinating adult protection intervention under the law in Scotland, and national policy in England, Northern Ireland and Wales.

**'Adult protection'** and **'adult safeguarding'**: the book uses both terms, noting the differentiation made by the Law Commission (2011), which is discussed in Chapter Four. Both terms are used to describe action by statutory, not-for-profit and private agencies to intervene to prevent or stop abuse of an older person. From the point of view of the abused older person, or their family, friends or loved ones concerned to stop abusive actions or behaviour, professional semantics as to whether this activity requires 'protection' or 'safeguarding' are unlikely to be their primary concern.

**'Elders'** and **'older people'** are used synonymously, to reflect the language adopted in international campaigning against elder abuse, and that used by international scholars whose work is discussed. (There, 'elder' is used as a courtesy to those writers). While 'elder' may not be a term most older people I have talked and worked with use, the book has tried to avoid unnecessary distractions: the issue is understanding and preventing the abuse and mistreatment of older people, and it is to that end the book is directed.

# TWO

# The need for theory, critical thinking and practice

This book is concerned with theory, policy and practice in safeguarding older people from abuse. The theoretical bolstering to this includes social gerontology and policy studies. The present chapter does not develop a case for one theoretical perspective over another. Rather its purpose is to make a case for theory-informed and critically driven understandings and interventions in safeguarding older people from abuse. The chapter's first section sets out 'the case for theory', describing what is meant in this context by 'theory' and why it matters. Its second section makes a call for critical perspectives, thinking and practice in elder abuse policy and practice. It suggests that without this, policy development and practice interventions run the risk of being *ad hoc* and at best without worth, but at worst damaging to an older person at risk of abuse.

## 'Theory' and why it matters

In the UK, the development of concern about elder abuse largely came, not from the academy, but from professionals such as social workers and health and medical practitioners, part of what Carroll Estes (1979, p 2) called the 'aging enterprise', that is, the '… programs, organizations, bureaucracies, interest groups, trade associations, providers, industries, and professionals that serve the aged in one capacity or another'. The early 21st century campaign in England and Wales for adult protection legislation has mostly come from the same quarters (for example, AEA, 2007a; Burstow, 2013). In its Social Services and Well-being (Wales) Bill introduced in 2013, the Welsh Government signalled commitment to merging its child protection and adult protection (adult safeguarding) systems, that is local safeguarding boards, adult protection committees, and so on) at some future date. Neither this, nor most of the policy, procedural or legislative developments in UK adult safeguarding generally, or the protection of older people from abuse specifically, has been driven directly by theoretically informed work, or by a critical appraisal of evidence, research or practice. This is not unusual in public policy. Policy choices are contested, political and politicised matters, rather than critically appraised, evidence-driven decisions. However, to understand some of the impacts and consequences of policy intentions and policy delivery on the protection or safeguarding of older people from abuse, the case for a critically driven dispassionate appraisal of assumptions, 'facts' and impacts on abused older people has to be made.

It is in that spirit that this book makes its case for conceptually and critically informed policy and practice in safeguarding older people from mistreatment. If we can locate elder abuse and safeguarding older people from abuse within theoretically informed frameworks, we may better understand why it occurs, what its consequences are, and what social, cultural and economic influences there are on the way professionals such as social workers, nurses and the police make decisions when dealing with suspected abuse. Like Katz (2003), this volume does not regard multidisciplinarity in research or practice as a precursor, and certainly not as a synonym, for critical thinking. Multi-disciplinarity can limit rather than enrich critical thinking, if findings from different disciplines are amalgamated *post hoc* without regard to the different theoretical paradigms from which they derive, if such were stated in the first place (see Bengtson et al, 1997, for discussion of this). Neither does the book make the clarion call for more research (although there is much that we do not know in safeguarding older people from abuse and need to find out). Rather its intention in making the case for theory-informed policy and practice in safeguarding older people from abuse, mirrored by practice-informed policy and theory development, is *practical*. As Lewin remarked (1952, p 169) 'there is nothing as practical as a good theory'; Lewin's advice was that theorists should try to provide new ideas for understanding or conceptualising a (problematic) situation, which may point up new ways of seeing and responding to it. Correspondingly, practitioners and policy-makers can provide theorists with information and facts relevant to solving a practical problem, facts that need to be conceptualised coherently for sense-making. For Lewin, 'theorists' should strive to create theories that can be used to solve social or practical problems, and practitioners and researchers in applied psychology should make use of available scientific theory (Vansteenkiste and Sheldon, 2006). As Estes et al (2003) observed, policy and theory are interpretive – they go beyond common sense to the *why* as well as *what* of a social phenomenon or behaviour. They are, as well, attempts to exert an influence on the politics of ageing. Both shape perspectives on ageing: neither is value neutral.

## Elder abuse, social gerontology and theorising

To date, elder abuse as a subject of study has been generally located within social gerontology in family violence studies and, to a much lesser extent, in research on domestic abuse. Social gerontology, the study of ageing in the social world, is a multi-faceted concept taking in the interpersonal, cognitive, emotional, economic and physical dimensions of life that influence functioning and wellbeing through the lifecourse (Hooyman and Kiyak, 2008). Social gerontology has come to mean the application of social sciences, for example, sociology, demography, psychology and social anthropology, to the study and understanding of ageing individuals and populations, and their interrelationship with wider social change and social forces generally (Dannefer and Phillipson, 2010). In 1988, commenting on the then state of theorising in social gerontology, Birren and Bengtson (1988, p ix) observed '… the data rich but theory-poor state of current research on aging'. This referred to an overemphasis on information-gathering to the exclusion of interpretation and meaning-making of the data; work was additive rather than integrative (Ray, 2003). While there have been theoretical developments in social gerontology since this was written (see Bengtson et al, 1997 and Alley et al, 2010 for analyses of the theoretical bases of peer-reviewed articles published in eight gerontology journals over two four-year periods), it is the case that policy development and implementation, and practice in adult safeguarding and elder abuse are, as yet, under-theorised. They may proceed without examination of the impact of the social, cultural and political context within which adult safeguarding takes place. They seldom question why things are the way they are. Work is frequently descriptive, less often critical.

In safeguarding and protecting older people from abuse, normative assumptions about, for instance, spousal and filial relationships in older age, in the author's experience, often feature significantly in professional discussion about what to do if abuse is suspected. The wider context to this discussion, for example, of the impact of socially and culturally reinforced economic dependencies on the power dynamics of intimate personal relationships, in the present and over the life course, may not over-inform this decision-making. The following section of this chapter considers what is meant by 'theory', in terms of understanding the phenomenon of elder abuse, and developing intervention and support to abused elders that derives from empirically and theoretically coherent and informed research and practice.

## The meaning of 'theory'

What is meant by 'theory' is often understood and used ambiguously. Bengtson et al (1999, p 5) suggested theory is 'the construction of explicit explanations in accounting for empirical findings', rather than some lofty, abstruse speculation. In essence, theory provides *explanation* or an *account* of an area under consideration, and often formulates or uses concepts to do this. In research, as well as policy and practice in human services, theory offers ways of looking at and making sense of what is observed. It assists the development of knowledge, understanding and sense-making of complex, confusing, 'messy' social phenomena.

At its simplest, then, 'theory' is an attempt to explain why things are the way they are or why things happen (Alley et al, 2010). Why are some older people abused? Why may professionals not 'see' elder abuse? Why does frailty and dependence in older age increase the risk of being abused? Why did the social problem of elder abuse come to be identified as such in the late twentieth century? These are matters on which professionals and policy-makers may deliberate and possess tacit knowledge, that is, things they know but do not know how to explain (Polanyi, 1967). But a 'fact' or a 'thing' cannot exist without a perceptual, or conceptual, organising system. Theorising, or organising facts, may happen at different levels from grand theory to smaller micro analyses; without such a framework, facts or events or circumstances have little cumulative meaning 'amounting to little more than a pile of bricks awaiting an architect' (Hendricks and Powell, 2009, p 5). Accumulating facts about this or that, as a magpie might retrieve shining booty to take to the nest, is not knowledge-building. Knowledge is more than the accumulation of facts, but seeks to explain and draw associations. It helps develop understandings of how values operate in practice (Holstein et al, 2010). Without theory we don't have a basis on which to develop and test hypotheses, interpret findings or generate questions to advance knowledge (Alley et al, 2010).

'Theory' is distinguishable from models and paradigms. Models are representations, sometimes maps, of sets of relationships that may approximate reality in varying ways. They describe how descriptions of phenomena may be related to each other. They aim to depict natural worlds, and the relationship between things. Paradigms exemplify aspects of reality, illustrating configurations of cultural or social assumptions. Kuhn's (1970) insights on the structure of scientific revolutions well-represented paradigms as patterns of thinking and background assumptions that are usually taken for granted and fix, for a time at least, the standard or normative manner in which scientific inquiry is carried out.

## The 'problem' of theory

In social gerontology, generally, and elder abuse, more particularly, the 'problem' with theory (that is, a dearth of theoretically informed policy and practice interventions) may be down to different factors. First, implicit understandings and assumptions in research or writing may not be spelled out, pulled apart, critiqued or challenged. They may lie unexplored or taken for granted, in the background rather than foreground of descriptive research that does not drill deeply to set out the bases from which it proceeds.

Second, theoretical development has sometimes been restricted to empirical generalisation that, because of policy-maker or practitioner scepticism about 'theory' as some esoteric abstraction for those not obliged to work in the 'real world', may lead to a substitution of empirical generalisation for theory. Thus empirical generalisations may become little more than a summary of some research findings that need some scaffolding – a theory – to prop them up. Bengtson et al (2005) said that such generalisations needed to be developed to an explanatory level to overcome the problem, in social gerontology, of research that generates rafts of generalisations, devoid of a complementary development of integrated knowledge.

Third, as Kuhn (1970) showed, theoretical and scientific development is a social endeavour. Like ageing itself, it is embedded in historical and institutional contexts that shape the research enterprise. Without recognition of this, the impact, influence and inter-penetration of those contexts into theory, policy and practice, in social gerontology, generally, and elder abuse, specifically, may remain invisible.

As a consequence, practitioners, policy-makers or academics searching for solutions to social problems without regard to theory have several problems. As Bengtson et al (1999 p 12) remarked, 'without theory, how can gerontologists decide which problems are caused by ageing itself, which are age-related phenomena, and which are not due to age at all?' 'Solutions' to 'problems' of ageing or elder abuse may end up as quick-fix responses that do not pay heed to previous work. Implicit theories, or questionable assumptions (that, for example, everyone over 80 is 'vulnerable' or 'lonely') are left unnoticed, unexplored, unchecked. An unquestioning call for 'more support' for 'older' (*sic*) people contains within it a taken-for-granted assumption that being 'old' equals 'need for more support' equals 'improved wellbeing'. In fact some empirical work has suggested that too much 'support' (this might involve the wrong intervention, at the wrong time, for the wrong reason to the wrong person) undermines a person's autonomy, and sense of privacy and self-direction (Bengtson et al, 1999).

In social gerontology, Estes et al (2003, p 9) considered the absence of theory to be apparent in various ways. They cited Crawford (1971) who drew attention to an historical tendency to treat a study of ageing in terms of social welfare policies that focus largely on the *consequences* of social arrangements, implementing *ad hoc* responses to social problems, and thus largely discouraging theorising about *why* or *how* those problems came to be problems at all. In the late 1970s, Estes (1979) observed gerontologists to be generally content with describing activity or disability in ageing, but mostly unquestioning about the way the lived experience of ageing is shaped by social and economic factors. For Bengtson and Schaie (1999), the problem of 'to theorise or not to theorise' was actually failure to build theoretical reasoning and scientific rigour into the research enterprise as a whole. As a result, a push for practical solutions to what we might call the 'burden business' – a view of ageing as a burden to be fixed, managed and marketised in intervention or entrepreneurial activity of one sort or another – may come to eclipse the development of theoretical frameworks.

Theory, in elder abuse, as well with social gerontology, can integrate knowledge and set out ideas, as well as facts, to develop explanations of how and why things are related. Theoretical understandings can illuminate the antecedents and consequences ('before' and 'after') of actions, behaviours or interventions. Theory can inform interventions (Bengtson et al, 1996). For Biggs et al (2003a; 2003b) the test of a good theory was its addition of logical coherence to a body of knowledge. Data, facts, pieces of information, swap stories of 'what worked here so it may work there', do not resolve debates about how to respond to the abuse of older people, any more than they do for other social problems. In its integration of knowledge, theory highlights linkages, connections and patterns between variables. Theory explains as well as describes. Theory can inform interventions and the alleviation of social problems (Bengtson et al, 1999). Theory can provide conceptual tools to help understand, interpret and question why things are as they are, and to evaluate critically the experience, understanding and reality of ageing and elder abuse (Biggs et al, 2003a).

Theorising can occur at several levels of work with abused older people or more generally. Theorising might involve questioning why some subjects – say, safeguarding older people from abuse – come to be regarded as social problems at particular historical junctures but others, for example, the impacts of economic inequality through the lifecourse for instance, attract less interest. Theorising might assist in seeing the downsides of quick and easy solution-driven approaches to elder abuse (for example, provide more domiciliary care and have the paid carer undertake some unspecified 'monitoring'), and instead permit a critical interrogation of decisions and their impacts on an older adult at risk of abuse. Biggs et al (2003a, p 10) were discussing social gerontology when they commented that 'knowledge advances to the extent that conceptual advancement and integration occur'. This could also be said of elder abuse. Without theorising and theoretical development, the result can be a 'piecemeal empiricism but relatively few insights' (Biggs et al, 2003a, p 10).

In elder abuse, like social gerontology more generally, there has been a tendency towards what Hagestad and Dannefer (2001) called 'microfication' – a disproportionate attention to micro-interventions and an emphasis on individual categories of, for example, psychological characteristics. Biggs, Hendricks and Lowenstein suggested that the classification of things into extensive categories, as 'has arguably happened in the study of elder abuse', contributes little to advancing understanding of the subject under concern. Investigators 'get lost among the trees', and a 'a sort of theoretical stamp collecting' results where 'different theories and traditions are grouped or re-grouped according to the collector's fancy, with little evident disciplinary progress and scant connection to the world of experience' (Biggs et al, 2003a, p 1).

Why does 'microfication' matter? A disproportionate focus on the micro, the picking and choosing this or that aspect of the object of concern to focus on, pushes out of vision various macro-level matters, such as social arrangements, socio-economic factors, power and conflict, social, institutional and cultural norms and values. From this micro-only perspective, the impact of structural factors such as ageism, poverty and inequality on health and wellbeing, and on rates of crime and domestic violence (see Wilkinson and Pickett, 2010), rarely impinge on the development of understandings of elder abuse, or challenge assumptions that ageing is synonymous with decrepitude and decline. Linking micro- and the macro-levels of analysis is needed, 'so that the pull of social inequalities can be identified and the experience and daily interpretation of them explored' (Estes et al, 2003, pp 146–7). Theory provides a critical lens with which to scrutinise assumptions, statements, contradictions around ageing and elder abuse. It is the conceptual grounding that makes knowledge cumulative, and prevents social gerontology (and elder abuse) from being just being bits of this and that (Hendricks et al, 2010).

## Critical perspectives, critical thinking, critical practice

In making a case for ethically driven practice in safeguarding older people from abuse, this book argues for both the use of theory and evidence-informed work to protect older people from abuse, and critical thinking in safeguarding practice, that is, careful, considered appraisals of facts and suppositions to arrive at well-reasoned safeguarding decisions.

In social gerontology, Estes et al (2003) regarded the development of critical approaches in the 1980s and 1990s as a response to three concerns. First, related to a need to understand more clearly the 'social construction of dependency' in older age, as an outcrop of welfare-ism, poverty in older age or ageism (see, for example, Townsend, 1981; Walker, 1981; 1982). Second, critical approaches questioned the individualistic focus of traditional gerontology, with its lack of attention to social structures, economic relationships and their impact on people through the lifecourse and in old age. Third, critical gerontology developed as a challenge to the predominance of bio-medical models of ageing that were concerned to rectify presumed decline. For Grenier (2012), a critical perspective on ageing was itself influenced by social, cultural and relational dimensions, including the effect of major social divisions and cumulative disadvantage on the experience of ageing, and the social and cultural construction of the process of ageing.

A 'critical approach' to gerontology or elder abuse is thus one that goes beyond everyday explanation and unthinking acceptance of 'common sense'. It is an approach that recognises and foregrounds as necessary the structural inequalities that shape human experience and daily life. For Estes et al (2003) a critical gerontology was one that considered both structural inequalities in society and in the personal experience of ageing, and that recognised that the voices and lives of people are fractured by class, race, social and economic inequality, and so on. Hence a critical approach regards so-called 'common sense' as a starting point not an end point; it is the raw material embedded in everyday attitudes and is observable in the effort put into constructing and maintaining such attitudes by powerful interests.

As an illustration, let us critically interrogate a common image of growing old in public policy. The 'European Year of Active Ageing and Solidarity between Generations 2012' had this to say to visitors to its website (presumably the worried over-60s):

> Worried about growing older? About your place in society when you're 60, 70 or 80?
>
> There is a lot to life after 60 – and society is coming increasingly to appreciate the contribution older people can make. That's what active ageing is about – getting more out of life as you grow older, not less, whether at work, at home or in the community. (http://europa.eu/ey2012/)

A critical approach to reading this would not be hard-stretched to unpack the assumptions bedded into 'worried about growing older?', and its reassurance that 'there is a lot to life after 60', as if a 60th birthday was a cause for concern, or poverty, inequality, ill-health, disability or experience of violence through the life course could be brushed away with a spot more 'active ageing'. By fashioning worry, offering reassurance that 'society is coming increasingly to appreciate the contribution older people can make' (as if 'solidarity between generations' was a one-way street) this manufactures images of ageing, and nails responsibility on those 'after 60' to get 'more out of life'.

'Solutions' to the so-called problem of ageing promise, as the European Year of Active Ageing and Solidarity between Generations 2012 might have suggested, to do away with age discrimination. Outputs (that is, the products) of biomedical and pharmaceutical interests promise drugs to tackle fears of cognitive and physical decline. Active ageing, doing paid work for longer, are offered up as solutions to socially generated 'burden of burden' fears and poverty in old age. As Estes et al (2003, p 4) noted, a critical approach sees these matters as 'sites of struggle' where images, narratives and understandings of ageing and ageism may find form in public policy on ageing. In elder abuse, a critical approach might be one that questioned why there was as yet little research on domestic violence in older age, few services to older people abused by an intimate partner, and why research endeavour, public policy and practice have overlooked this. The questioning of why certain subjects or social problems are 'not seen' is one side of a critical coin. The other side is the need for critical approaches to remind research, policy and practice interests that dominant paradigms shape theoretical construction, public policy and practice (Lynott and Lynott, 1996).

In elder abuse, a critical perspective would be one that is alert to social constructions of ageing and their ideological underpinnings. Bengtson et al (1999) offered suggestions to social gerontologists that also speak to policy-making and decision-making in safeguarding older people from abuse. The first was advice not to act without considering and explaining the 'why' behind decisions. The second suggestion was don't confuse theories with empirical generalisations and models. Theory means explanation and explanation develops knowledge. Third, Bengtson et al (1999) advised paying attention to what went, or happened, before. In safeguarding older people from abuse, this might include the hinterland to the decisions, what influenced what was not said or considered, as well as what was said to reach agreed decisions. In short, critical awareness and critical thinking involves the use of reason, and reflective processes and skills focused on deciding what to believe or do. Critical approaches do not rest on an assumption that good intentions are enough to protect people who are abused or mistreated.

## Critical thinking in practice

As suggested, a critical approach to the study of ageing, generally, and the abuse of older people, more specifically, is concerned to expose, lay bare, interrogate the taken-for-granted assumptions that permeate a business-as-usual approach to care and support of older people and safeguarding older people from abuse. Decision-making is at the heart of adult safeguarding practice. In the UK, staff and professionals from agencies such as social services, the police or NHS as well as others, come together to consider evidence of abuse and action to take. Decision-making or problem-solving in safeguarding an older person from mistreatment may be uncertain. It may concern the nature of the problem or alleged abuse, disputed facts and information about what happened or didn't happen, about what is needed, the likelihood of the alleged abuse stopping, or whether a crime has been committed.

Gambrill (2007; 2012) has set out elements and features of critical thinking and the discussion that follows draws on these. Critical thinking and scientific reasoning are closely linked. Both seek clarity, a critical appraisal of claims and recognise criticism as essential for developing knowledge, or information that reveals or decreases uncertainty about how to achieve an outcome (Nickerson 1986, cited in Gambrill, 2012, p 210). Critical thinking is necessary but not sufficient to arrive at well-reasoned decisions: that requires knowledge, which is needed to make accurate inferences. Knowledge includes facts and know-how, as well as self-knowledge and a capacity to see above and beyond what Gambrill (2012) called 'propaganda'. (In gerontology this might include the selling of 'solutions' to the inevitability – the fact of life from the moment of birth – that ageing is.)

In general, critical thinking involves both the possession, use and careful application of relevant knowledge and skills. It requires alternative perspectives to be relished and close attention paid to the process of reasoning, not just its product. Critical thinking and critical practice involve drawing on research-informed information, and the conscious, explicit, and judicious use of current best evidence in making decisions about the care of clients. Critical thinking can assist registered professionals such as nurses, social workers and medical doctors come to well-reasoned decisions, to be evidence-based and thus honour ethical obligations to citizens for whom they have a statutory duty of care (Gambrill, 2012).

Critical thinkers question what others do not; they challenge taken-for-granted assumptions. In elder abuse, for example, a critical thinker would question *a priori* assumptions that older people 'die anyway' (without, for instance, questioning why a 90 year-old man living in a care home lost 20 per cent of his bodyweight in the last six months of his life), or that illness and frailty are to be expected after a certain age. Critical thinking would involve questioning what others take for granted; in adult safeguarding meetings, for example, asking 'what's the evidence for this?'

Developing these critical, practical thinking faculties rests on learnable, acquirable affective qualities and skills. These include a flexibility and open-mindedness in thinking that is open to different ways of analysing circumstances or concerns. Such open-mindedness manifests a relish of self-questioning and views mistakes as powerful ways of learning (rather than failure, and a source of professional shame carrying a threat of regulatory chastisement). The latter may result but is more likely when patently poor practice has not been questioned, challenged or debated by those in a position so to do. The threat of professional humiliation and shame are more certain when contexts to practice are ones that lay down rules, regulations and standards as the only measures of professional endeavour. These elevate obedience to rules and standards as an end in itself, rendering critical thinking and challenge less rather than more likely. Rules, numerical targets and standards cannot embrace, and thus on their own terms, 'measure' aspects of care and safeguarding such as kindness, attention, affective responsiveness. Chapter Nine discusses this further.

Critical thinkers value well-reasoned accounts that may diverge from their own, as an opportunity to test, open up and tear apart, unexposed areas of supposition and assumption in reasoning. Such thinkers are motivated by doing the right thing by the older person, rather than just following the rule book, or going along with powerful voices in multi-agency safeguarding even when they disagree. They are not motivated by the personal need to feel liked, but by the need for respect of their professionalism, integrity and humility (that is, their willingness to say 'I don't know', or 'I got it wrong', or 'I'm scared of this').

Critical thinkers ask others to explain why they have come to the view they have. They use, and want others to use, findings of research and evaluation to inform practice. They are able to evaluate critically the quality of information and research, and question conclusions from research that are based on flimsy evidence, or are over-stated. Critical thinkers can ask 'good questions' that help colleagues weigh up information and clarify misconceptions and flaws in arguments.

Critical thinking may assist individuals and groups being bamboozled by conventional wisdoms. Critical thinkers identify and confront flawed arguments and recognise a difference between persuasive rhetoric, suppositions and facts. They are confident in saying when the emperor is wearing no clothes. In groups, decision-making can result in group members going for premature closure in reaching a decision. Members of a group may come to it with different organisational priorities, from varied professional cultures and management styles. They may approach decision-making divergently. Individuals may have conflicting skills and styles when dealing with disagreement, ranging from relish of exploration of various perspectives to withdrawal, upset or aggression. Individuals and group cultures may associate critical debate and challenge as confrontation, rather than a reasoned process trying to reach well-constructed and well-supported decisions.

Critical thinking is alert to problems of 'groupthink', or the 'deterioration of mental efficiency, reality testing, and moral judgement that results from in-group pressures' (Janis, 1982, p 9). In groupthink, a group of people may overestimate the rightness of its decision-making; it may ignore counter-factuals that call into question its assumptions. High group cohesiveness becomes prized more than a disinterested pursuit of 'truth' or, more prosaically, alternatives to come to a reasonable decision. For Janis (1982), high cohesiveness in groups was present in examples of groupthink, although cohesiveness itself did not produce groupthink.

A 'groupthinking group' may stereotype others, or make *ad hominem* attacks on those outside (or inside) it who criticise its work or findings. Individuals may self-censor what they say, views and opinions that are not the norm may be out-casted, and direct pressure to fall into line may be put on a member who questions the hegemonic hold of group norms and views. As a result, alternatives are not debated, no effort is made at disconfirmation, that is, an active attempt to disprove as a way to test the rigour of a viewpoint. Consensus-driven decision-making may ignore, criticise, blame or attack disconfirming information or evidence that calls into question the 'groupthink'. High-risk situations, with a real threat of public humiliation if 'failure' is exposed, may drive groups to create high solidarity among group members. Boat-rockers are not welcome guests at the groupthink party.

In safeguarding older people from abuse, an uncritical, business-as-usual approach to elder abuse might take for granted a welfare response to, say, repeated assault ('physical abuse') of an older woman by her spouse, rather than the zero tolerance and prosecution of the perpetrator, as would be a more likely (but not a certain) response to incidents of domestic violence involving younger protagonists in the home. A critical – one that was disinterested, dispassionate, informed – safeguarding response would question gender assumptions about perpetrators and victims of domestic abuse in old age, for example that the victim is likely to be the woman. (Domestic violence in old age, and the abuse of older men, is discussed in Chapter Three.) A critical approach would be one that asked what research-informed information there was on lifetime domestic violence in a relationship and its impact on the people involved, and what information there was that indicated how best to respond. In work exploring the differing accounts and theoretical constructs used in understanding and responding to abuse and neglect by different protagonists such as the older person, the social worker and a family member, Eisikovits et al (2013) concluded that health and social work professionals should be reflective of their own role and attitudes towards the abuse they are working with. This would involve being aware of their own attitudes towards old age, to the abuse, to the older person and their family, and probing the influence of these on what they do, feel and say, as … [t]he social workers' attitudes and emotions need "bracketing" in order for them to be reflective '… [t]he construction of intervention is related to what and how professionals perceive elder abuse and neglect' (Eisikovits et al, 2013, p 7).

Groupthink, uncritical thinking and the challenges of group decision-making may well be familiar territory for the reader. It would be unusual to work in health and social care, adult safeguarding, research and academia, policy-making or political life (or any other sector of organisational endeavour) and not to have encountered decision-making and behaviours exemplifying an ideal type of groupthink. If critical thinking and ethical practice in policy or practice to safeguard older people from abuse are to find form, traits that decision-making groups might reinforce and valorise include intellectual autonomy, humility, curiosity and integrity. Those working at any level of those organisations, agencies and institutions with a role in adult safeguarding would model and cultivate workplace cultures that reinforce thinking and critical questioning. Not being a 'team player' would be recognised as an important counterweight to an unthinking fitting-in or keeping quiet with safeguarding colleagues, if discussion or decision-making about the protection of an adult at risk was shallow, ageist, ill-informed or lazy.

Creating cultures of critical thinking involves practice, actions and behaviours that expect a questioning, challenging and informed appraisal of situations, facts or uncertainties. Such appraisals would actively challenge quality of care or support to an older person that is known to be marginal. Ethical and critical thinking and practice may stand more chance of taking root in open workplace cultures, where people paid to work with and safeguard older people from abuse are free to raise questions and express criticism about current practices and policies and their outcomes. Those cultures are hard to conceive and develop where wider regulatory, policy and political contexts are ones where rule-expansion, rule-tightening and naming and shaming of failure are preferred *modi operandi*.

This chapter has set out a case for theory and critical thinking and practice in policy and practice to safeguard older people from abuse, and has suggested that without these, safeguarding policy development and practice interventions run the risk of, at best, being worthless, but at worst harming an older person at risk of abuse. Aspects of groupthink are described in the case study that forms Chapters Six and Seven of this book, and in discussion of safeguarding failures and cultures of complicity in Chapter Eight. Ethical dimensions of this discussion are considered in Chapter Nine.

# THREE

# The abuse of older people

This chapter considers the process and outcome of the 'naming of elder abuse' in the UK and internationally, and the focus and findings of some research on the prevalence and nature of elder abuse. This material is indicative of themes and findings: it is not intended to be systematic or comprehensive. This chapter trails the book's later discussion of an apparent *de facto* blindness to abuse in a lifeless jabbering of the 'choice' refrain in public policy and professional safeguarding practice. Finally, ageism and its manifestations and consequences for older people who are at risk of abuse are discussed. The chapter closes by enveloping the foregoing with reference to the human rights of older people, founded on a framework of the fundamental values that are dignity, autonomy, equality, fairness and respect.

## 'Naming' elder abuse in the UK

Blumer (1971) suggested that social problems, far from being objective 'facts', become named as such through a process of collective definition. To situate and analyse policy responses to a social problem, it is necessary to understand the construction of the 'matter of concern' to which policy is responding. Different layers of meaning are nested in ways in which a problem is viewed, and in its underlying ideology. Atkinson (2000) observed that whether or not a situation is regarded as a political (or social) problem depends on the narrative in which it is discussed. Social issues that become defined as a problem are:

> ... rarely self-evidently problems as such. For an aspect of the real to be defined as a 'problem' it needs first of all to be constructed and articulated as an object amenable to diagnosis and treatment in and through a narrative discourse which carries with it an 'authority', or in Bourdieu's (1991) terms is enunciated by an individual or organization possessing the relevant symbolic capital to make performative utterances, i.e. to develop a narrative which will be 'listened to' and heeded. (Atkinson, 2000, p 214)

Biggs (2001, p 304), drawing on the work of Bourdieu (2000) and Foucault (1980), put it thus:'policies not only respond to social ills, they also consecrate them. They contribute to the constellation of ideas and evidence that create the problem itself'. For older people, the collective creation of elder abuse as a matter of social concern started to take shape in the UK in the 1960s, although as Brammer and Biggs (1998, p 285) had observed 'the British experience shows a relative absence of concern' about elder abuse. In 1965, the Dickensian conditions of mental hospitals (as they were then called) in which some older people lived out their last days had been exposed in a letter to the UK newspaper *The Times*. Signed by ten people, including psychiatrists and academics who formed AEGIS (Aid for the Elderly in Government Institutions), this letter described 'the evil practice in certain hospitals – general as well as mental hospitals – of stripping geriatric patients of their spectacles, dentures, hearing aids and other civilised necessities, and of leaving them to vegetate in utter loneliness and idleness' (Robb, 1967, p xiii). The first attributed UK reference to what he called 'granny battering' was by Baker (1975). In North America, Butler (1975) had named the 'battered old person syndrome'.

In 1988, the British Geriatrics Society convened the first UK conference on the abuse of older people, attended by 400 professionals including those from the British Association of Social Workers, Carers National Association and Age Concern (BGS, 2005). Following this, the document *Abuse of Elderly People: Guidelines for Action for those Working with Elderly People* was published, to assist staff to identify older people who may be abused, or at risk, in domestic situations (Decalmer and Glendinning, 1993). In 1990, the UK Department of Health commissioned the Age Concern Institute of Gerontology to produce the first UK scoping study of elder abuse. This 'exploratory study' described the 'stirrings at the grass roots' about elder abuse, and identified key players (just twelve) involved in this work in England and Wales (McCreadie 1991, pp 2, 15). These were professionals working in medicine, health and social work. It was largely professionals, or the part of the 'aging enterprise' (Estes, 1979) who drove the issue of elder abuse onto policy-makers' agendas (Slater 2002).

McCreadie's (1991) study drew attention to a lack of guidelines, policies and procedures in this area; her report's six-page reference list identified the main UK and US published research – the latter far exceeded the former. When she updated her report five years later, McCreadie described the development of interest in elder abuse as an 'explosion' (McCreadie, 1996, p 1). Professional concern was largely focused at this time on the treatment of older people, and care-giver stress. In 1992, the Social Services Inspectorate published *Confronting Elder Abuse* (SSI,1992), followed in 1993 by *No Longer Afraid* on safeguarding older people in domestic settings (SSI, 1993). Thus it was in the 1990s that the coalescence of policy and professional concerns in the UK developed into the social policy 'naming' of elder abuse as a social problem (Penhale and Kingston, 1997). In the US this occurred a decade earlier when 'elder abuse "came of age" as a recognized health and social problem during the 1980s' (Anetzberger, 2005, p 1).

Even so, development of local policies on abuse of older people within the UK in the 1990s remained *ad hoc*, and no national policy guidance was published in either England or Wales until 2000. Elder abuse periodically attracted media attention, if only for the day on which a story or scandal was reported. Then, as now, these typically concerned institutional care of older people. Such scandals resulted in inquiries, reports and the ritual of 'learning of lessons' (Stanley and Manthorpe, 2004); with media coverage generally 'superficial and transient' (Podnieks et al, 2010, p 139). As the final report of the Public Inquiry into serious failings at the Mid Staffordshire NHS Foundation Trust in England observed:

> The experience of many previous inquiries is that, following the initial courtesy of a welcome and an indication that its recommendations will be accepted or viewed favourably, progress in implementation becomes slow or non-existent. (Francis Report, 2013a, p 24)

The findings of the Francis Report, and the ethical and moral issues for older people its findings raised, are discussed further in Chapters Eight and Nine.

## Defining elder abuse

Defining elder abuse has not proved straightforward, either for the 'aging enterprise', or policy-makers or legislators, and definitions and descriptions of abuse used by older people have not always corresponded to those used by professionals or researchers (Brandl and Cook-Daniels, 2002; Mowlam et al, 2007), or have failed to address the significance of the social context within which abuse occurs (Dow and Joosten, 2012). It has been argued that the 'vain search for definitions' (Brogden and Nijhar, 2000, p 40) and dichotomous categorisation of 'abuse/not abuse' can be diversionary or distracting in terms of promoting the citizenship rights of all older people (Wilson, 2004).

Nonetheless it is the case that definition and prevalence data carry unique weight in mobilising public concern and resources to support older people who have been mistreated, and in assisting their access to criminal justice systems.

As at 2013, the term 'elder abuse' had no legal definition in England and Wales (CPS, 2008). National adult protection policy guidance first introduced in England and Wales (DH, 2000; NAfW, 2000) did not differentiate elder abuse from abuse of other vulnerable adults. (This is discussed in Chapter Four, which considers the development of adult protection or adult safeguarding policy in the UK.) Elder abuse was located in that guidance within a policy framework of protection for all vulnerable adults, where a vulnerable adult was defined as a 'person aged 18 years or over who is or may be unable to take care of himself or herself, or unable to protect himself or herself against significant harm or serious exploitation'. Abuse was defined as 'a violation of an individual's human and civil rights by any other person or persons', and national policy guidance in England and Wales referred to five categories of abuse: physical, sexual, psychological, financial and neglect (DH, 2000, pp 8–9; NAfW, 2000, p 14). The World Health Organization (WHO), on the other hand, defined elder abuse as a 'single or repeated act or lack of appropriate action occurring within any relationship where there is an expectation of trust, which causes harm or distress to an older person' (WHO, 2002). This definition emphasises a relationship and an abuse of *trust*. The term 'elder maltreatment' is one used more in Europe and North America; defined by the WHO as 'physical, sexual, mental and/or financial abuse and/or neglect of people aged 60 years and older' (WHO, 2011, p viii).

All definitions used internationally include physical abuse; and most include neglect, financial abuse and psychological abuse. Some definitions include sexual abuse under physical abuse, and abandonment within 'neglect'. As Anetzberger (2005) noted, this variety raises a number of questions. What is included, or not, as abuse? Must there be intent for an act of omission or commission to be called abuse? Does elder abuse always require a perpetrator? Who decides if the act is abuse? Should vulnerability of the victim be required in defining abuse? Do the effects, frequency, duration and severity define the problem?

These questions illustrate some controversies and complexities that underlie the lack of an internationally accepted definition of abuse. In their analysis of a selection of elder abuse literature published between mainly 2003 and 2013, Goergen and Beaulieu (2013) identified common elements in principal definitions of elder abuse used internationally. They found consensus that elder abuse: was individually and socially undesirable and caused harm; included acts of omission as well as commission; involved someone other than the victim (hence self-neglect was excluded); was a status offence (it could not be perpetrated against anyone); included different types of action, non-action and effects, such as physical or financial abuse. Unresolved definitional matters include the nature of the victim–perpetrator dyad, for example, whether or not a pre-abuse relationship of trust has to be in place. (Financial scams, for example, are perpetrated by strangers who have elicited a feeling of trust before conning their victim out of money or possessions.) Goergen and Beaulieu (2013) concluded that the concept of elder abuse has two specific characteristics. First, it is connected to particular perpetrator–victim relationships, in a private or paid, professional sphere where the perpetrator has assumed a responsibility (or duty) towards the older person, who has placed trust in the other. This includes those with criminal intent who create a façade of trust. Second, the potential for neglect presupposes an elevated vulnerability of the older person; this is linked to being older but old age does not equate to vulnerability. Vulnerability is a key variable; it increases the risk of elder abuse and may compromise an older person's ability to deal with it. The authors concluded that discussion of conceptual clarity and measures of vulnerability were required in elder abuse research (Goergen and Beaulieu, 2013).

These issues and this 'definitional disarray' (Pillemer and Finkelhor, 1988, p 52) are far from simple matters of semantics or standardisation. They are directly relevant to attempts to measure the prevalence and incidence of elder abuse, because of their implications for survey design, survey instruments and interview questions and topic guides (Goergen and Beaulieu, 2013). Words can be powerful signifiers of how acts of commission or omission are interpreted by professionals such as nurses, doctors and social workers, the police, adult safeguarding and legal systems, and hence the response made to the abused older person. Words frame understandings and responses: 'financial abuse' for example, is not a term used to describe crimes like stealing, theft or fraud committed against anyone who has not been labelled a 'vulnerable adult' or an 'adult at risk'. Physical harm to any citizen would be called assault or grievous bodily harm (depending on the act, severity or circumstances), not 'physical abuse'. The 'euphemisation' (Bourdieu, 1977) of the term 'abuse' with its appended epithets, can serve to soften and sanitise understanding, and the response and support offered to an older person. It may pave the way to 'welfarist' services rather than criminal justice responses to acts which, if committed against anyone else, would be labelled a crime (Williams, 1993).

## Prevalence of elder abuse

Elder abuse prevalence rates are similar to those of child abuse but are much less likely to be reported (Stolee et al, 2012). As noted above, the size of a social problem matters if resources are to be secured and supportive responses to it developed. The first decade of the 21st century saw a proliferation in the number of prevalence surveys completed internationally, including the UK (O'Keefe et al, 2007); Ireland (Naughton et al, 2010), US (Laumann et al, 2008); Spain (Iborra, 2008), Israel (Eisikovits et al, 2004), New York (Lachs and Berman, 2011). One of the first was a stratified random sample of the prevalence of physical abuse, psychological abuse and neglect reported by 2020 people aged 65 and over living in the community in the Boston Massachusetts area of the US (Pillemer and Finkelhor, 1988). The reported rate of abuse in three categories investigated was 3.2%. In Canada, a national random sample using similar methods found a rate of 4% of those over 65 reported experiencing maltreatment since the age of 65 (Podnieks, 1992). In Ireland, the national elder abuse prevalence survey (which used the same operational definitions of mistreatment, abuse and inter-personal violence and similar methodology as the UK survey reported below), found an overall rate of mistreatment (physical, psychological, financial, sexual abuse and neglect) of 2.2% (Naughton et al, 2010).

The 2007 UK study surveyed the prevalence of abuse within the previous year among 2,100 people aged 66 and over living in private households across the four UK nations (O'Keefe et al, 2007). People living in care homes did not take part, neither did older people whose mental capacity or ill health would prevent participation in interview. There were no proxy interviews. Abuse by strangers was not surveyed. A rate of 2.6% of abuse was reported in relationships where there was 'an *expectation* of trust, namely family, friends and care workers'; when neighbours and acquaintances were included along with those in a '*position* of trust', the reported rate of abuse within the previous year was 4% (O'Keeffe et al, 2007, p 17. Emphases added).

The conflation of '*expectation* of trust' with '*position* of trust' was not explained in the UK prevalence report; it presented an intriguing elision of understandings, the clarity and distinction of which, *from an older person's point of view,* was unclear. The difference in the impact of abuse perpetrated by, say, a neighbour providing informal care whom the elder may see several times a day, and a paid care worker doing intermittent shifts, is opaque; the more so as the report went on to comment on the difficulty of distinguishing care provided by 'friends' from 'acquaintances' or 'neighbours' (O'Keeffe et al, 2007, p

17). Qualitative findings from survey interviews with 36 older people contacted as a linked part of the UK prevalence survey acknowledged the difficulties presented in using researchers' definitions rather than older people's experiences of abuse. The authors of this qualitative report concluded that the definitions of elder mistreatment and of perpetrators used lacked clarity for the older people they interviewed (Mowlam et al, 2007). It is not unreasonable to assume that this lack of clarity may have affected rates of reporting.

In terms of its findings, the UK prevalence survey found neglect was the most common form of abuse reported. Women were more much more likely (5.4%) to report abuse within the year prior to interview than men (2.1%). Prevalence was higher when respondents reported declining health, poor health, living with a limiting long-term illness, poor quality of life or depression, or feeling lonely in the week prior to interview. The risk of abuse increased with age, living alone, receiving services, being in poor health; being an older woman; and being a woman who was divorced, separated or lonely (O'Keefe et al, 2007). The headline abuse prevalence figures in the UK of 2.6% and 4% referred to abuse *only* in the previous year. When respondents were asked about physical, sexual and financial abuse (not about neglect or psychological abuse) since the age of 65, rather than just in the previous year, the abuse prevalence rates were between 50% and 100% higher depending on the types of abuse (O'Keefe et al, 2007, p 68).

Higher rates of reported abuse were found by Cooper et al (2008) in their systematic review of studies measuring prevalence of elder abuse and neglect, reported by older people themselves, or by family and professional care-givers, or investigated using objective measures. Of 49 studies meeting the authors' inclusion criteria, just seven used measures that had been assessed for reliability and validity. In these, 6% of older people in general population studies reported what Cooper et al (2008) described as significant abuse in the previous month, and 5.6% of couples reported physical violence in their relationship in the previous year. In research using valid instruments, almost 'a quarter of vulnerable older people dependent on carers reported significant psychological abuse'; and one fifth reported neglect (Cooper et al, 2008, p 158). Over one third of family care-givers reported perpetrating significant abuse of the cared-for older person; 5% reported physical abuse towards care recipients with dementia in the previous year. A total of 16% of care home staff reported committing psychological abuse; over four fifths had observed abuse occurring but rates of abuse reported to care home management or adult protection services were low – just 1–2%. From this systematic review, the authors concluded that one in four older people were at risk of abuse, only a small proportion of which was currently detected; and that, critically, older people, care-givers and families were willing to report elder abuse and should be asked about it routinely (Cooper et al, 2008).

## Risk factors of elder abuse

Because of international differences in the definition of abuse, variations in what prevalence surveys have included or excluded from survey questions, and the scientific quality of some studies, the identification of risk factors – whether of the perpetrator, the older person or the setting – requires some caution. That said, the risk of elder abuse appears to increase with disability, cognitive impairment and dependence (WHO, 2011); there is now consistent evidence that having dementia places an older person at risk of mistreatment.

As with other types of family violence, living with others at home can be risky for an older person. Risk factors of elder abuse include situational or contextual factors, such as living arrangements. Older people who live with another, or others, in a shared domestic dwelling are at greater risk of abuse than older people who live alone (Pillemer and Finkelhor, 1988; Lachs et al, 1997). Living with the perpetrator increases the risk of abuse (WHO, 2011): tensions of living with another person can escalate into abuse (Wolf and Pillemer, 1989). Being connected to the community and having positive experiences of life seem to prevent or mitigate the impacts of abuse (WHO, 2011); while social isolation, implicated in the risk of other types of family violence such as the sexual abuse of children, increases the risk of elder abuse. Weak social networks, and impoverished social capital, significantly increase the risk of mistreatment (Wolf and Pillemer, 1989; Lachs et al, 1994).

If prevalence rates of elder abuse are generally in the 2–4% region then, as noted, older people living with dementia are at greater risk of mistreatment than those without a cognitive impairment. This was found to be the case in Lachs et al's (1997) longitudinal study, which did not use care-giver accounts. Earlier research of mistreatment by paid or unpaid carers of people with dementia also found this to be the case; Coyne et al (1993) had reported 12% of care-givers admitted physical abuse of an older person, while Homer and Gilleard (1990) found 14% of care-givers reported physical abuse of older people with dementia in respite care.

Carer stress and anxiety associated with caring for a family member living with dementia are strongly associated with a carer reporting they have mistreated the older person. Beach et al (2005) found potentially harmful behaviour by a care-giver towards the older person they cared for was more likely in care relationships where one spouse cared for another, and where care-receivers had greater needs for care. Cooper and her colleagues found family carers of an older person with dementia were likely to report they behaved 'abusively' towards the older person. (Very few of these reports were at a level that professionals would consider abusive, that is, as requiring intervention under adult protection procedures.) Abusive behaviour by the family carer was associated with, for example, carers' experience of anxiety and depression, the number of hours they spent caring, and being abused themselves by the person with dementia (Cooper, 2013).

Factors that may be associated with increased risk of perpetration of elder abuse include the perpetrator's history of mental illness, particularly depression; (Wolf and Pillemer, 1988; Pillemer and Finkelhor, 1989; Homer and Gilleard, 1990; Coyne et al, 1993); drug and alcohol misuse by the perpetrator (Wolf and Pillemer, 1989; Anetzberger et al, 1994) and the perpetrator having a history of physical violence against others (WHO, 2011). In the Beach et al (2005) study referred to above, potentially harmful care-giving behaviour was likely when care-givers were more cognitively impaired, reported more physical symptoms, or were at risk of suffering clinical depression.

Inter-personal violence and abuse of an older person may, of course, have been an established feature of relationship, personal or family dynamics. To consider the risk of abuse over the life course, a Canadian survey using a purposive sample of 267 people aged 55 and over, examined the prevalence of perceptions of abuse at three life stages: up to the age of 17; between the ages of 18 and 25; and between 5 and 12 months prior to the date respondents were interviewed. Psychological abuse was most frequently reported by people who had experienced abuse at different life stages. The authors concluded that a childhood history of abuse among the respondents surveyed 'had a deciding influence on later mistreatment, over and above what happens in later life' (McDonald and Thomas, 2013, p 1235). Similarly, in Germany, secondary analysis of the national survey on violence against women aged 50–86 years, found women who had experienced violence during childhood, and non-partner physical or sexual violence after the age of 16, had a higher likelihood of experiencing current partner violence (Stöckl et al, 2012).

## Institutional abuse and mistreatment of older people

The risk of abuse to vulnerable older people relying on institutional care of one sort or another has been the subject of many inquiries, reports and periodic expressions of 'disgust' by elected politicians (for example, by the then Conservative Secretary of State for Health in England, reported in *The Guardian*, 2012). In the academy, McDonald et al (2012) reviewed research to identify gaps in knowledge and methodology in the study of institutional abuse. In their search of 22 databases for qualitative or quantitative research published between 1998 and 2008 (seminal research conducted prior to 1998 was also included), these authors identified 49 studies reported in English, and 20 in French that met their inclusion criteria. They found larger nursing homes were associated with higher rates of abuse allegations. In Israel, Cohen et al (2010) surveyed 71 older people who had been screened in two hospital units for abuse, after admission from the long-term care facilities they used. Of these, 31% reported some mistreatment, mostly disrespectful behaviour. Signs of abuse, mostly neglect, were detected in over 22% of the sample. Greater dependency on others for help with activities of daily living was significantly associated with reported abuse, as were increasing age, being female, and having poor nutritional or health status. The authors found that direct questioning mainly disclosed examples of disrespectful behaviours and humiliation, while assessment of signs of abuse was more sensitive to cases of neglect.

Similarly, Cooper and her colleagues in their qualitative study involving focus groups with 36 paid carers working in four London care homes, found carers disclosed many examples of poor care, and situations with 'potentially abusive consequences' were a common occurrence (Cooper et al, 2013, pp 1, 7). These included older people waiting too long to be helped with personal care, institutional regimes that mitigated against a carer having longer than a few minutes to help an older person eat a meal (hence the older person had barely a couple of mouthfuls of food); carers not having a moment to sit down and chat. Others were more blatant mistreatment: threats; dangerous lifting and moving practices; improper restraint (Cooper, 2013). Reports of deliberate abuse were rare. The researchers judged that lack of resources, under-staffing and under-resourcing of elder care, underlay many of the examples care workers gave. An important finding of this study was the preparedness of paid carers to provide examples of institutional poor care they had witnessed. This suggests more assertive engagement with paid workers, to get a routine conversation going about sub-optimal practice, could encourage more constructive challenge to poor care, in real time and not weeks or years later when abusive institutional cultures have taken root.

Although there is evidence of positive health and social outcomes when people receive dignified care (Tadd et al, 2011), being treated with dignity and respect when receiving acute hospital care in England or Wales is not something all older people have been able to rely upon. Tadd et al (2011) reported a marked variation in the level and provision of dignified care for older people in 16 wards in four acute hospital Trusts in England and Wales. Forty older people recently discharged from hospital and 25 of their unpaid carers contributed views to this study, as did 79 frontline NHS staff and 32 NHS middle and senior managers. The researchers also carried out non-participant observation on hospital wards.

The findings painted a dismal picture of what older people might expect if they could not avoid acute hospital admission. Acute hospital ward routines could be frenetic with no time or opportunity for engagement with the patient. Encounters of healthcare staff with the older person could be patronising and disrespectful. The dignity of care provided varied depending on the time of day, and who was in charge and on duty. Influences on dignified care included environmental factors such as: mixed sex wards; staff who were not trained or educated in the care of older people; the perpetual movement of people within and across wards; and a view held by some working in the NHS that older people should not be in acute hospital care anyway. Features that promoted dignified care were hardly remarkable: signage (what and who was where); safe walking spaces; communal areas for having a chat with other people; space between beds (so that confidential medical discussions were not overheard); courtesy and respect shown by NHS staff; ward managers who fostered collaborative work; and senior Trust managers who demonstrated genuine involvement in the quality of dignified care provided to vulnerable people who used hospitals they were paid to run.

Tadd et al (2011) concluded that motivation of the majority of hospital staff to represent patients' interests was compromised by systemic and organisational factors that included the management focus on measurable performance indicators; a perceived culture of blame; and local cultures on some wards. On the other hand, key elements of dignified care were the human, relational qualities of kindness and compassion: respectful communication; a respect for privacy; promoting the older person's autonomy and a sense of control,; and addressing basic human needs (to eat, drink, eliminate) with sensitivity (Tadd et al, 2011; Calnan et al, 2013). None of these, of course, costs money.

Neither are they numerical targets or performance indicators that staff are expected to meet.

## 'Domestic violence grown old'

The occurrence of violence in intimate personal relationships of older people, and especially domestic abuse suffered by men, have not been focal features of research, policy or practice in elder abuse, certainly in the UK. It is the case, paradoxically, that while there are data indicating the extent of domestic violence and intimate partner violence involving older people, public and policy awareness and the development of service responses have largely remained oblivious to 'domestic violence grown old' (Vinton, 1991).

There is no standardised definition of intimate partner violence, in general, or of that of older people, specifically. Band-Winterstein and Eisikovits (2009) derived a definition from the work of others, as follows:

> Interpersonal violence (attack) is a nonlegitimate forceful tactic, intentionally employed by one party (action) to cause physical and/or psychological harm to the other (consequence), in the attempt to control a situation. It includes the use of physical force an infliction of injuries as well as emotional and sexual abuse, sexual harassment, and financial exploitation. The definition focuses attention on the acts of violence themselves, along with the intention of the perpetrator, the experience of the victim, the consequences of the violence, the patterns of violent episodes, and the overall climate of the relationship. (Band-Winterstein and Eisikovits, 2009, p 165)

This definition identifies *intentionality* and *control* as key features of intimate partner violence. It does not indicate the relationship of the perpetrator and the abused, or the domestic arrangements where abuse may occur. This differentiates intimate partner violence from elder abuse where acts of omission as well as commission can be abusive if they result in significant harm.

In terms of prevalence of domestic abuse in older age, the European Commission-funded five country (Austria; Belgium; Finland; Lithuania; Portugal) AVOW (prevalence of abuse and violence against older women) study found over 28% of 2,880 women (aged between 60 and 97 living in private households) reported some kind of violence.

Emotional abuse was the most common form of violence, and the perpetrator in most cases (apart from neglect) was the woman's partner or spouse (Luoma et al, 2011). Bonomi et al (2007) found similar levels of intimate partner violence reported in their random sample of 370 English-speaking women aged 65 and over who used a particular healthcare system in the US. In this study, lifetime partner violence was estimated at 26.5%. Over 18% of the women experienced physical and sexual violence; almost 22% experienced non-physical violence, such as threats or controlling behaviour. The proportion of women rating the abuse as severe ranged from over 39% (forced sex or sexual contact) to 71% (threats). Only 3% of the women had been asked by a healthcare practitioner about physical or sexual violence by an intimate partner since the age of 18.

If domestic violence in older age has received relatively little public attention, then rape and sexual assault of older women, or men, remain generally invisible. The nature, extent, prevalence and incidence of sexual assault of older women is largely hidden and thus unreported (Jeary, 2004), for reasons that include fear, denial, ageism, or societal myths about sexual assault (for example, that only young, 'attractive' women are at risk of attack). In a US study, Baker et al (2009b) identified risk factors in the living situations of 198 older women, aged between 50 and 98, who had presented to emergency services following alleged sexual assault. Of these women (where data were available), 58 lived in an institution; 70 in their own home; and 21 women were homeless. The researchers found that risk factors in the living arrangements of the women may combine with their particular vulnerabilities to increase the risk of their sexual assault. Women who lived in a domestic setting or who were homeless reported coercion by overt or threatened physical violence (for example, being hit, choked, kicked, punched). Women living in an institution were more likely to report coercion through the abuse of authority. Older women were more likely to be vulnerable to sexual assault if they had a temporary or permanent disability, and in most cases they knew the alleged offender (Baker et al, 2009b).

The feminist discourse and analysis that have driven the development of public awareness and statute on domestic violence have typically been lacking in elder abuse (Penhale 2003). To trace a theoretical path between the elder abuse and domestic violence perspectives, Band-Winterstein and Eisikovits (2010) analysed interview material from some of their previous work, along with in-depth interviews with 25 older Jewish women subject to violence at the hands of their partners. They found, first, that the body was central to the way older women remembered experiences of being beaten, violated or humiliated.

Second, the women measured time as their time away from death, not birth. A central theme of the spatial experience of these women was limitation and constriction due to age, and physical and social constraints that lead to a static experience of space, experienced as a limitation on freedom, a powerless sense of rage, a sense of not belonging, alienation, aloneness, being '... emotionally homeless and undefended, lost in space' (Band-Winterstein and Eisikovits, 2010, p 211).

Band-Winterstein and Eisikovits (2009) found older women subject to intimate partner violence reported feeling trapped in ambiguous situations: on one hand, wanting the violence to stop and, on the other, to maintain the relationship with the abuser. Older women remained in this double-bind because of a social expectation that they should, coupled with the social stigma and shame they feared would be visited upon them if they left. Four themes running through this conflicted torment were found by Buchbinder and Winterstein (2003) in their in-depth interviews with 20 women. First, women experienced themselves in two contradictory ways, as either, or both, heroes or fools for staying in the relationship. Second, the sense of self that had been sacrificed for the sake of the children was apparent. Motherhood had been central defining aspect of their lives but feelings towards the children could be ambivalent, with pride mixed with disappointment and betrayal. Third, women had perceptions of temporal dislocation and loss: of feeling lost in time between the painful past and a trap-like future. The stories of the women could be structured on two dimensions: awareness of their suffering accumulated over many years of violence, and their awareness of the limitations of their chronological age.

In other work on the psychological abuse of older women by an intimate partner, Montminy (2005) interviewed fifteen women aged between 60 and 81 who had experienced psychological violence within marriage in the previous 24 months. All the women lived in the community. The husband's psychological violence fell into categories that included control, denigration, threats, abdication of responsibility, manipulation, blame, harassment, indifference, sulking and infantilisation. Control was the central category, with the incidence of control behaviours increasing at retirement, when the children left home and when husbands experienced a decrease in health status. The violence had started early in the relationship, when the couple were dating or first married. This extended patterning of abuse had long-term destructive consequences for the woman: '... living for several decades with a contemptuous husband can cause a woman to devalue herself, which then makes it difficult for her to act because she feels powerless to take life into her own hands', Montminy observed (2005, p 15).

## Domestic violence or adult protection?

If the 'distinctions between domestic violence and elder abuse are ambiguous and blurred' (Kilbane and Spira, 2010, p 165), the question arises as to whether abused older women are abused elders (an adult protection perspective), or 'battered' women (a domestic violence perspective) (Vinton, 1991). Arbitrary chronological cut-off points can influence public and professional awareness of domestic violence in old age although, as Goergen and Beaulieu (2013) commented, the dynamics of intimate partner violence do not suddenly transform into elder abuse when the victim has their sixtieth birthday.

In the adult protection perspective on domestic violence, intimate partner violence involving older people is regarded as a feature of the wider incidence of elder abuse (Penhale, 1999; 2003), and thus covers a wider range of exploitation. In the second paradigm, the domestic violence perspective, most literature has been concerned with younger women. Some earlier clinical research (for example, Davis, 2002) has not found a common profile of old or young women subject to domestic violence. Harbison questioned if feminism had been concerned about older women: older women in Harbison's (2008) study largely stayed in long-term abusive relationships because they believed no one would believe them, or be sympathetic. Older women typically saw themselves as having few or no other choices available. They did not have enough cash to leave, their lives had been spent home-making and child-rearing. Their not walking away from that could be viewed by others as collaboration with their abuser – a distortion of the lived experience of these older women that implied a choice that they seldom identified as theirs to exercise, as is discussed further below.

Whether or not domestic violence in older age is understood in one perspective or another is not just a matter of taxonomy. Understandings and perceptions shape responses. Band-Winterstein and Eisikovits (2010) noted that the two perspectives, adult protection and domestic violence, were not integrated. Neither took older people voices into account. The drive for each had come from different interests: in elder abuse from health and social care professionals; in domestic violence, from feminists. This dichotomy has led to either a focus on age and vulnerability, with a welfare or medicalised response in the elder abuse perspective; or a push for statute, policy and social justice in the domestic violence perspective. Band-Winterstein and Eisikovits (2010) considered both perspectives homogenised the issue of older women who were beaten and abused by an intimate partner: the elder abuse paradigm by merging them within a cohort of vulnerable older people;

and the domestic violence perspective by rendering age invisible. The elder abuse perspective acknowledged spouses were mostly the perpetrators, but 'masks the problem of domestic violence through its focus on caregiving, risk and vulnerability' (Montminy, 2005, p 5).

Rather than the is-it-elder-abuse-or-domestic-violence dichotomy, Yan and Chan (2012) have suggested that intimate partner violence involving older people is a complex phenomenon linked with other manifestations of domestic violence, for example, child abuse, elder abuse and other intra-familial violence. Their survey of a population representative sample of older couples in Hong Kong found the characteristics of victims of domestic violence in older age were more often 'younger' older people with a criminal record, a low level of social support and who had a substance misuse problem, and who had grown up witnessing family violence. Yan and Chan (2012) came to the view that this should be treated as a distinct category of family violence rather than being subsumed under either an adult protection or domestic violence perspective.

## Domestic violence through the life course: 'choice' laid bare

How continuous intimate partner violence is experienced through the lifecourse is likely to shift over time. In their qualitative study, Band-Winterstein and Eisikovits (2009) used a lifespan perspective to explore the effects of violence on the women at every stage of life. Exploring the experiences of twenty mixed-sex couples in Israel (forty older people aged between 60 and 84) who had lived with domestic violence through adult life, Band-Winterstein and Eisikovits (2009) identified four conceptual 'clusters' of living in violence over time.

In one cluster, where violence was alive and active, different types of violence of varying degrees of severity were perpetrated on the woman by the man. At various points, this violence had been directed to the children, not just the mother. This heavy load of conflict continued into older age; the authors observed that 'such effects are usually conducive to an ecology of terror associated with emotions, such as fear, repression, humiliation, shame and anxiety' (Band-Winterstein and Eisikovits, 2009, p 170). A second cluster, 'violence in the air' manifested in continual conflict and threats directly aimed at the children, and covertly at the woman. A third cluster, 'more of the same but different', involved long-term physical violence, in older age transformed into other forms of violence (emotional, financial) but with the threat of physical violence always present. In the fourth cluster, 'violence to the end', physical violence to the woman continued but increased to the end of life. The authors concluded that there was no empirical support to suggest that violence 'ages out' or disappeared as women became older: '… the violence always remains experientially in the present' and '… acts as a barricade between the past, present, and future, which impairs [older women] from placing time limits on violent events' (Band-Winterstein and Eisikovits, 2009, p 177). In this, intimate partner violence had a cumulative dimension, with the woman's suffering and terror increasing as the result of long-term entrapment. The manifestations of violence and control may shift but were experienced continuously: terror perpetuated itself.

In reality, the 'you've made your bed so lie on it' cliché can possess enormous power to maintain the suffering of an older woman abused by an intimate partner or spouse. Older women are not just young women who've lived a bit longer. Socialisation, education, economic activity levels are all profoundly influenced by history, and the cultural and political contexts of the time of birth and experiences through the lifecourse. When they entered the workforce for the first time, women born before the 1950s in the UK will not have had any statutory protection from losing their job if they married, or from being sacked if they became pregnant. They had no statutory right to equal pay with their male counterparts doing the same job. It was not until the 1970s that women won legal rights to return to work after having a child, and the right to keep a job after marriage. These landmark historic markers of social justice were not part of the landscape of life of women born in the first half of twentieth century UK, where abortion was illegal, and rape within marriage lawful.

To understand the impact and imprint of the lifecourse on how a woman might see herself and her life options requires a degree of humility and empathy that a vacuous chanting in policy discourse and professional practice of the 'choice' mantra somehow doesn't quite grasp. For older women who are beaten, held in contempt, bullied and controlled by their life partner, the death of every friend, the onset of new disability or deteriorating health, may mean another lock on the door of their life: the chimera of their 'choice' laid bare.

## Disclosing and responding to elder abuse

While the exercise of 'choice' to leave domestic violence may be hard, and some older people find it difficult to disclose abuse by an intimate partner or spouse, there is evidence that elders who are being abused or mistreated will, if asked, tell someone (Cooper et al, 2008). Ockleford et al (2003) reporting on interviews with their opportunity sample of 149 older women in the UK, Italy and Republic of Ireland, found just under one quarter reported a type of abuse lasting years, with a 'substantial proportion' reporting multiple types of abuse (Ockleford et al, 2003, p 1457). A total of 76% (26 women) disclosed the abuse to someone; very few said they found this helpful. Older women experiencing domestic abuse were simply not visible to professional and voluntary support services: no demographic data on age or gender of service users, or reasons for older women contacting the services, were recorded.

The 2007 UK prevalence study strongly indicated the levels of domestic abuse older people were experiencing *and* that these were reported to others. This pattern of disclosure held with other types of abuse, for example, neglect and financial abuse. Of those reporting abuse in the previous year 70% had told someone such as a family member or friend, a health professional or social worker. Only 6% reported abuse to the police. It was estimated that just 3% of reports of abuse by older people reached adult protection services, although the survey did not ask what happened after that reporting (O'Keefe et al, 2007).

What happens after disclosure would depend in part on the experience and training health or social care professionals had received and their awareness of elder abuse and obligations upon them to report it. McCreadie et al (2000), in surveys of GPs in Tower Hamlets and Birmingham in England conducted before the national adult protection guidance *No Secrets* was implemented in England (DH, 2000), found just under half had 'diagnosed' (the authors' word) elder abuse in previous year. The strongest factor predicting this GP recognition of elder abuse was GP awareness of five or more risk factors for elder abuse.

In their systematic review, Cooper et al (2008) found professionals consistently underestimated prevalence of elder abuse. One third of professionals in this meta-analysis had detected a case of elder abuse in the previous year; about half of detected cases were reported. Professionals who had received training were no more likely to detect abuse than those who had not, but they were more likely to report it. The majority of professionals did not know that most abuse did not involve major injuries.

In a later study of the effectiveness of an educational intervention designed to measure the knowledge about managing and detecting elder abuse, Cooper et al asked 40 trainee psychiatrists in two London NHS Trusts how often they considered, asked about, detected and managed elder abuse; and inquired as to their confidence in doing this, both before and three months after a brief group education session (Cooper et al, 2012). Immediately after the educational intervention, participants' knowledge of abuse increased and they identified more abuse and potential abuse. Three months later, they reported having more confidence in managing abuse and they considered it more frequently when seeing older people and their carers, but *they did not ask older people and their carers about abuse any more often than they had pre-intervention.* The education intervention had not resulted three months later in these trainee psychiatrists raising the topic more often with patients and their families. Hence, while family carers appeared willing to give examples of mistreating those they cared for, professionals in this research seemed reluctant to open up the area for discussion, and thence to consider what improved and enhanced support might be needed by these family carers.

## Older male victims of domestic violence

The needs and circumstances of men who are abused by an intimate life partner remains an under-reported and under-researched area. If professional and public awareness of domestic violence in older age is low, and the availability of suitable and acceptable support impoverished, then the experiences and voices of abused older men have been largely absent. Abuse of older men has been described as a 'taboo' subject (Pritchard 2007, p 109), although it has received occasional, intermittent research and practice attention (for example, Pritchard, 2002; Kosberg, 2005; 2007). Thompson et al (2007, p 146) were critical of a lack of consideration given to what they called the 'upstream' determinants of older men's risks of abuse and neglect, that is, gender issues inherent in the mistreatment of men and the gendered policy and social context within which abuse is perpetrated. Abuse and violence perpetrated against older men may not be on the commissioning radar for government-funded research. For example, research carried out in three areas of England for the UK Home Office on the abuse of typically under-researched and hard-to-reach victims of domestic violence (including heterosexual, gay, bi-sexual and transgendered men) did not provide data on age (Hester et al, 2012). In Canada, Poole and Rietschlin's (2012) secondary data analysis of two government surveys found over 15% of reported cases of physical or sexual domestic violence concerned people aged over 55. The prevalence rate of abuse by a former or current partner for men and women aged 60 and over was 6.8% (considerably higher than a 2–4% elder abuse rate discussed above). Poole and Rietschlin (2012) found the risk of being emotionally or physically abused was not different for men and women over 60. Even so, it is the case that what is known by practitioners, professionals, policy-makers and researchers about the incidence and characteristics of abuse and mistreatment of older men is, as yet, limited.

## Impact of elder abuse on the older person

The impacts on older people who are abused and mistreated are stark. Violence shortens lives. Violence has a profound, negative impact on the health and wellbeing of older people (Walsh et al, 2007). Violence results in a poorer quality of life and increased morbidity (Lachs et al, 1998; Lachs et al, 2002; Lachs and Pillemer, 2004). Violence can hasten death. Baker et al (2009a) undertook a retrospective study of 169,676 woman living in the community aged 50–79 and enrolled on one of two women's health studies, who responded to baseline abuse questions. Total mortality was measured between 1993 and 2005. The prior year self-reported abuse prevalence rate was 11.3%. Women who reported physical abuse had the highest age-adjusted mortality rate, followed by women who reported both abuse types. Abuse independently predicted mortality risk after controlling for age, education and ethnicity. The authors concluded that community-dwelling middle-aged and older women who reported physical, verbal, or both types of abuse in the previous year, had significantly higher adjusted mortality risk than women who did not report abuse. In Europe, the AVOW study also found a significant association between abuse and violence perpetrated against the 2880 women it surveyed in five countries, with impaired physical health, poor mental health and loneliness (Luoma et al, 2011). Other research, whether large or small-scale, has reported similar findings, for example, Fisher et al, 2011; Lafferty et al, 2012.

## Support to older people who have been abused

Most abuse older people experience is not reported into adult protection or safeguarding systems, and public awareness of elder abuse may be skewed by periodic media flare-ups focused on poor hospital care. In their survey of the knowledge of abuse and neglect among 1,000 adults in the UK, Hussein et al (2007), for example, found people identified care homes and hospitals most commonly as the location for mistreatment, suggesting that elder abuse and violence in domestic settings were less likely to be publicly perceived as such.

Whatever the levels or accuracy of public perceptions of elder abuse, older women and men wanting to stop abuse are faced with where to try to get help. Personal, emotional, practical and legal support and assistance are typically needed by an older person seeking help to stop abuse and mistreatment (Lundy and Grossman, 2004). Meeting affective, practical and legal needs requires significant collaboration between legal and adult protection systems. However, these two paradigms mostly operate on parallel tracks, without integration. Domestic violence workers are seldom trained in issues of ageing or adult protection; nor adult protection workers in domestic violence.

As to sources of support and assistance older people escaping abuse have identified, while family and friends are important, older women subjected to long-term violence may be less likely to confide in others than women for whom the violence had more recent onset (Leisey et al, 2009). Leisey and her colleagues found abused older women they interviewed had trust in healthcare doctors, but not in clergy (who presumably viewed the woman's predicament as God's will). Involving the police was regarded negatively, and leading to more not less trouble. Women wanted information about appropriate outreach and support services, and more information about their legal rights. Leisey et al's (2009) study highlighted the need, from the older person's point of view, for help, support and advice that was integrated across criminal justice and human service systems.

Relatively little research attention has yet been paid to the support needs of older people in black and minority ethnic communities, for example to identify how abuse is understood in different communities. Bowes et al (2012) cautioned against over-assuming the particular significance of cultural differences in the occurrence of elder abuse. They observed that cultural normative differences, for example in the role and social position of women, might be unquestioningly be linked to the risk of harm, while the impact of contextual factors such as poverty and inequality on individuals and families are down-played. Ageism, and a wider devaluing or social denigration of 'being old', may be ignored. Care-giver stress and dysfunctional family dynamics may be overlooked. The social exclusion, marginalisation and poverty suffered by some black and minority ethnic communities are structural, societal problems, rather than artefacts of minority cultural characteristics. Bowes et al (2012) concluded that services to abused older people should be alert to both *differences within* communities, and *similarities across* different communities and groups.

## Evidence about effectiveness of interventions

If older adults seek help to stop abuse and mistreatment, as yet there is little evidence of the effectiveness of various intervention. Most published work is descriptive, observational and uses case studies; there are no meta-analyses and what research is available is not strong science (Daly et al, 2011). Pillemer and his colleagues (2006) identified a number of problems that beset an understanding of the nature, extent and responses to elder abuse. Research may not clearly define its object of study, and many studies are scientifically weakened by an undifferentiated treatment of various types of abuse and neglect. Some research has focused on abuse of an older person living with other people; some on older people living alone or in institutions. Rare are studies that include a control group, or a comparison group. Published research has used a range of methods of greater or lesser scientific strength, including documentary analysis, interviews with care-givers, proxies to older people, surveys of staff. Few studies use reliable or valid measures of the indicators of risk. Retrospective studies may not take account of the timing and duration of events, and their progression over time. They run the risk of introducing bias; for instance, recall bias (interpreting facts or feelings from a later vantage point), or information bias (cannot recall or provide reliable information, problematic for someone with a cognitive impairment).

In their systematic review of elder abuse interventions, Ploeg et al (2009) found only eight studies in 183 articles they examined (from 1,253 potentially relevant identified) met their inclusion criteria: an English-language paper concerned about person aged 60 and over; the intervention was described and addressed physical, psychological and financial abuse, and neglect; it included an assessment of outcomes and was primary research using quantitative methods and a comparison group. This review found evidence about the reoccurrence of abuse after intervention was limited and insufficient evidence to support particular interventions. Where there was evidence, the intervention may have increased rather than decreased the likelihood of reoccurrence. Interventions had no significant effect on the resolution of the abuse. These findings derive from just eight studies; they could be due to methodological differences, or it could be that the intervention groups contained the most intractable cases of abuse.

Thus, at 2013, there was minimal research evidence to support current elder abuse assessment and intervention strategies. Stolee et al (2012) looked at current processes to identify and communicate 'best practices' in elder abuse, including literature and online searches, stakeholder surveys and key informant interviews. They concluded that professionals' efforts to detect elder abuse and respond were hampered by limited access to knowledge, resources and expert consultation. As it is, '[t]he weak evidence base of what works needs to be improved' (WHO, 2011, p ix).

## Ageism, elder abuse and human rights

Awareness of abuse of older people, and its nature and extent are, arguably, predicated on ageist attitudes, responses and reactions to old age itself, and to the frailty, increased dependency and incapacity that may accompany the journey to the end of life. A social and cultural devaluation of growing old and being old underpin ageist attitudes to older people, 'making elder abuse and neglect more tolerable' as Dow and Joosten (2012, p 854) remarked. In their discussion of elder abuse, ageism and human rights discourse, Biggs and Haapala (2013) suggested that elder abuse discourse had typically been located within the private or personal sphere of interpersonal relationships, while that of human rights was conceptualised within the impersonal public sphere, and in the relationship between the person and the state. They suggested that instead of this dichotomy, the personal, interpersonal and impersonal dimensions of elder abuse required reconnection: '[f]or older people to be free of mistreatment the state should create conditions where abuse and neglect need not take place, in other words, where interpersonal relationships do not occur in the context of ageist prejudice' (Biggs and Haapala, 2013, pp 1, 4).

The term 'ageism' itself has generally been attributed to Robert Butler (1975, p 4), who considered 'ageism allows the younger generations to see older people as different than themselves; thus they subtly cease to identify with their elders as human beings'. In this, Butler implied 'younger generations' perceived 'difference' from those older than themselves. This begins to, but does not quite, grasp the pernicious permeation of ageism into self and social identity, a process starkly captured by Nelson (2005, p 207) as 'prejudice against our future feared self'. Bytheway set out a more elaborate description:

1. Ageism is a set of beliefs originating in the biological variation between people and relating to the ageing process.
2. It is in the actions of corporate bodies, what is said and done by their representatives, and the resulting views that are held by ordinary ageing people, that ageism is made manifest.

In consequence of this, it follows that:

a. Ageism generates and reinforces a fear and denigration of the ageing process, and stereotyping presumptions regarding competence and the need for protection.

b. In particular, ageism legitimates the use of chronological age to mark out classes of people who are systematically denied resources and opportunities that others enjoy, and who suffer the consequences of such denigration, ranging from well-meaning patronage to unambiguous vilification. (Bytheway, 1995, p 14, developed from Bytheway and Johnson, 1990)

Here, Bytheway identified some processes, mechanisms and outcomes that result in ageism. First, he suggested ageism originated in 'a set of beliefs' about the ageing process. Second, transmission mechanisms for those beliefs were 'corporate bodies' and those operating within them, whose actions resulted in those views being held by 'ordinary ageing people'. Third, the consequences of the transmission process were fear, denigration, stereotyping; and the use of chronological age, negatively, to apportion resources and opportunities.

Bytheway's 'actions of corporate bodies' cannot adequately portray the complex interpenetration of the minute, casual, intended, unintended, institutionalised manifestations of ageism. Crimes like assault, rape, and theft for example, when committed against an older person may be construed as mistreatment, and dealt with by social services 'concerned to *rectify* problems rather than to *enforce legislation*' rather than through the criminal justice system (Brogden and Nijhar 2000, p 13. Emphasis in original). Awareness of elder abuse in the UK, and recourse to the criminal justice system to safeguard older people, have lagged far behind provision and legal remedies for victims of domestic violence (Filinson 2006). The Crime Prosecution Service (CPS) of England and Wales has acknowledged 'that ageism may provide the backdrop where crimes against older people are tolerated' (CPS, 2008, p 10).

In what may yet come to be labelled 'institutional ageism' is day-to-day practice in health and social care where a person's age may determine the treatment or response they receive, rather than the condition or presenting need they have, irrespective of age. A GP may not be called to a care home when an older person has breathing difficulties until the situation becomes an emergency, which initially it was not. Ageism underpins an inert acceptance that 'old people die anyway', militating against finding out *why*, for example, an older person died of septicaemia. A death certificate can passively record septicaemia as cause of death, without reference to the neglect that caused acute pressure sores, and the subsequent onset of septicaemia (AEA, 2007b).

In April 2012, the medical journal *The Lancet* published an open letter from 13 scholars, journal editors and campaigners who expressed their collective concern at the way in which the health implications of population ageing were misrepresented in the media; in particular, the framing of ageing as negative, as a burden on health, welfare and economic systems. Blame was laid at the door of the trite use of dependency ratios that assumed that anyone over the age of 65 was non-productive – the 'burden' fallacy. Similarly, the authors criticised the uncritical use of disability-adjusted life years to capture the health of a population, which explicitly regard older people as a social and economic burden. They concluded that 'depictions of older people remain stereotyped and generalised, distorting public opinion and skewing policy debates' (Lloyd-Sherlock et al, 2012, p 1295).

Just as negative stereotypes of ageing become internalised by older people (Minichiello et al, 2000), the way health and social care services and professionals work, and what they expect of service users, can powerfully shape the behaviours and responses to them by older people. Non-challenge by an older person to patronising or discourteous forms of address, for example, may be construed as 'old people don't like to complain'. Evidence to the UK parliamentary Joint Committee on Human Rights (JCHR), found this reflected the powerlessness of the older person, relative to service systems that operate to *condition* passivity in those they are paid to support, treat and care for (AEA, 2007b).

The principles and articles of the European Convention on Human Rights (ECHR), the UN Declaration of Human Rights and the UN Principles for Older Persons (2000) based on it, neatly encapsulate the gulf between those principles and the day-to-day lived reality for many older people. Human rights are fundamental and irreducible rights. They represent moral and ethical principles, founded on a framework of fundamental values: dignity, autonomy, equality, fairness and respect. The state has positive obligations actively to promote and protect rights guaranteed by the ECHR, including duties to prevent breaches of human rights; take measures to deter breaches; to respond to breaches (for example, to investigate); and to provide information to people to explain the risk of their human rights being eroded, if such a risk exists. Hence the 1998 Human Rights Act (HR Act) lays duties on public authorities with responsibility for designing, commissioning or delivering social care to perform those functions in a way that is compatible with the ECHR. The NHS Constitution, for example, requires commissioners and providers of NHS care to respect individuals' human rights (EHRC, 2011).

Ellis (2004), in a study carried out between 2001 and 2003 on welfare providers' attitudes to the 1998 HR Act found a conditional, individualistic, view of human rights existed amongst social workers who worked with older and disabled people in three local authorities in England. Social workers emphasised service users being self-reliant, autonomous and reducing their dependence on services. The views reported were striking for their lack of understanding about the potential of the 1998 Act to safeguard and promote the rights of vulnerable older people, or of the local authorities' statutory duties under the 1998 HR Act.

A decade later, the Equality and Human Rights Commission (EHRC), in its inquiry into older people and human rights in home care in England, found many local authorities had a patchy understanding of their human rights obligations and, moreover, older people and their families had little or no information about what their human rights were (EHRC, 2011). The EHRC (2011, p 79) found some older people endured distressing treatment 'which in certain cases breaches their human rights'; it came to the view that 'current systems for exposing problems are either insufficient or not operating properly'.

The JCHR (2007, paras 66–95) had, in any case, noted before the EHRC (2011) reported, a 'significant distinction' between the 'duty to provide' under the Care Standards Act 2000 of England and Wales (and its associated national minimum standards), and the 'right to receive' under the 1998 HR Act. National minimum standards (NMS) of care in England or Wales had not made explicit that people living in care homes have a legal right to be treated with respect for their dignity – a right conferred by the 1998 HR Act, and enacted before the introduction of NMS. None of the professional codes of practice of doctors, nurses and allied registered professions or social work refers explicitly to human rights principles; yet it is to these codes that professionals are expected to adhere as a condition of registration.

Human rights, arguably, matter most to those who are vulnerable and dependent on public services for healthcare and for meeting basic needs for nourishment, hygiene, and using a lavatory. The JCHR said:

> In our view, elder abuse is a serious and severe human rights abuse which is perpetrated on vulnerable older people who often depend on their abusers to provide them with care. Not only is it a betrayal of trust, it would also, in certain

circumstances, amount to a criminal offence. (JCHR, 2007, p 92)

This chapter has discussed the naming of elder abuse as a matter of social and policy concern in the UK and internationally, and has reviewed some findings of international research on the prevalence and nature of elder abuse, particularly the nature and impacts on an older person (both women and men) of domestic violence in older age. As the UK parliamentary Joint Committee on Human Rights (2007) concluded, elder abuse is an abuse of human rights. Social and professional awareness, and legal and professional responses made to elder abuse, have to be rooted in an inviolable obligation to safeguard the right of older people to live free from violence, harm and exploitation.

# FOUR

# Adult protection, safeguarding and personalisation

The development of policy and practice, and adult protection and safeguarding older people from abuse, has taken place against a backdrop of the unrolling of personalisation and individualisation of care. This chapter considers, first, adult protection legal and policy development in the UK, and the various terms in use to refer to the abuse of adults. Second, features of the development of personalisation policy, in its various guises and manifestations, is considered across the four UK nations. Third, the chapter discusses the impacts on older people of this policy trajectory, and on safeguarding older people and other adults at risk. The uncritical development of personalisation, particularly in England, has not, it will be argued, been unalloyed good news for older people at risk of abuse, or for those who are frail or highly dependent. The description and detail about policy and statute in adult protection and personalisation in the UK in this chapter is intentionally brief, to avoid the inevitable rapid outdating of material as legislation on adult safeguarding and policy on personalisation are variously agreed and implemented across the four UK nations.

## Adult protection law and policy in the UK

Across the UK, statute and national policy to protect older people from abuse have been introduced at different times following devolution of health and social care to the four UK nations in the constitutional settlement of 1998. As at 2013, the UK government at Westminster retained dual responsibilities both as government and parliament for the four nations in some areas of government (for example, defence) and also government and parliament for England. (The shape of these constitutional arrangements may change further as in September 2014, the people of Scotland vote in an referendum to decide if Scotland should become an independent country.) While, in 2013, the UK government retains ultimate authority over devolved institutions, and is responsible for financial allocations and for constitutional legislation (Birrell, 2012), health and social care, and thus adult protection and adult safeguarding, are devolved matters. So although the development of adult safeguarding policy and practice has had similarities across the four nations, its speed and focus have differed since devolution.

To start with, the terms 'adult protection' and 'adult safeguarding' have come to be used differentially across the UK. The Law Commission (2011, p 109) said that safeguarding could be viewed as part of a general approach to be taken by professionals and staff in assessment and service delivery; while the more focused term 'adult protection' may be used to refer to the action taken to intervene and investigate when abuse is suspected. Certainly, 'safeguarding' has come to denote, in Wales and Northern Ireland, particularly, a wider focus on the person's welfare and on the prevention of abuse. In Scotland, the terms 'adult protection' and 'support' are most in use; in England 'adult safeguarding' has gained common currency.

In 2000, England and Wales each introduced national guidance on the protection of vulnerable adults from abuse. *No Secrets*, the national guidance in England, and *In Safe Hands* (Wales) were similar in content and length (the groups advising the development of each country's guidance had had overlapping membership). As noted, both sets of guidance defined 'a vulnerable adult' as a person aged 18 years or over 'who is or may be in need of community care services by reason of mental or other disability, age or illness; and who is or may be unable to take care of him or herself, or unable to protect him or herself against significant harm or exploitation' (DH, 2000, para 2.3; NAfW, 2000, para 7.2). Abuse was also defined in the same way, as 'a violation of an individual's human and civil rights by any other person or persons' (DH, 2000, para 2.5; NAfW, 2000, para 7.4). The five categories of abuse stated in each set of guidance (physical, sexual, psychological, financial or material, neglect) were similar; discriminatory abuse was also included in *No Secrets*. Both sets of guidance contained the same information about a threshold of abuse, stating that 'significant harm' should be taken to include not only ill-treatment (including sexual abuse and forms of ill-treatment that are not physical), but also 'the impairment of, or an avoidable deterioration in, physical or mental health; and the impairment of physical, intellectual, emotional, social or behavioural development' (Lord Chancellor's Department, 1997, para 8.11).

The Law Commission's (2011) report on adult social care law reform in England also considered the terms used to describe the adult at risk of abuse. Its 2010 consultation paper had noted that the use of categories, such as 'vulnerable adults' or 'adults at risk', were attempts to move beyond mental incapacity as a way of defining adults who are or may be unable to protect themselves from abuse or neglect. In noting the stigma and obsolescence of the term 'vulnerable adult', the Law Commission (2011, p 116) proposed use of the term 'adults at risk' instead, which it defined as 'persons who appear to have health or social care needs, including carers (irrespective of whether or not those needs are being met by services); be at risk of harm; and be unable to safeguard themselves as a result of their health or social care needs'.

## Scotland

Scotland was the first UK nation to introduce distinct adult protection legislation. The Adult Support and Protection (Scotland) Act (ASP(S) Act) was passed by the Scottish Parliament on 15 February 2007, received Royal Assent on 21 March 2007, and was implemented from 29 October 2008. The Act provides protection for adults who cannot safeguard their own interests; an 'adult at risk' is defined as a person unable to safeguard their own wellbeing, property, rights or other interests, who is at risk of harm and, because they are affected by disability, mental disorder, illness or physical or mental infirmity, are more vulnerable to being harmed than adults who are not so affected. In this definition, disability, mental ill-health or old age do not automatically mean the person becomes an 'adult at risk'. All three elements of the definition must be met: it is the adult's circumstances *in toto* that are considered (Scottish Government, 2009).

In Scotland, the definition of 'adult at risk' requires an assessment to be made about the risk of harm to the person, and the Act's definition of harm is both detailed and broad. An adult is at risk of harm if another person's conduct is causing or is likely to cause the adult to be harmed; or the adult is engaging or likely to engage in conduct that causes or is likely to cause self-harm. 'Harm' includes all harmful conduct, particularly that causing physical and psychological harm; unlawful conduct that appropriates or adversely affects property, rights or interests (for example, theft, fraud, embezzlement or extortion); and conduct that causes self-harm. Intervention must provide benefit to the adult that could not be reasonably achieved without intervention, and any intervention must be the least restrictive option to the adult's freedom (Scottish Government, 2009).

Significant duties and powers are included in the 2007 ASP(S) Act. These include a duty on councils to make inquiries to establish if action is needed, when it is known or believed that an adult is at risk of harm; and a duty to cooperate with other councils, the NHS and police. Council officers have rights of entry to places where adults are known or believed to be at risk of harm. Under Section 11, a council may apply for an Assessment Order to conduct an interview in private, or a health professional to carry out a medical examination in private. The adult at risk may refuse consent; this may be overridden in certain circumstances. Section 14 of the 2007 ASP(S) Act allows the council to apply to the sheriff for a removal order that, if granted, allows the adult at risk to be moved, within 72 hours, to a specified place. A banning order bans its subject from a specified place and lasts for a period of time up to six months.

The duties and powers contained in the 2007 ASP(S) Act are thus considerable. In the six months following the Act's introduction, the number of adult protection referrals in Scotland doubled and, in the following seven months, once more doubled. De Souza attributed this to the increased awareness of professionals as a result of preparation before the Act's implementation in October 2008. In the year following implementation, just one in five adult protection referrals led to an investigation; de Souza believed this to be because professionals worked with the adult at risk between referral and investigation to offer support and enable individuals to protect themselves from conduct that may be harmful, thus reducing the number of investigations and, consequently, interventions (de Souza, 2011).

## England and Wales

In England and Wales, progress towards placing adult protection on a legislative footing has been slower. During 2013, bills including provisions on the protection of adults at risk of abuse were debated in parliament for England and in the Assembly for Wales: respectively, the Care Bill in England, and the Social Services and Well-being (Wales) Bill. In relation to adult protection, the England Care Bill, introduced in parliament on 9 May 2013, was concerned mostly to place the existing national guidance *No Secrets* on a legislative footing. It did not contain provision (as does Scotland's adult protection legislation, the 2007 ASP(S) Act), to give designated agencies powers of entry if it were believed an adult at risk may be abused; neither did the Care Bill propose a duty on specific agencies to notify a local authority if they believed an adult was at risk of abuse (although these and other matters were subject to lobbying on proposed amendments as the bill proceeded through its various stages). In Wales, the Social Services and Well-being (Wales) Bill introduced on 1 February 2013, proposed, among other matters, a fresh definition of an adult at risk of abuse, duties on public bodies to investigate, report, cooperate and to provide information if they suspected abuse or neglect; and powers of entry for designated officials if abuse is suspected. Both the England and Wales bills proposed adult safeguarding boards should be put on a statutory footing. The actual shape and provisions in adult protection legislation in England and Wales will become clear once the respective statutes have received assent and secondary legislation and procedural guidance are in place. However, at mid-2013, it appeared that neither England nor Wales was minded to adopt wholesale the provisions of the Scotland adult protection legislation.

### Northern Ireland

In Northern Ireland (NI), regional adult protection policy and procedural guidance was issued in 2006, some six years after national guidance in England and Wales. This guidance was produced by Northern Ireland's Regional Adult Protection Forum, whose establishment in 2002, to promote, develop and improve arrangements for the protection of vulnerable adults, had been supported by the Department of Health, Social Services and Public Safety in NI. A familiar set of statements underpinned the implementation of work to protect and safeguard vulnerable adults, including the calls for cooperation between agencies, consistency in response, coordination of action against alleged perpetrators, and information sharing between agencies. The definition of vulnerable adult used was the same as England and Wales, with the explicit addition of an adult 'resident in a continuing care facility' (NHSSB, 2006, p 10).

In March 2010, the NI Department of Health, Social Services and Public Safety set out the structures to support the development of adult safeguarding arrangements. The multi-agency and multi-disciplinary Northern Ireland Adult Safeguarding Partnership (NIASP), which brings together adult safeguarding organisations and interests, was set up along with Local Adult safeguarding Partnerships (LASPs) in each of the health and social care trusts. As at 2013, NIASP's role included the determination of a strategy for safeguarding vulnerable adults, developing and disseminating guidance and operational policies and procedures, and monitoring trends and outcomes in adult safeguarding (HSC, 2012; NIASP, 2012).

## Personalisation and its manifestations

The state of flux surrounding adult social care was acknowledged by the Law Commission in its report of the adult social care law reform project. The Law Commission observed that 'law reform must operate within the broader context of government policy...one key development is the Government policy of personalisation' (Law Commission, 2011, p 4). In England, Wales and Scotland, the introduction of policy on personalisation in one form or another, whether direct payments (DPs), personal budgets (PBs), individual budgets (IBs) or self-directed support (SDS), accelerated from the 1990s (Stevens et al, 2011). The introduction of the 1996 Community Care (Direct Payments Act) by John Major's Conservative government the month before Labour's UK election victory of 1 May 1997, marked a decisive shift in the provision of support to social care users. However, the different policy terms and programmes constituting 'personalisation' have been understood, operationalised and implemented in increasingly divergent ways across the UK.

Searching for a definition of personalisation is not a pursuit for the time-pressed. Definitions can be tentative and qualified, for example:

> [personalisation] *appears* to approximate the idea of person-centred support. It *generally seems* to be used to draw a distinction between service-led arrangements where people are fitted into a range of existing provision and more person-centred approaches where arrangements for support are tailored to individual need. (Boxall et al, 2009, p 504. Emphases added)

Personalisation has been referred to as *new, different* and *a break with the past*, or as '... a way of thinking about public services and those who use them, rather than being a worked-out set of policy prescriptions' (Needham, 2011a, p 22). Whatever its definition, different types of policy provision have come to be included under the personalisation umbrella. Personalisation may involve more than individual budgets (IBs); a direct payment (DP) is one form of personal budget (PB) (Tyson et al, 2010). PBs are the social care component of IBs; IBs include all funding streams in one funding pot and are complex and considered more costly to administer (Needham, 2011a, p 31).

However defined, personalisation, in one form or another has, as noted, developed at different speeds and with different emphases across the four UK nations. In England, personalisation policy pronouncements and developments have proceeded apace; it has not always been easy to see if policy presaged personalisation or if personalisation led policy development. From 2003, DPs became supplemented by PBs (Glasby, 2012), which had been invented and piloted in six local authorities by the social enterprise In Control. In Control started its work in

2003 in England with 31 people in six pilot local authorities areas; the pilots focused on people with learning disabilities (Poll et al, 2006). In Control's stated focus was 'to explore ways in which the current system of social care might be reformed, in particular to develop a pragmatic and universal model of Self-Directed Support to progress the personalisation of social care services … with the specific intention of promoting active citizenship' (Hatton et al, 2008, p 9). The speed of roll-out of PBs was fast. In 2006, In Control reported 60 people in six local authorities in England had a PB; three years later this had increased to 30,000 people in 75 local authority areas.

The 2006 White Paper in England, *Our Health, Our Care, Our Say: a New Direction for Community Services*, proposed the introduction of IBs for service users to build their own care packages, and bring together funding from, for example, community care purchasing budgets, equipment budgets, disabled facilities grants or Supporting People funding (DH, 2006). This White Paper was published before completion of the Department of Health-commissioned evaluation of IB pilots in 13 local authorities (this 'IBSEN' project ran from November 2005 to December 2007). A year later, again before completion of the IBSEN evaluation, the Department of Health published *Putting People First*. Six government departments and various health and social care bodies in England were signatories to this commitment to greater personalisation of services and a 'system-wide transformation' to give people 'maximum choice, control and power over the support services they receive' (HM Government, 2007, pp 2–3).

The change of UK government in June 2010 continued this push to personalisation in England. England's White Paper *Caring for Our Future*, published on 11 July 2012 by a Conservative–Liberal Democrat coalition government, side-stepped the bother of defining personalisation, instead cutting straight to an end-point: 'personalisation is achieved when a person has real **choice and control** over the care and support they need to achieve their goals, to live a fulfilling life, and be connected with society' (HM Government, 2012, p 18. Emphasis in original).

In Wales, by contrast, development of personalisation has been distinctly differently from England, especially in the Welsh Government's questioning and critique of personalisation. The 2010 report of the independent commission on social services in Wales, *From Vision to Action*, identified principles of 'good personalisation'. These included tailoring support to needs, finding new collaborative ways of working, and developing the right leadership and organisational systems to enable staff to work in creative, person-centred ways. The independent commission recommended the Welsh Government gave stronger commitment to principles of self-directed support (ICSS, 2010, pp 28, 29). Following its acceptance of this report, the Welsh Assembly Government published its social services paper *Sustainable Social Services for Wales: A Framework for Action* in 2011 (WAG, 2011). Personalisation was mentioned just once: '[w]e believe that the label "personalisation" has become too closely associated with a market-led model of consumer choice ...' (p 15). On 9 March 2011, shortly after publication of *Sustainable Social Services for Wales* the National Assembly debated personalised budgets, and agreed that:

> The National Assembly for Wales 1. [r]ecognises the importance of individually tailored care services but rejects any approach based on markets or that would put the responsibility for having to sort out solutions to their problems on individuals...3. [s]upports the developmental approach outlined in (*Sustainable Social Services for Wales: A Framework for Action*) which offers service users greater voice and control without fragmenting services or placing an unwelcome burden on them. (NAfW, 2011)

On 18 October 2011, announcing intention to introduce a social services bill, the opening paragraph of a written statement by the Welsh Government underscored its commitment to cooperation not marketisation: '[c]ollaboration and multi-agency working are pre-requisites to the effective delivery of our responsibilities to safeguard and protect ...' (WG, 2011, p 1).

In Scotland, the focus of personalisation has been distinct again. Scotland's self-directed support national strategy described SDS as the:

> support individuals and families have after making an informed choice on how their *Individual Budget* is used to meet the outcomes they have agreed. SDS means giving people choice and control. The process for deciding on support through SDS is through *co-production*...support that is delivered in equal partnership between people and professionals. (Scottish Government, 2010, p 7. Emphases in original)

This strategy was followed by the Social Care (Self-directed Support) (Scotland) Act, 2013, which requires local authorities to offer people four options about the way their social care is managed: via a direct payment; through self-directed support; with support arranged by the local authority; or by a mixture of any of these. The Act gives local authorities the power to support unpaid carers, and councils have a duty to provide information to citizens to assist them to decide how to arrange their support.

Finally, Northern Ireland's health and social care commissioning plan, published in 2012, committed the government to 'greater impetus' in SDS, with government 'exploring the models of self-directed support or personalisation' developed in England and Scotland and giving this work (HSC, 2012, p 75).

## Personalisation stories

With the exception of the IBSEN project, referred to above, the roll-out of personalisation in one form or another was not informed by rigorous evaluation or systematic appraisal of people's experiences, or of implications for care and support to older people in particular and their safeguarding from harm. In Control's own reports on the phases of its work were described as a 'snapshot' and 'not the result of a large-scale formal research project investigating the effectiveness of Self-Directed Support compared with the prevailing system of social care'. Instead, they formed part of 'an ongoing collaboration that attempts to develop low-cost methods for routinely monitoring Self-Directed Support as it develops' (Hatton et al, 2008, p 9). In the report of the third phase of its work, In Control said that 70 per cent of the 30,000 people then receiving a PB were living in just ten local authorities. The report's authors counselled caution: 'it is clear that Self-Directed Support is still a fledgling technology and one that needs to be adopted and implemented with care' (Tyson et al, 2010, p 36).

As to the level of any critical scrutiny of these developments, Needham (2011a) found little opposition to the idea of personalisation, apart from some trade unions and academics (neither constituency being one that policy-makers or governments are typically much in thrall to). In any case, appearing to question policy claiming to provide choice and control to adult social care users can seem curmudgeonly (Ferguson, 2007) or, in the simplistic 'either/or' of political debate, as a tacit defence of institutionalised service provision. The elusiveness of a definition of personalisation referred to earlier may underlie this critical silence. Its 'all things to all people' *cachet* is an asset that exploits that ambiguity: '[p]ersonalisation does not qualify as a philosophy. When it used rhetorically or used by civil servants its very virtue is that *it manages to embrace competing philosophical positions in a way that is attractive to some and unobjectionable to most*' (Duffy, 2010, p 256. Emphasis added). Objections to such virtue, if made, struggle to get traction on precisely what it is that is under scrutiny.

As it would seem foolish to argue against 'choice and control' (both warmly comforting apple pie words), Boxall et al, (2009, p 508) recognised an 'in-built bias towards – rather than away from – policy change that supports personalisation'. Lymbery (2010) commented on a 'messianic' feel to personalisation, while James described this as 'evangelical and persuasive' rhetoric, remarking that 'it seems churlish to question any aspirations to facilitate independence and the litany of terms that accompany it' (James, 2008, p 23).

As a definition has been both elastic and elusive, and its embrace in public policy not over-informed by evidence, Needham suggested personalisation could be best understood as a *narrative* with potent storylines:

> Personalisation does not seem to be coherent or wide-ranging enough to constitute an ideology or indeed a philosophy (despite sometimes being described in those terms), nor is it a broad buzzword in public policy like community and responsibility. It is not a category that bestows roles and identities like citizenship or consumerism. However, it is more than a specific policy programme. ... Personalisation is best understood as a narrative of public service reform, endorsing a set of relationships and policy goals in a way that is compelling and emotionally resonant, but also multi-interpretable. (Needham, 2011a, p 157)

As a narrative, Needham identified a number of storylines: that personalisation works, transforming lives for the better; personalisation saves money; person-centred approaches reflect the way people live their lives; personalisation is applicable to everyone; and people are experts in their own lives. Each storyline could be evoked to different audiences:

> It is interesting to observe that ways in which the individual stories and claims of self-evidence are layered onto policy evaluations, such that when the formal evidence proves somewhat ambiguous, the story teller can deploy common sense and/or resonant stories about individual transformation to make the case. Organisations such as In Control and the Office for Public Management have played a key role here in weaving together these different strands

of support, acting both as evaluators of and advocates for personalized approaches. (Needham, 2011b, p 60)

The point of this rhetorical process is not serendipitous. Duffy (2010, p 255) identified 'rhetoric is an important part of policy-making, it demands finding ways of picturing the world which are attractive and which guide different people to necessary collective decisions'. Story-telling, Needham's (2011a) construction of narratives as noted earlier, are vital in creating these ways of 'picturing the world'. The following quote from a chief executive encapsulates the process involved – as well as its distaste for evidence:

> We need more storytellers, not more evidence. What will change minds is people telling stories about changed lives. If I was Tsar for personalisation – I would quickly work out how to audit it. Then I would get In Control telling great stories all over the place, not in social care but telling finance directors how much can be saved... (A chief executive discussing personalisation, quoted in Needham, 2011a, p 169)

This quote illustrates beautifully the selling points of the 'marketing exercise, [in which] the In Control approach has proved outstandingly effective ...' (Boxall et al, 2009, p 508). Contained in these stories is the need to break with the past and, in England, for new Labour and its coalition successor government, the relentless quest to modernise (DH, 1998), transform (HM Government, 2007), in realising this break with the past. For Du Gay, these 'epochalist narratives provide a simple and easily digestible set of slogans through which to catalyse the demand for "change"' (Du Gay, 2003, p 671, cited in Cutler et al, 2007, p 854). The later Blair administrations and, to a lesser extent, that of the Brown-led government, placed great emphasis in England on epochal narratives to signal their intention to reform social care. The end of one 'bad' era – and the start of a new – 'good' – epoch deployed the rhetoric of binary opposites to make the case for change. For example:

> In the old system of social care a disabled person who accepted support from the state would find that they could only receive support if they were prepared to: (a) sacrifice control over that support and thereby large parts of their lives; and (b) accept services that then excluded them from meaningful engagement in community life (that is, they

would often be placed in residential care or segregated in day centres). Self-directed support turns this old paternalistic system on its head. (Duffy, 2010, p 257)

This pitching of one 'good' counter-posed against a demonstrable 'bad' is a persuasive rhetorical device. There can be no defence of welfare provision that warehouses disabled adults in purposeless day centre activity, or ensconces an adult in segregated, regimented, post-workhouse provision that masquerades as a 'home'. However, setting up the rhetorical 'bad' against which to pitch the intended 'good' of policy change itself is part of Duffy's (2010) 'old system of social care', that is, the criticism of what went before becomes the engine for future change.

## Choice and control

The coalition government's *Vision for Adult Social Care* in England had this to say about choice and control:

> People not providers or systems should hold choice and control about their care. Personal budgets and direct payments are a powerful way to give people control. ... With choice and control, people's dignity and freedom is protected and their quality of life enhanced. Our vision is to make sure everyone can get the personalised support they deserve. (DH 2010, p 15)

Choice demonstrates the social care consumer at work; it underscores individualism but pays scant attention to power relations between the citizen and the state, social and economic inequality and the impact these have upon on a person's exercise of 'choice' (Stevens et al, 2011). Neither choice nor control may be central defining features of everyday life of an adult at risk who is being abused. As noted, there was little empirical work completed before the roll-out of personalisation in one of its various guises. Such discussion as there has been on the impacts on older people, and on adult safeguarding more particularly, has been from professionals and those involved in adult safeguarding (for example, Morgan, 2013). Questioning the hegemonic, unquestioned acceptance of 'choice' and 'control' as 'good things' is not to suggest that an older person's life is better taken over by institutional care or intrusive adult safeguarding surveillance intent on removing reasonable risk along with potentially abusive care and support. Rather it is to expose some of the reality of the personalisation versus safeguarding rhetoric.

First, the elevation of individual choice may well be at the expense of the collective good. Roulstone and Morgan (2009) reviewed self-directed support for disabled people. They argued that disabled people's movements and government ideas of SDS may have a superficial similarity, but they were not the same. Without their own disabled people's own organisations, users of day services would have faced moving from the enforced collectivism (of institutional provision) to enforced individualism. Disabled people (like anyone) will be at very different points in their lives in terms of their readiness for self-determination. Without financial and organisational support to set up and manage SDS, it 'takes on distinctly neo-liberal characteristics', with the risk of dependency, say, on a day centre, shifting to, for example, the family of origin (Roulstone and Morgan, 2009, p 343). As a consequence, with its implied shift to atomised consumerism and privatisation, individualised support may erode the advantages of risk-pooling and cross-subsidy across the lifecourse, which welfare provision funded by taxation can provide (Needham, 2011a). Personalisation may replace the rights of citizenship with the sovereignty of the market:'[p]ersonalization is not generally held to be synonymous with individualism, yet its key contribution to policy thus far has been to encourage individual ownership of budgets, with reduced scope for risk pooling and collective service allocations' (Needham, 2011b, p 64).

Second, the 'choice and control' theme of public policy is not new. Richard Titmuss (1976, p 73) advised that '[r]eality begins with history'. If that is so, the 'break with the past' line in personalisation does not quite stand up to scrutiny. There is long historical provenance to the 'out with the old, in with the new' discourse in social policy. For example, the 1989 White Paper *Caring for People* (DH, 1989) put forward six objectives for change, the main rationale being the introduction of a new means of funding social care (Lewis and Glennerster, 1996). Then as now, apart from pilot work on case management carried out in Kent, England (Challis and Davies, 1986), there was no underpinning research or evidence base for the changes that resulted in the 1990 NHS and Community Care Act (NHSCC Act) (Lymbery, 2010). Again, then as now, the call was made for services to meet individual needs and empower service users. Guidance to managers on implementing the 1990 NHSCC Act stated: 'care management and assessment emphasise adapting services to needs rather than fitting people into existing services. ... Care management is the process of tailoring services to individual needs' (DH, 1992, p 11). 'Empowerment' then, as personalisation now, was the response to the Thatcherite problem of the 'bad state'– that is, to liberate people from it (Clarke, 2005).

Means (2012) considered four major reports covering over more than 60 years of social care history in the UK to examine main assumptions made about social care at the time they were written. These were the Rucker Report on break up of Poor Law, the 1968 Seebohm Report on personal social services, the 1988 Griffiths Report on community care, and the 1999 Sutherland Report of Royal Commission on long-term care. Means found in these an endless struggle to define social care, not least because of the drive from the NHS to offload costs and calls on health budgets. Means said the Griffiths Report 1988 in many ways set out the personalisation agenda pursued by new Labour and coalition governments in England in the early 2000s, and observed that 'we forget our past history at our peril' (Means, 2012, p 318).

## Public policy, personalisation and older people

Personalisation has delivered mixed blessings as far as older people are concerned. Manthorpe et al (2011) reviewed literature on the barriers and facilitators to SDS for the Scottish Government. This review found some staff considered IBs inappropriate for older people (for example, Ellis, 2007; LAC 2008, 1), possibly due to professional uncertainty about risk posed to an older person who is vulnerable (Scourfield, 2005; Davey et al, 2007; Glendinning et al, 2008; Henwood and Hudson, 2008; James, 2008;). This review also described some older service users found managing the budget and the personal assistants onerous (Smyth et al, 2006; Arksey and Kemp, 2008). Older people may underestimate their own needs (Glendinning et al, 2008), and carers may be overlooked in the self-assessment process (Glendinning et al, 2008; Rabiee et al, 2009). Putting these findings alongside each other, it seems there have been significant gaps in the understanding the impacts on older people of personalisation.

As noted, the IBSEN evaluation (Glendinning et al, 2008) had not reported before the Department of Health in England published a white paper for its expansion (DH, 2006). IBSEN was a large-scale evaluation of the impacts of IBs on older people and other adult social care users piloted in 13 local authorities in England between 2005 and 2007. A mixed methods design, with a randomised controlled trial at its centre, IBSEN considered the costs, outcomes and cost-effectiveness of IBs for all adult service user groups, compared to traditional types of service delivery. Service users were randomly assigned to the IB group, and received an IB, or to a comparison group, where they received conventional social care services or a DP. Over the 25 months the IBSEN evaluation ran, less than a half of those in the IB group had IB-funded support in place at the time of the follow up interview. Of those with an IB in place, one fifth did not have it all in place, or it had been in place less than one month (Netten et al, 2011). Nonetheless, at the end of the IBSEN pilots, the then Labour government said personal budgets were to be put in place for everyone eligible for publicly funded adult care support. Support for cash-for-care schemes continued under the coalition that formed government in 2010, showing what Moran et al (2013, p 846) called 'remarkable consistency' in England, despite changes in political administration.

For older people, the results of the IBSEN study were telling. IBSEN found no evidence of cost effectiveness differences between IBs and conventional support arrangements in terms of social care outcomes. Outcomes for older people were poorer than for younger IB holders; there was no improvement in social care outcomes for older people receiving an IB (Moran et al, 2013). Older people were less satisfied with IBs than other user groups. Older people did not experience greater control with IBs; they reported experiencing greater anxiety about planning and managing IBs than other user groups, and felt less safe than those receiving mainstream services. The experiences and outcomes for older people contrasted with the clear benefits of IBs identified for younger user groups: '[f]or the largest group of service users nationally – older people – there clearly are important challenges to be met if personal budgets are to prove an effective means of personalisation' (Netten et al, 2011, p 14).

Whether in the IB or the comparison group, older people consistently received lower levels of financial support than a younger disabled person with similar restrictions on their activities of daily living (Moran et al, 2013). The mean value of an IB an older person received was less than that of a younger person with physical disabilities, and was much less than that received by people with learning disabilities. Over half of older people receiving an IB used it to buy conventional social care services. Only a minority of older people had a large enough budget to spend cash on wider social activities (Moran et al, 2013). The IBSEN evaluation itself reported that 'many older people supported by adult services do not appear to want what many of them described as the "additional burden" of planning and managing their own support'. The report authors commented 'it may take time for older people to develop the confidence to assume greater control' (Glendinning et al, 2008, p 19).

Arguments that 'older people' need to be confident to use IBs, or overcome some generational deference to professionals (as Moran et al, 2013, reported some IB lead staff in the IBSEN evaluation considered to be the case), homogenise older people, and risk giving an impression that 'older people' are an undifferentiated mass needing to sharpen themselves up to make it in the new world of cash-for-care. Such arguments ignore the particular, and divergent, needs and circumstances of a cohort of people whose age may span 30 years and more. They overlook the systemic inequity at work when older people on IBs receive, on average, smaller budgets than younger people with similar functional restrictions. IBSEN data indicated that older service users would need a 25% increase in support for these age differences relative to younger people to be removed (Forder, 2008, p 27). A randomised-controlled German study (Arntz and Thomsen, 2011, cited in Netten et al, 2011, p 15) found that older people achieved better outcomes using PBs, but that these too were associated with much higher levels of formal care expenditure. Older people's confidence in IBs might be more forthcoming (and deference to professionals less apparent) if those needing social care could rely on IBs resourced at a level that would buy social and leisure activities as well as personal care, and that were on a par with the level of budget a younger person in similar circumstances received.

## A distaste for dependency

Despite the intention that personalisation should mean thinking about social care differently, there seems to have been oblivion, particularly in England, to the types of support and care that may be needed by those who are frail and dependent. While personalisation in one of its manifestations is said to be suitable for any user of social care services, the reality has been that the stories, so popular in the narrative of personalisation (Needham 2011a), have seldom featured very old, highly dependent, or cognitively impaired people. Indeed, policy in England (DH, 2010, p 10) set itself against such undesirable 'dependency'; its approach to social care required 'unleashing the creativity and enthusiasm of local communities to maintain independence and prevent dependency'. Highly dependent people are not priorities for state spend on social care; as Kittay (2001a, p 546) has remarked, 'the labor of care always seems too expensive'.

The social stench that surrounds dependency contrasts with the 'happy shiny people' good news stories about personalised services for empowered and independent adults. The 'active ageing' imperative brings with it an uncritical stigmatisation of elders who fail to 'age well' (Minkler, 1996). (Who would want to age 'badly'?). It is in this aversion of the social gaze – in this failure to 'bear witness', as it were, to the human inevitability of ageing and dependency – that we may understand how 'dependence has become a dirty word: it refers to something which decent people should be ashamed of' (Bauman, 2000, p 5). Being ill, old and dependent ranks pretty low on any index of wellbeing.

Just as the status of those dying is liminal (neither in the world nor departed from it), very dependent older people become socially liminal. They don't quite fit the 'sixty is the new 40' meme of the moment, where energetic, sexually active, physically attractive old age is packaged as an aspirational social goal of 'the new aging', around which 'a buoyant and optimistic cultural imagery has rallied' (Katz and Marshall, 2003, p 4). Very old, frail, highly dependent people are rendered invisible. It is these invisible older people (disproportionately women), without wealth, without mental capacity, and possibly without family, who are at greater risk of abuse.

Policy preferences reflect the values of the society that produce them. Ageism is subtle; apparently unquestioned ageist assumptions dig deep into policy discourse. In the dualistic, either/or world of professional dilemmas ('has mental capacity, can make bad choice'), the valued trinity of 'choice', 'control', 'independence' have as their obverse the devalued 'high dependency', 'can't make choices', 'needs constant care'. 'Care' can have a warm and fluffy feel to it; 'dependency', on the other hand, is a description never used warmly (Fine and Glendinning, 2005).

When this distaste for dependency (Lloyd, 2006) is written into social policy, written out of it is a recognition and a capacity to respond to the lived, day-to-day reality of hundreds of thousands of citizens in the UK. Dependency and frailty are, of course, inevitable facts of life at some point for anyone, irrespective of age. The policy rhetoric of active, informed consumers exercising the ubiquitous 'choice' does not embrace this that well. When dependency and frailty are exceptionalised – put outside the valued social mores of being young, active, independent – older, frail, dependent beings become deviant, different, easily devalued. Personalisation may well mean 'thinking about public services and social care in an entirely different way', but awareness of dependency or frailty is not foregrounded in this. A 32 year-old man disabled in a road traffic accident is not the same as a 90 year-old woman with fluctuating mental capacity, disabled by arthritis whose main carer is a spouse who has abused her throughout their marriage.

## Risks and rights

Consideration of potential risks to the adult at risk of abuse did not feature a great deal in the development of personalisation. In Scotland, Hunter et al (2012) examined self-directed support in Scotland and adult safeguarding, using data from interviews at two time points with three adult protection lead officers involved in the national evaluation of self-directed support in three pilot sites. The authors concluded that, like IBSEN, consideration of adult protection implications were little considered when rolling out that particular personalisation programme. Manthorpe et al (2010), in a qualitative interviews with 14 adult safeguarding coordinators in the 13 pilot sites involved in the IBSEN study, had earlier found the views, experiences and expertise in adult protection had not been regularly drawn upon in the roll-out of the IBSEN pilots.

In England, In Control's report of its third phase commented that 'risk is an important aspect of a full life' (Tyson et al, 2010, p 73). Like having choice and control over one's life, it is hard to disagree with this of course. In the personalisation discourse, abuse and mistreatment have tended to be framed only as matters of risk management. In Control said their experience was that people using SDS felt safer, and contrasted this with institutional forms of service and the risks that total institutions may pose to those who use them.

The consultation paper, *A Vision for Adult Social Care,* issued by the Department of Health in England, six months after a coalition government assumed office in 2010, mentioned safeguarding, in relation to people who were unable to maintain their own safety:

> Personalisation is about enabling people to lead the lives they can choose and achieve the outcomes they want in ways that best suit them. It is important in this process to consider risks, and keeping people safe from harm. ...Risk should not be an excuse to restrict people's lives. Safeguarding is a range of activity aimed at upholding an adult's fundamental right to be safe. ...Safeguarding is of particular importance to people who, because of their situation or circumstances, are unable to keep safe. (DH, 2010, p 5)

Within public policy that elevates personal choice and the 'right to make bad choices' at the same time as playing down contextual, social and cultural factors (such as ageism, poverty and inequality, a distaste for dependency), there lies the danger that dogmatic assertion may eclipse dispassionate scrutiny. This can be seen in examining circumstances in which some adults at risk have come to harm.

## Dangers of dogma

As at 2013, there was no requirement on adult safeguarding boards or adult protection committees in any of the four UK nations to commission a serious case review (SCR) if an adult at risk came to serious harm, nor any obligation to publish the review if they did. As a result, the adult safeguarding serious case reviews in the public domain are those a safeguarding board or adult protection committee has agreed to put there. They may not be representative of cases where an adult at risk has come to serious harm. Nonetheless, findings of serious case reviews may throw light on themes related to discussion on risk, vulnerability and the superordinate elevation of 'choice'.

The 'dogma of choice', identified in the review of circumstances leading the death of Steven Hoskin (Cornwall Adult Protection Committee, 2007, p 25), tracks through other serious case reviews. Margaret Panton's was one of the first published SCRs concerning an older person. Mrs Panton was 78 when she moved home to live with people to whom she was related. Mrs Panton was well-known to health and social care services. This decision to move was seen as her right to make choices, her self-determination. Within five weeks of that move she had died, suffering serious injuries of burns, lacerations and bruises. The hinterland to this case, and the risks Mrs Panton was exposed to, were known by professionals but not systematically appraised through adult protection systems (Vickers and Lucas, 2004).

In a case reviewed by this author, a woman in her late 70s was badly beaten by her son. The review found the risks the son posed to his mother were documented and well-known to mental health and social services with whom both mother and son had contact. Professionals described the mother's 'choice' to see her son, despite his past history of violence and extortion of money from her. *Choice and self-determination* were the uncritical guides to the action social workers and nurses took or failed to take in their work with both mother and son. The theme woven through professional decision-making was the woman's 'right to make bad choices'. The problem was that the warm words of 'choice' and 'self-determination' missed the lived reality of this frail mother's life, and the complex dynamics typically present in situations of family violence. (The findings of this case review led directly to the research reported in Chapters Six and Seven.)

Steven Hoskin's death, referred to above, illustrated this is harrowing detail. Steven was a man with learning disabilities who was murdered, aged 39, after being tortured and thrown over a railway viaduct by several young men and a woman who had moved in on his life. A serious case review was commissioned following the convictions for Steven's murder of a 29-year-old man and a 16-year-old woman, and the manslaughter conviction of a 21-year-old man. Those convicted, and other young people, had moved into Hoskin's bed-sit and engaged in various illegal activities. Both Steven Hoskin, and those who tortured and murdered him, were well known to the police, health, social care, housing and emergency services.

On the 'choice' staff and agencies saw Hoskin as exercising, the serious case review was excoriating. Hoskin's 'choice' to stop contact with some services was not explored; the potential implications and risks of 'choices' – indeed if they were choices rather than fear-based withdrawals – were not explored by agencies. The police reported Steven's circumstances in the months preceding his murder as follows: 'Steven Hoskin had lost all control of his own life within his home. He had no say, choice of control over who stayed or visited his flat …' (Cornwall Adult Protection Committee, 2007, p 24). Hoskin had wanted friends; his so-called 'choice' to let his tormentors and murderers take over his life was driven by this very human need. As a result, his life became one of 'joyless enslavement' challenging the 'dogma of choice' for adults who are apparently 'able" (Cornwall Adult Protection Committee, 2007, p 25).

In England and Wales, 'the right to make bad choices' has underpinned the delivery of tens of thousands of trainings to health, social care, legal and criminal justice staff since the introduction of the 2005 Mental Capacity Act. Before that Act's implementation, in their research of how adult protection procedures were used when elder abuse was suspected in domestic settings, Preston-Shoot and Wigley (2002) found many staff privileged self-determination over protection. Considerable weight could be given to a person's views, described by social workers as their 'choice' – even when this left the adult exposed to risk.

Of course, 'self-determination' and 'choice' are pre-eminent human services work values, although not ones always critically interrogated in practice. Professionals may hide behind 'choice' to avoid risking their relationship with a service user (Pritchard, 2001; 2002). In the US, Bergeron (2006) suggested the notion of 'self-determination' (as well as 'competency') were not sufficiently questioned or explored in social work or in elder abuse. The simplistic binary thinking behind the either/or of 'has mental capacity/can make bad choice' could mean an abused older woman remaining in a life-threatening domestic situation. Bergeron found mental incapacity was cited as the only reason for professional intervention; she called for social workers to think more critically about the conflicting values often at play in decision-making in cases of potential elder abuse. Upholding the principle of self-determination may demand their making a judgement of how intervention might *both* uphold individual choice *and* provide protection from harm (Bergeron, 2006).

The findings of Preston-Shoot and Wigley's (2002) study also raised questions about far the exercise of 'choice', and 'self-determination' is possible if an elder is frail, dependent on their abuser for care, has suffered domestic violence for most of their adult life, or is living in impoverished, isolated circumstances. As discussed in Chapter Three, choice is not an absolute concept, but is shaped by social and cultural factors, inequalities and contradictions. It is those contradictions that health and social care workers face when judging whether or not to use the adult protection procedures.

If the alternative to domestic abuse is 'a home', what view of that does the older person have of care homes? If the older person has been physically harmed, chastised, belittled or threatened by others, how realistic is it to think they can assert the wish to up-sticks and leave? How will they manage to effect that departure and find somewhere else to live? If the older person is worried about what family will think of the violence, or how they will be judged by others for their plight, how likely is it that they will disclose abuse? Bergeron (2006) argued that good decision-making needed practice. Understanding the concept, still less envisioning what 'self determination' might be, may be challenges too far for an abused older person who just wants their mistreatment to cease (Ash, 2013).

The title of Fyson and Kitson's (2007) commentary on the abuse of people with learning disabilities in a NHS facility in Cornwall, UK – 'Independence or protection – does it have to be a choice?' – questioned this binary thinking. Fyson and Kitson argued that abuse could only be minimised if policies reflecting choice and independence were mediated by effective measures to protect. The social policy imperative that emphasised choice and independence mostly ignored the need to be protected from harm. As a result, a woolly pre-eminence of 'choice' over a human right to live free from abuse, can result in a passive professional head-shaking about the mistaken options vulnerable people may 'choose', and the continuation of abuse for the older person.

This chapter has considered the development of adult protection law and policy in the UK, against the backcloth of public policy development of personalisation and individualisation of care and support to older people. Professionals engaged in adult safeguarding work are required to use adult protection or adult safeguarding policies and procedures to deal with the potential abuse of an older person or any adult at risk. The influences on the way they use that policy and the actions they take including, for example, the degree to which risks are identified and managed, are key variables in outcomes of work to safeguard an older person. Chapter Five, which follows, looks at some of the theoretical underpinning of policy implementation, and particularly at the work of Michael Lipsky on street-level bureaucracy. That discussion leads, in Chapters Six and Seven, to report and discussion of a case study that considered the influences on social workers working to protect an older person from abuse.

# FIVE

# Public policy implementation in street-level bureaucracies

What happens to an older person when abuse is alleged will depend to a considerable extent on the way in which professionals and practitioners such as social workers, police officers or nurses understand, use and implement safeguarding policy. This chapter seeks to lay out a conceptual backcloth to the research reported in Chapters Six and Seven. This sought to identify the constraints and dilemmas social workers and their managers faced when implementing public policy on adult safeguarding. The resonance Lipsky's theory of street-level bureaucracy has to understanding professional dilemmas in adult safeguarding has been reported by Ash (2013). The present chapter considers the exercise of discretion by public servants using public policy; in particular it focuses on the significance of *context* to understanding both the actions adult safeguarding professionals may take when dealing with potential abuse of an older person, and the constraints and realities they grapple with when weighing up what to do. The significance of context also underpins Chapter Eight's discussion about cultures and contexts of complicity in adult safeguarding, and that on the need for ethically driven safeguarding policy and practice in Chapter Nine.

## Michael Lipsky and street-level bureaucracy

In his landmark work on street-level bureaucracy, Lipsky (1980) argued that public policy is made, in effect, in the day-to-day activities of 'street-level bureaucrats'. Street-level bureaucrats are paid staff and professionals employed to deliver public services, such as health, social care, education or criminal justice. For Lipsky, understanding policy implementation in practice, called for an understanding of the dilemmas street-level bureaucrats encountered in their day-to-day work. To this end, Lipsky argued that the decisions, devices and routines these street-level workers use to cope with work pressures – the uncertainties about what to do and how to do it in the face of the complex, unpredictable demands of human services work, as well as the ambiguities inherent in the policies they had to use – in reality become the policy delivered to the public.

Lipsky identified the processes involved in this. Street-level bureaucrats made policy, both in the discrete acts of discretion they exercised, and in the aggregation of those individual acts to become, to all intents and purposes, the policy operated at the local or street level. This discretion was shaped by various factors, including the degree of freedom an agency allowed its street-level bureaucrats or, conversely, street-level bureaucrats' need to make their own decisions when agency policy was abstruse, uncertain or simply not stated.

Lipsky (1980) said the exercise of discretion by street-level bureaucrats could not be eliminated because human service work was unpredictable and complex. Lipsky dismissed the possibility of removing the exercise of individual judgement by a street-level bureaucrat, observing that 'we are not prepared as a society to abandon decisions about people and discretionary intervention to machines and programmed formats' (Lipsky, 1980, p xv). This was written, of course, decades before computerised case management systems started to shape what and how information was recorded about people using social services (see, for example, Broadhurst et al, 2010; Wastell et al, 2010), but it captures the persistence and nigh impossibility of eliminating discretion from decision-making that characterises street-level work in public agencies.

For Lipsky (1980), the greater the discretion street-level bureaucrats exercised at the local level, the greater the relevance his analysis had in understanding why local policy implementation may be different from what policy-makers intended. Aside from requirements of compliance reporting, street-level bureaucrats control the flow of information upwards to managers, itself an act of discretion. Managers rely on the goodwill of street-level bureaucrats to deliver human services and to work longer than their contracted hours without pay when needed. Services are delivered in situations of uncertainty (for example, when there are no clear-cut answers about what to do; or when social and political demands on public servants are unrealistic and unrealisable), and at times of scarcity (when human and cash resources are under pressure or just not there).

Lipsky recognised that street-level bureaucrats may experience dissonance as they grapple with the dilemmas inherent in the system and structure of their work. (The subtitle of his 1980 book was *Dilemmas of the Individual in Public Services*.) Here, his analysis takes up the central significance of *context* to the work of street-level bureaucrats. Dissonance, Lipsky (1980, p xiii) said, lies at the heart of a street-level bureaucrat's work, and what he called the 'corrupted world of service' in which they operate. Recognising that people usually enter public sector work with some commitment to service, he commented that 'the very nature of this work prevents them from coming even close to the ideal conception of their jobs' (Lipsky, 1980, p xii). Professional and occupational aspirations to deliver the rhetoric of public policy – in the early 21st century UK this would include 'choice' and 'control' – become defeated by large workloads, inadequate resources, and ambiguous or conflicting agency policies. Public agencies devote energy 'to concealing lack of service and generating appearances of responsiveness' (Lipsky, 1980, p 76), and creating the 'myth of altruism' (Lipsky, 1980, p 71) where a helping façade masks a very different experience for people in need of their services (and indeed those who deliver them).

Lipsky argued that street-level bureaucrats develop different coping strategies to manage the dilemmas and dissonance they experienced. One such strategy was self-protection with a 'cognitive shield', where clients or users of services were blamed for their predicament, thus 'shielding' the worker from responsibility to do anything about it (Lipsky, 1980, p 153). Dissonance leads some employees to walking away from their jobs, or to others becoming ill or burnt out. Street-level bureaucrats may deploy survival strategies that reflect their reduced expectations of themselves and service users, and the intentions of public policy. They may rationalise these compromises and trade-offs, for example, as a reflection of their greater professional maturity or their appreciation of the 'real world' of human service work; or by admitting their original aspirations were unrealistic. This dissonance is magnified as many street-level bureaucrats – certainly doctors, nurses and social workers – have professional and bureaucratic status, both of which require compliance with the rules of their professional code and their statutory duties. Some of these rules may be contradictory, such as 'promote the needs of service users', as well as the unwritten (but nonetheless well-understood) 'ration services because budgets are tight'. Professionals may operate these implicit and explicit rules selectively or in accord with the 'norms and practices of their occupational group' (Lipsky, 1980, p 14), practices that may not accord with the rules of the agency.

Once more pointing up the significance of context on what public service professionals do, Lipsky argued that the greater the dissonance street-level bureaucrats experience, the more important their workplace and its culture became in keeping morale up and reducing stress. Local workplace or team routines, group norms, 'war stories' and other peer survival strategies assume greater significance in influencing the behaviour of colleagues than policies, set procedures or the written-down requirements of managers. Street-level bureaucrats come to rely on their workplace mates, the water-cooler stories, and their workgroup workarounds to get by.

For Lipsky (1980), the relationship between managers and street-level bureaucrats was both conflictual *and* reciprocal. Each saw the job of delivering services to the public differently; each had different imperatives. Even so, they needed each other. Street-level bureaucrats mostly work outside any direct oversight by their managers, just as managers work away from those they manage. Workers may act autonomously by having different priorities from their managers, or by not accepting rules and resisting control put on their discretion. Managers, on the other hand, want consistent results. Their concern is with performance, and how much it costs to deliver that performance, along with 'those aspects of process that expose them to critical scrutiny' (Lipsky, 1980, p 19). In the first part of the 21st century, such critical scrutiny could well entail professional humiliation – typically, character assassination by a frenzied tabloid press – if missed targets, budget overspends or other symptoms of public sector malfunction reached the public domain. From a Lipskian perspective, managers may turn a blind eye to informal work processing strategies or practices by frontline workers if they protect the organisation from overload or public criticism, even though these may not entirely line up with agency policy. In essence, resistance, rule-bending and rule-breaking by street-level bureaucrats become tolerated by their managers because they need street-level bureaucrats to deliver the service.

In one of the few pieces of work to use Lipsky's concept of street-level bureaucracy in research on the protection of older people from abuse, Clark-Daniels and Daniels (1995) considered the impact of street-level decision-making by social workers in cases of elder abuse. In this US study, Clark-Daniels and Daniels examined what difference the exercise of discretion and the caseloads of workers made to the decisions they reached on four aspects of adult protection activity with older people at risk: initiating an adult protection investigation; filing the final report; deciding if the allegation had validity; and final placement of the alleged victim. These are parts of the adult protection process that vary in the amount of discretion a worker can exercise throughout adult protection process. The authors hypothesised that: compliance with deadlines would reflect available resources and administrative constraints; placement of the older person would put pressure on social workers to differentiate between clients to limit access to limited services; and differentiation would reflect normative biases and professional assumptions. Clark-Daniels and Daniels found that moving from compliance decisions to substantive regulatory or distributive decisions by social workers produced greater rationing of services of the sort predicted by Lipsky, reinforcing the importance of the context to decision-making to explain street-level decision-making. This is discussed further later in this chapter.

## The problem of the street-level bureaucrat

The public opprobrium that greets failure by street-level bureaucrats to protect a child or adult at risk of abuse, is often met with apologies by those in charge of the street-level bureaucracy, and promises that lessons will be learned (see Ash, 2013 for a fuller discussion of this). What has become a ritual re-view and re-vision of policy, and re-training of remaining (that is, those not removed from their posts) staff, may turn on tightening up systems, structures and processes of care and safeguarding. The implication is that policy, if followed and shown to be followed, will mean those lessons have indeed been learned, and whatever it was that should not have happened, will not happen again.

In this way, the 'problem' of the street-level bureaucrat has frequently turned on ways to control their actions so that the implementation of 'policy as intended' takes place. Pressman and Wildavsky's (1984) memorably titled book, *How Great Expectations in Washington Are Dashed in Oakland; Or, Why It's Amazing that Federal Programs Work at All, This Being a Saga of the Economic Development Administration as Told by Two Sympathetic Observers Who Seek to Build Morals on a Foundation of Ruined Hopes*, came to a view that the more links there were in the policy implementation chain, the bigger the implementation deficit, that is, the greater the risk that policy would not be implemented as intended. 'If things don't turn out as expected and there were resources to do it, then something has gone wrong with implementation', a common line of reasoning proceeds. Hupe (2011) called this the 'thesis of incongruent implementation', or the gap between policy intention and achievement. A central tenet of this is that policy determines execution; hence Pressman and Wildavsky (1984) made a plea for fewer links in the policy implementation chain. Hupe (2011, p 68) cited the quantitative study of the implementation of Danish employment policy carried out by Winter et al (2007), which tested whether fewer links in the implementation chain secured congruence between intention and execution of policy. Winter et al (2007) had hypothesised that the goal of policy reforms would be more internalised in actors in the national agency than in a relatively autonomous local municipality (because they were closer to the source of policy – there were fewer links in chain); and that more direct lines of authority in central government would secure greater commitment, attention to rules and adherence by street-level bureaucrats. The research findings supported these hypotheses; actions of street-level bureaucrats in the national agency were more in line with policy intention than were those of their counterparts in local government.

Observing the 'lasting functionality' of the top-down view of policy implementation Hupe commented on the normative assumptions of policy-making, stemming from Weber's ideal-type bureaucracy; that is, that the written intentions of law and policy 'should in an immediate way direct and prevail in action in the real world', manifesting as 'the primacy of policy on paper' (Hupe, 2011, p 65). The political nature of policy-making means that policy goals are often political compromises, differentiated by Hupe (2011) as party politics, idea–politics and bureaucratic politics. The interaction of these social dynamics and the interplay at the contextual level of policy implementation, can mean policy outcomes become ambiguous and open to various interpretations in order to appeal to a wide range of interest groups. 'Opposite cognitive limitations, unclear instructions, and insufficient compliance, may stand, for instance, professional behaviour and the use of common sense', Hupe (2011, p 72) observed, and '[i]f there is anything the study of Pressman and Wildavsky has drawn attention to, it is the fact that public policy implementation does not take place in a normative vacuum' (Hupe, 2011, p 77).

If street-level bureaucrats are key players in making public policy, then a managerial imperative – from a top-down view – demands influence over how they work. Shaping and directing discretionary practices at the street-level might be attempted through a range of performance-based incentives. A significant contextual fact of life for public sector professionals such as nurses, doctors and social workers – Lipsky's street-level bureaucrats – is performance management of their work and regulation of their profession. However, ambiguities inherent in public policy, or the non-availability of sufficient cash or human resources to deliver it, problematise performance management and complicate accountability. Performance measures selectively identify pieces – or parts – of street-level bureaucrats' work and set these as measurable targets. Other parts of the professional task may be ignored (these may, of course, be the goals of the service user). In adult safeguarding, a woman abused by her life partner throughout that relationship, may fear intervention by an adult safeguarding team if it exposed the violence in the home to her children, grandchildren or the neighbours. The pressure on the street-level bureaucrat to meet their target of making a safeguarding referral within, say 24 hours of abuse being suspected or witnessed, may not be the wish of the woman. If reporting suspicions of abuse of an adult at risk became mandatory, the street-level bureaucrat's discretion about such reporting reduces, and the wishes, fears and concerns of the woman potentially over-ridden. The pressure to meet targets, the tempering of professional discretion and the wish of the citizen may not always coalesce.

As Brodkin (2011) noted, a key assumption of this top-down strategy is that these performance indicators are the equivalent of the bottom line; attaching incentives and penalties to them, assumes street-level organisations and their street-level bureaucrats can be left to get on with their work as they do what they are told. Brodkin (2011) argued that these strategies of new public management are based on flawed assumptions about *how* street-level discretion interacts with performance incentives and *how* those strategies relate to policy intentions. She elaborated a framework for understanding street-level logic of choice and constraint under new public management, and suggested that street-level bureaucrats not only respond to performance incentives but they use their discretion to adjust them, which leads to informal practices that are different from those policy-makers intended. A simple response-to-incentives model does not explain (or indeed try to understand) the weighing up street-level bureaucrats do when faced with targets or policy mandates. Discretionary choices derive from specific organisational conditions, and interact with performance incentives to create a street-level 'calculus of choice' (Brodkin 2011, p i272). New public management performance measures will view 'what counts' as if it were apolitical – on the street it may be anything but. Brodkin (2008, p 318) observed 'quantitative measures of inputs and outputs tend to reconstruct policy in its own terms rather than illuminate the qualitative content of what bureaucrats do and how they "make" policy on their own terms'. Street-level bureaucrats don't do what they like, in other words, they do what they can (Brodkin, 1997).

Further, a 'top-down' compliance model of policy implementation does not have the systems and structures that contextualise policy implementation as its focus. Rather its concern is to understand how frontline workers (street-level bureaucrats) can be held to account in the execution of policy-as-intended. Here, policy implementation is regarded as a linear process, one proceeding from political idea or policy intention, through primary and secondary legislation, to rollout. Policy evaluation work in this mould generates bullet points of advice to managers charged with securing street-level bureaucrat compliance, including instructions such as, agree simple policy goals, employ exceptional leaders, keep communication channels open. These are now the commonplace bread-and-butter stuff of management development programmes.

Such exhortations are all consistent with normative notions of an authoritative political hierarchy aiming to secure compliant delivery of policy goals. A difficulty with this perspective lies in its implicit assumption that policy implementation is like a transmission belt, with policy directives passed and processed down a chain of command that ends with the citizen recipient of the policy intention. The perspective ignores the influences, and the messiness, of contexts on human and organisational behaviour, and the social systems and structures that surround that process. As Brodkin (2008, p 320) asked, 'if bureaucracies were the graveyard of good intentions, were they the cause of death or simply its location?'

In a US study, Sandfort (2000) examined frontline conditions in the delivery of welfare in five public and private sector welfare organisations, considering how each of the two schools of public management – traditional public administration and new public management – operated in the organisations trying to direct frontline work. She found a disjuncture between both management frameworks and the day-to-day work of frontline staff delivering welfare provision; street-level workers in both contexts exercised more discretion than was recognised by either management framework. Street-level worker day-to-day experiences of welfare delivery meant they collectively generated understandings that enabled them to do the work. Sandfort argued this social process had structural significance. These structures were not imposed by organisational charts, procedures or rules that staff passively enacted, but arose from a collective experience shared by front-line workers.

To understand the disjunctures between management frameworks and front-line conditions, Sandfort drew on other work, including Giddens (1984) and Bourdieu (1990), to consider the way in which people can constitute, and be constituted by, structures: in other words, how people exert agency while operating in larger structures. This thrust of thought suggests people live and work in contexts without an inherent structure, but structures emerge from the desire to make sense of circumstances. Structures are constituted by, first, schemas (the norms, beliefs, shared knowledge people develop when operating in particular social context) and, second, resources (concrete objects, authority and tools that are valued within the particular context). By drawing on both schema and resources, people create the structures of social systems; front-line staff depend on both collective knowledge and organisational resources to develop the structure within which they operate. Sandfort (2000) suggested the generalisable social process that develops in the frontline of organisations is not recognised by performance management tools and techniques that purport to be objective. Instead, how this performance apparatus is understood by people on the frontline requires examination, as does the exercise of professional discretion within these performance management frameworks.

## Discretion and its discontents

A key insight Lipsky's (1980) work provided was the understanding of both why and how discretion comes to be exercised by street-level bureaucrats working in a street-level bureaucracy. This section considers the exercise of discretion in human services and social work widely, before returning to discussion of adult safeguarding at the end of this chapter.

Since the 1980s in particular, the UK social work profession has debated whether or not the scope for the exercise of professional discretion has been reduced. While this debate can become polarised into a 'yes-it-has', 'no-it-hasn't' stalemate, a more sensitised appraisal is needed to look at what influences the decisions taken in adult safeguarding work to protect an older person from abuse. Baldwin (2000) suggested there was an in-built tension between the rationalist, top down policy tenets of UK community care and care management in the 1990s (with its implied *rationality* and *objectivity*), and the reality of assessing need and providing services, all of which required the exercise of discretion (with its implied *subjectivity*). Baldwin interviewed care managers and managers in two English authorities and found many examples of resistance to procedures; care managers could and did subvert the intentions of agency policy. Different workers interpreted guidance differently; this exercise of discretion meant the intentions of policy became distorted. Baldwin found social workers and their managers to be venomous in their opposition to community care administrative processes and procedures but, when challenged, could not substantiate their feelings beyond 'prejudice' (Baldwin, 2000, p 48). Baldwin's findings supported Lipsky's proposition that street-level bureaucrats modified client demand where resources were scarce. In other words, care managers tailored their assessments to resources without recording unmet need, which had been a core design feature of assessment and care management.

Like Lipsky, Dworkin (1978) viewed discretion in relative terms, that is, its meaning is influenced by, or is contingent upon, its context. That context takes in the standards and requisite authority bounding the discretionary space, or the professional room to manoeuvre. Dworkin (1978, p 31) explained discretion in terms of action or decisions made 'subject to standards set by a particular authority'. Discretion could be exercised in the space left open by the standards, which Dworkin likened to the hole in a doughnut. 'Weak' discretion was available when, for example, some superordinate authority had final sanction. 'Strong' discretion existed when judgment is needed to apply standards, but where there was no further scrutiny of that judgement. Strong discretion also existed where an official was not bound by the standards, although that would not constitute a licence to act in any way at all, as criticism of that discretionary decision could be made. Neither did it mean an official reached decisions of judgement that were outside standards of fairness and sense, but rather that the decision was not controlled by standards. Hence, returning to the same metaphor, Dworkin (1978) said such a decision, reached through the exercise of strong discretion, still lay within the doughnut's perimeter.

In the long-running debate in UK statutory social work about whether discretion remains or has diminished, Howe (1991), for example, argued that social workers had lost discretionary power in that much social work was practised in welfare bureaucracies where managers sought to reduce social work discretion. With a nod to Lipsky, Howe (1991, p 219) conceded that 'pockets of freedom' might exist as some work could not be routinised as it required judgement. Lymbery, too, held that social work discretion had been reduced by the 1990 NHSCC Act, arguing that this increased managerial control of social workers had 'potentially serious' consequences for social work with older people. Lymbery maintained social work's location in bureaucratic professional hierarchies (which required accountability to procedural processes, frameworks and standards) reduced the autonomy of an individual worker (Lymbery, 1998; 2001).

As Evans and Harris (2004) noted however, this assumed managers could control workers' behaviour in ways that dampened down their discretion and autonomy. In reality, managers may be ignorant of the detail of operational policies and the realities of day-to-day practice. Most social work practice, as well as the work of other street-level bureaucrats (such as nurses or police officers in adult safeguarding), is done far away from a manager's eye, as Evans and Harris (2004) observed. The strength of local team cultures (or 'the way things are done here') means professional autonomy can be exercised in policy implementation (Preston-Shoot, 2001). Salman's (2007) interviews with British social workers illustrated how practitioners 'played the game', for example: 'you bend rules by talking up clients' needs, in order to help them; it's called the rationing game' (a former social services director); or, 'I need to bend the rules because my employer has raised the barrier to eligible needs' (social worker with older people).

Other empirical work suggested the exercise of professional discretion in decision-making survived the community care reforms of the 1990s, although social workers may have thought otherwise. Ellis et al (1999) looked at how far 'bottom-up' decision-making by social workers was controlled by the 1990s community care changes. In their research with six social work teams, the discrete steps of assessment and care management were 'experienced as an assault on professional identity' (Ellis et al, 1999, p 274), and a threat to good practice. The researchers found, however, that the team with the heaviest referral rates was driven by assessment and eligibility criteria and, despite their claim to provide needs-led assessments, this hospital social work team focused on the provision of personal care, that is, a *service*-led response. The authors concluded that professional discretion had been used defensively in the past to ration services and social workers' professional autonomy then was 'something of a myth' (Ellis et al, 1999, p 277). They identified similarities with the circumstances (scarcity and uncertainty) Lipsky had described, saying that in some ways community care changes recreated some of the conditions of an earlier era, when frontline staff had ultimate responsibility for managing overblown and conflictual policy objectives, with insufficient resources and little management oversight.

In other research, Taylor and Kelly (2006) examined how far Lipsky's observations about discretion still applied to public sector bureaucrats, in light of the introduction of greater managerial control over professionals. They differentiated three forms of discretion – rule, task and values – and assessed how far each had been compromised by public sector reform. They found rule-making capacity to be much less influential than before. It was questionable if targets had removed the dilemmas public sector workers faced before their introduction. High levels of accountability generated by new public management added to the street-level bureaucrat workload. The increase in rules and accountability had reduced rule discretion; hence, in Lipsky's terms, reduced the policy-making role of street-level bureaucrats. There was less scope for workers to deviate from formal controls. However, rules may not be operable in unpredictable situations. There remained a high level of task discretion, as the way in which complex tasks are performed cannot be specified precisely. Values discretion, or the beliefs workers bring to the job, were harder to influence. Task-based discretion may have increased as professionals were required to consider the implications of their tasks, for targets, managers and customers. Taylor and Kelly (2006, p 640) concluded that the policy-making discretion Lipsky wrote of 'is, for the most part, over'.

Evans and Harris (2004) came to a somewhat different conclusion. They suggested that increased rules and procedures do not automatically result in greater control – more rules may in fact create more discretion. For Evans and Harris (2004) discretion was not either there or not there in decision-making; the existence of discretion was not the absence of rules. Professional judgement has to be exercised in relation to a standard, to a procedure, to the legislation and regulation applying to a particular situation: professionals have to decide what rule operates in what situation at what time. Rules can open up scope for the exercise of discretion rather than the reverse. In any case, discretion is neither inherently bad nor good; it may be important in some situations, in others it may be a cloak for professionals to hide behind, or an opportunity for misuse of professional power. Maynard-Moody and Portillo (2011), for instance, argued that excessive rules contribute to (rather than limit) the exercise of discretion. Extensive rules introduce discretion into prescriptive systems, as the applicability of each rule has to be decided upon: street-level workers decide which rules to follow and which to ignore (Prottas, 1979). Further, as Evans and Harris (2004) asked, who decides where and when the shift from individual discretion to formal procedures actually occurs? As professionals make this judgement, they concluded, '… by creating rules, organizations create discretion' (Evans and Harris, 2004, p 883). As for social work, even in the highly rule-bound places in which they practise, Evans (2012) maintained social workers retained significant freedom in their work .

Perhaps because of that, the inevitability of discretion being exercised in street-level work, and the democratic control issues this raises (that is, the question of whether the democratic mandate is being carried out by the people paid to implement public policy) have been of longstanding interest to policy-makers. In their primary research carried out in five agencies ('street-level bureaucracies' in the language of Lipsky) in two US states, Maynard-Moody and Musheno (2000) identified a dominant academic narrative, which viewed self-interest as guiding street-level choices, in other words, street-level workers used discretion to make their work easier, safer and more rewarding. A second, very different story was told by street-level workers who regarded themselves as citizen agents acting in response to individuals and circumstances, basing their decisions on the worth of the individual citizen agent. Here, street-level workers discounted self-interest to meet individual needs, and in so doing made their own work harder. In this research, street-level workers described themselves as decision-makers who based those decisions on normative choices, not rules, procedures or policies. They defined those normative choices in terms of their relationship to citizens, clients, co-workers and the systems they worked within. From their perspective, street-level workers saw themselves acting responsibly, defining their work in terms of relationships not rules. Discretion was thus exercised in a context of social relations. Maynard-Moody and Musheno (2000) characterised street-level work as bound by a chain of hierarchical relationships, where discretion permeated every level: '[s]treet-level work is, ironically, rule saturated but not rule bound' (Maynard-Moody and Musheno, 2000, p 334). This street-level discretion was generally tolerated or ignored by managers, but when discretion led to scandal or public concern the response was always to enhance bureaucratic control.

## The exercise of discretion in adult safeguarding

The exercise of discretion in adult safeguarding and in decisions taken to protect an older person from abuse is diffused across the professional groups and agencies involved. Social workers, healthcare professionals, police officers and other adult safeguarding colleagues, have influence over aspects of their work that are not measured, monitored and reported upon by adult safeguarding systems. In adult safeguarding in England and Wales, local policies set out time limits for completion of different stages of the adult protection process, for example, a time limit for raising an alert when abuse is suspected or alleged, and for holding the first multi-agency meeting (often called strategy meetings. See, for example, *Wales Interim Policy & Procedures for the Protection of Vulnerable Adults from Abuse*, 2010). In Wales, StatsWales collect national adult protection data on the total number of adult protection referrals in a year, the number that led to investigation, and the number that were risk-managed. Aggregated and disaggregated local data will indicate the throughput of a case, what meetings were held when, with what outcome. They do not (and cannot) indicate, though, how professionals weighed up information, what drove their decision-making to risk-manage, investigate, or do nothing.

In Scotland, as discussed in Chapter Four, the 2007 ASP(S) Act requires local authorities to make enquiries about an adult's well being if it is known or believed that the person is an adult at risk, and that intervention may protect the person's well being, property or financial affairs. Nonetheless, even within this statutory framework, there is scope for discretionary action. Deciding if the adult is an 'adult at risk' is open to discussion and interpretation. Age or disability are not of themselves markers for being at risk: being aged 89, for example, does not in and of itself imply vulnerability or need. Thresholds of intervention are fluid and influenced by custom and practice, including how workers construct, view and see the situation in front of them. That, of course, is an exercise in discretion.

## Understanding policy implementation, understanding the street-level bureaucrat

Lipsky's work in street-level bureaucracies was carried out in the US in the second half of the twentieth century. His book *Street-level Bureaucracy: Dilemmas of the Individual in Public Services* fundamentally altered the way organisational hierarchies and policy implementation are regarded, shifting focus to the context, structure and systems that saturate rule-based human service work. The concept of 'street-level bureaucracy' has engaged academics and practitioners internationally (for example, Hill, 1987, 2012; Barrett, 2004; Dunér and Nordström, 2006) although, with some exceptions (for example, Clark-Daniels and Daniels, 1995; Ash, 2010), generally not in elder abuse research. Since the book's publication in 1980 (and its updated edition of 2010 to mark 30 years of unbroken publication) considerable attention has been focused on the exercise of discretion and, in both adult and child safeguarding, on professional failures to follow procedures. As noted earlier, this is not an either/or matter – 'either professionals exercise discretion or they follow a rule-book'. Rather, discretion is context-contingent: it is structured by, and in turn structures, the rule-bound organisations within which it is exercised. As Ellis (2013, p 14) observed, exercising discretion implies 'in theory ... the power to choose between models of practice'; however 'the nature and scope of that power can only be understood by reference to the contexts within which it is generated'.

In adult safeguarding, rules and procedures do not protect older people from abuse, nor do they in and of themselves improve professional practice. They may be necessary but they are not sufficient to ensure an older person is safeguarded from mistreatment. Procedures may exist, but not be read, used or understood. Local cultures may shun close attention to procedural detail, and the power of the workplace norms, as Lipsky (1980) said, may well override policy intentions. The existence of procedures, guidance and training does not resolve the tension between proceduralisation and the exercise of professional discretion. Even if 'the best' procedures and training could, firstly, be developed and, secondly, protect elders from abuse – patently absurd propositions – dilemmas remain for the street-level bureaucrat in their exercise of judgment and discretion to protect a vulnerable elder.

In Chapter Two, this book set out a case for the use of theory in understanding elder abuse. With Lipsky's work on street-level bureaucracy, Maynard-Moody and Portillo (2011) have queried whether this was a theory, in a narrow meaning of specific predictions amenable to hypothesis-testing. However, Lipsky's concept and explication of street-level bureaucracies and the behaviours of the street-level bureaucrats working in them, offer a coherent and grounded set of observations and principles that themselves have generated a wide range of generalisable empirical work, in a many street-level bureaucracies internationally. The nature and funding of the public service systems in which those street-level bureaucracies have been located have varied greatly; that Lipsky's conceptual framework has 'spoken to' the street-level bureaucrats' experience of public service in those organisations is strong rationale for the salience of the concept in understanding organisational decision-making, discretion and policy implementation.

The following chapter reports on a case study that used Lipsky's concept of street-level bureaucracy to identify constraints and factors social workers and their managers grappled with when they dealt with potential abuse of an older person.

# SIX

# A case study of street-level policy implementation to protect older people from abuse

For the older person at risk of abuse, the ins and outs of adult safeguarding policy are likely to be of less immediate concern than the impact on them of the actions or behaviour of professionals and staff who are paid to implement it. As described in Chapter One, the case study reported below arose directly from the findings of a number of cases the author had been asked to review since the agreement of national policy on adult protection in England and Wales (DH, 2000; NAfW, 2000). In these cases, two common themes seemed to be present. First, professionals placed superordinate importance on the service user's exercise of 'choice'. If the adult had mental capacity they could, as discussed in Chapter Four, make all the bad choices they wished. In one particular case, which led to the research reported in this chapter, a woman in her seventies was badly beaten by her son; her refusal to complain to the police was deemed by social services and NHS staff involved to be 'her choice', and left at that.

Second, as noted in Chapter One, professionals, when confronted with potential abuse of an older person often seemed reluctant to use adult protection policy. This could have been explained in the immediate aftermath of agreement of national adult protection policy as their lack of awareness or understanding of either or both elder abuse and adult protection. However, as time wore on and adult protection trainings had been delivered to many thousands of staff, this explanation seemed a little thin. If there was something else going on, what was that? How did it influence the action paid workers and professionals took when presented with an elder abuse allegation or suspicion?

These questions found form in a case study carried out in a social services department ('The Department') in Wales. The questions were asked, first, to find out what constraints and realities influenced social workers' decision-making when they were dealing with potential abuse of an older person; and second, to find out if Lipsky's concept of street-level bureaucracy offered anything by way of understanding factors that influence local implementation of adult protection policy by social workers and their managers. Every social worker and manager working with older people or in an adult protection role in The Department was interviewed or took part in a focus group, and The Department's adult protection monitoring statistics and documents (such as annual reports, minutes of adult protection committee meetings) covering a two year period were analysed (see Ash 2013 for further information about research design, methods and data analysis). The research was confined to local authority social services (rather than taking in the multi-agency adult safeguarding system and its component partners) because of limits on time and funding. To safeguard the anonymity of respondents in a small country, detailed respondent identifiers are not included in what follows, other than indicating whether a respondent was a frontline social worker (Lipsky's 'street-level bureaucrat'), or a departmental manager.

This chapter discusses five themes that emerged from the research: social workers' awareness of elder mistreatment; The Department's culture and organisation; dilemmas of resources that social workers and their managers grappled with; dilemmas of care for older people; and the exercise of professional power; and discretion in the implementation of adult protection procedures. This chapter develops previously reported discussion of three of these themes (Ash, 2010; 2011b; 2013), and considers some broader implications of the findings.

## 'Seeing' elder mistreatment

Considering the first UK prevalence survey on the prevalence of elder abuse in the UK found Wales to have the highest reported rates of mistreatment of the four nations (O'Keefe et al, 2007), the relatively low number of adult protection referrals concerning older people in The Department was puzzling. In The Department, adult protection referral rates concerning older people were on a par with other groups of vulnerable adults. The national picture in Wales has shown older people referred more often (followed by adult protection referrals concerning people with a learning disability); and this pattern has been the case for a number of years (CSSIW, 2013). In addition, levels of adult protection referrals made by social workers in The Department were low relative to the national picture.

If social workers were making relatively few adult protection referrals this raised the question of how aware they were of elder abuse, and of the thresholds they may have used to decide if concerns were dealt with in or outside the adult protection procedures. Were social workers seeing questionable practices and behaviours but not querying these as potential mistreatment, or were they simply not seeing these practices at all? This question of 'seeing', and challenging abuse came to prominence in The Department when a large-scale adult protection investigation of a care home was instigated by the social care regulator (reported in Ash, 2013). This care home had been discussed by social workers and their team manager in the first focus group held at the start of the research. One social worker said of this regulated care home: "the whole place was an abuse … it was awful". Conversations about how bad this place was were familiar topics of conversation between social workers and their colleagues in The Department, and in other agencies such as the NHS. However, as the care home was regulatorily compliant, social workers and nurses had continued to place older people there.

Social workers and nurses periodically went to this care home to carry out statutory reviews of the care plans of older people to whom they had a duty of care. During the research, some social workers spoke of their guilt in not having picked up what was, apparently, everyday life for older people, where as one described, "if a person got out of their chair because they were trying to attract the attention of someone… before they (could) say anything they were told to sit down".

Once the adult protection alert had been raised, a large-scale adult protection investigation commenced. One Department manager said this investigation

> '… shocked a lot of people. There's a lot of guilt around these situations. I've talked to nurses who say 'I did a review there two months ago why didn't I pick up these things?' I've talked to social workers who say we've known for ten years (the home) is not a very great place but we've placed people there. There's a lot of guilt and discomfort around that.'

These expressions of shock were puzzling, given the standard of care provided by this home was known about. Social workers talked about it the office. One manager acknowledged that: "people have come back and talked…about examples of swearing in front of people and things like that, [not] treating people with respect really". The social worker, quoted above, who described the care home as 'the whole place was an abuse' had returned to the team and spoken about their latest visit, but had taken no further action. No witness statements were made of what had been seen and heard, nothing was said to the person-in-charge of the care home at the time, no discussion or decision about taking action (other than describing events to colleagues) had occurred.

This 'not raising an alert' raised several thorny questions. Were social workers confident and competent to challenge poor care when they came across it? One manager wondered how assertive social workers were when a care home presented a particular 'front' to them, when they undertook a care plan review with an older person:

> 'How confident do social workers feel to probe, and also when you're reviewing how much do you accept what you're told? It [the large-scale abuse alert] has raised a few questions I think, as to how we review, how you can get a more accurate picture from reviews. ...How do you get a really good view of what's going on when you've got a very limited window of opportunity, how do you get behind that stage management?' (Department manager)

Another manager wondered if the reticence about raising concerns was because social workers had very little ongoing contact with an older person they placed in a care home: they didn't have much chance to get behind any stage management. Social workers simply did not go to care homes often enough to know what was going on and what life was like for people living there. Unless a social work service was part of an agreed care plan (and this seldom was), as care managers their role was typically one of periodically reviewing care plans. Even if a social worker did not personally witness poor care, the care plan review system was designed to identify what life was like for the service user, and if assessed needs were being met by a service. However, these reviews seldom generated concerns about standards of care. One Department manager described care plan reviews as "cursory at the best", and another social worker observed:

> 'I don't remember a single example of a POVA-type [protection of vulnerable adults] enquiry or concern being realised by a social worker as a result of their visit to a particular home. Our involvement with a home, once someone's in there...it's set piece really – reviews.' (Social worker)

In this 'whole-place-was-an-abuse' care home, low-level yet observable abusive practices were tacitly tolerated by social workers and nurses who placed older people in it. Older people, at the end of their lives, who may have been frail, highly dependent or cognitively impaired, were likely to die in that place or in another institution such as a hospital. Their last days would be spent in surroundings where coarse speech and swearing by paid staff were the everyday norm, where they were fed roughly, not given their dentures, or told to 'shut up' if they asked for help.

### Domestic abuse in older age

As discussed in Chapter Three, the prevalence of domestic violence in older age is an under-recognised but very real aspect of family violence. In this case study, there were no examples of social workers using domestic abuse referral and support systems and procedures to protect an older person from abuse by their intimate partner. Instead, there seemed to be a feeling of professional impotence:

> 'A gentleman had admitted he had hit his wife. She was very upset but having spent a lot of time with them with one of my colleagues we discovered that this was how their marriage had been for 35 years. Their children were now grown up [and said] 'oh yeah, that's quite normal behaviour' [for them].' (Social worker)

Social work intervention was seen as limited as:

> 'We can only do so much as social workers because it does get to that point where the only way you can solve the problem is get a divorce and if they choose to live like this in their marriage then we can't control that.' (Social worker)

Social work intervention in domestic abuse seemed much more likely where there were younger partners and children involved; as one team manager commented "it tends to be much more domestic violence as being seen for younger people (sic)" while domestic abuse with older protagonists was more likely "to go down the POVA route".

Social workers placed significant emphasis on an older person's exercise of choice. When considering a situation concerning the contact a mother had with her adult son who was known by health and social services to take his mother's money, hit and threaten her, a team manager commented: "for me the issue is whether she is making informed choices...what is she weighing in her decision-making. ...We should be prepared to endorse the individual's right to make choices."

For the social workers and their managers, informed choice flowed from whether the person had mental capacity to make a particular decision. 'People have the right to make unwise decisions' was a phrase repeated many times in The Department. The extent to which concepts such as choice, control, independence could embrace, say, dependency or ill-health, was not questioned. Discussion of cases where there were long-term poor relationships between the older people involved did not consider 'domestic violence grown old' and the power relationships within those, as would have been more likely with a younger couple. It was not surprising, therefore, that there were few, if any, support services that older victims of domestic abuse could access.

The whole-place-was-an-abuse institutional adult protection investigation described above had raised uncomfortable questions for managers about the unit cost they paid for beds in care homes, as well as assumptions about what care could be provided to older people, and how, at that price level. Considering this, one manager had begun to think about the ageism implicit in service design:

> 'We know it's blatantly ageist in terms of what we spend on residential and nursing care compared to learning disabilities and things like that. The cost differentials are not just linked to levels of need, they're linked to an assumption about what you provide for older people who no longer need *dot, dot, dot.*' (Department manager)

## Organisational culture

Gareth Morgan (1997, p 138) described organisational 'culture' as:

> Shared values, shared beliefs, shared meaning, shared understanding, and shared sense making are all different ways of describing culture. In talking about culture we are really talking about a process of reality construction that allows people to see and understand particular events, actions, objects, utterances, or situations in distinctive ways.

Eldridge and Crombie (1974, p 89) described the 'unique configuration of norms, values, beliefs and ways of behaving' as characterising organisational culture and the way people and groups work together to get things done. This strongly shapes how professionals practise (Preston-Shoot, 2011). In The Department managers and social workers shared stories, messages and belief systems about services to support care of older people, and had a shared recognition of the factors that constrained the work they did. This homogeneity was striking (and not like the conflicted relationships between managers and staff that Lipsky (1980) had described in the street-level bureaucracies he studied). Both managers and social workers saw the cash-strapped reality of their work with older people as a fact of life – the 'real world' of social services to older people, a challenge that required their creativity, resourcefulness and capacity to make small pots of money go that extra bit further. A cultural message, which both Department managers and community care teams recognised, was the need for social workers and team managers to draw on expertise and knowledge within and across adult services, as there were no in-house specialist posts or units. A manager summed this up "it's you or it's nobody, cock, you know, I'm sorry but it's you or nobody. There's no vulnerable adults team, no reviewing team, no intake team. It's you!"

Rather than simply making the best of a bad deal – a virtue out of necessity – this lack of budgets had become part of a unifying *esprit de corps* that shaped how people described the culture of The Department, and how they worked together. With an evaporation of funding for specialist teams and posts, the pitfalls of specialisation were seen to be avoided (for example, segmenting expertise away from the core, or meeting the transaction costs of trying to get discrete parts of the service system working together):

> 'It puts a lot of pressure on social workers but I do genuinely believe that we've got a staff team who may move slowly but they *all* (respondent emphasis) move because there isn't anything out there that's additional. The more specialised people you get it [expertise] stays with those people, whereas protection of vulnerable adults work has to be like the writing in the rock.' (Department manager)

Social work teams recognised the general supportiveness of The Department. Social workers valued their working culture, which encouraged discussion and tolerated the 'messiness' of decision-making in situations where facts may be few, but anxiety levels acute. One manager, who had worked in The Department for some years prior to promotion, commented, "I've always found the culture supportive in decisions that you've made, and if you can demonstrate you've thought about things, and you've done what you can and you've recorded what you've done, that's supported in the culture."

### Residential care bad, community care good

Staff at all levels in The Department spoke of their goal to support older people at home. Numbers of older people living in care homes in the authority were falling, "which generally we would see as a good thing" as a Department manager observed. Another manager summed up The Department's approach to service and care planning for older people: "we've always felt the last resort is a nursing home. It's not where we feel older people should be living."

Although social workers spoke of this emphasis as a policy that originated with the 1990 NHSCC Act, maintaining older people at home has, of course, had a much longer history in policy intention and service design for older people. 'The importance of enabling older people to go on living in their own home where they most wish to be…is now generally recognised' was the view in 1955 of the then Ministry of Health (Ministry of Health, 1955, p 38. Cited in Means and Smith, 1998, p 319). The large-scale institutional abuse investigation in The Department referred to above catalysed reflection on the cultural mantra described by one manager as "residential and nursing care bad, community good"; the belief that "there will be a day when there's no such thing as residential and nursing care, we don't need it if we were good enough at community care" (Department manager). The questioning of *why* and *how come* the care home subject to a large-scale abuse investigation provided such a dismal quality of life for older people, led to some pondering about the hegemonic hold of the 'residential care bad, community care good' refrain . As one manager reflected, "I think we all know there are times when that type of communal living is … well first of all it's necessary to make it work, but also actually it is in some people's interests …".

As noted, the large-scale abuse investigation had led to questioning of the level of fees paid by the authority for care home placements. It also sparked considerable questioning of the value and purpose of the regulatory and commissioning infrastructure of care home provision for older people. That searching found this infrastructure wanting:

> 'All this [regulatory, commissioning and reviewing] activity that goes on often doesn't seem to get to the heart of how people are living and being cared for. [When a report] throws up quite serious concerns about the place, we think well hang on a minute, we've had contracts with individual people there for a long time. We've had bits of POVA cropping up now and again, why don't we have a full picture of what its like to live in a place like that where the people are subject to abuse and so on?' (Department manager)

## Challenging poor practice

If social workers had not challenged the known poor care of the whole-place-was-an-abuse care home, this raised the matter of how far the organisational culture – as in Gareth Morgan's (1997, p 138) 'shared process of reality construction that allows people to see and understand particular events, actions, objects, utterances, or situations in distinctive ways' description quoted earlier – encouraged or discouraged challenge to poor care practices.

As to how much challenge social workers made to poor care, a manager commented:

> 'Like with everything in management you want to get to a consistent position and we are not at that I would say. There are some people with the confidence to (challenge) and we've seen that recently. Some staff are very good at going in and gently saying that. Other staff say it in a way that isn't productive, or just don't have the courage to say it.' (Department manager)

The same manager could not be certain that staff would recognise and thus challenge some situations that, at best, illustrated poor care practices. They gave an example of prolonged non-interaction by care staff with older people living in a care home, and asked if social workers would challenge a situation where "people are left just sitting in a chair for four or five hours a day without any interaction at all". Another manager was more explicit in saying challenge to this was precisely what managers expected and required:

> 'I can see the staff out there who are doing it [challenge] and I can see the others that aren't and those are the ones we have got to say [stay or go]. Unless they can come up to the mark in terms of really ... holding people to account, unless they can do that and have support to do that then we can't really manage this profession with those people.' (Department manager)

Social workers were aware of the organisational expectation and 'permission' to challenge, as one remarked "you are encouraged to challenge the quality of care and you will be supported in that and the organisation will be very pleased you've done that". Challenging poor practice, though, required confidence as well as practice. Within the multidisciplinary framework of the adult protection procedures, a manager did not find professionally assertive social work to be strong:

> 'One of the things we're not good at is we lose the social work perspective sometimes in the [POVA] process. The bit I don't think we're good at, whilst we're in that process of strategy meetings and potentially an investigation, [is] enabling the social worker to work alongside the [alleged victim] more to support them, to make sure they're involved. I don't think we release the [social work] resource to do that well enough.' (Department manager)

This lack of professional 'uncertainty' – whether to challenge poor practice or take a strong professional role in the adult protection process – reflected the nature of the day-to-day working life of social workers. Social workers who had been in the profession for many years, and who had chosen to stay in frontline practice, mostly spoke confidently about using their role, experience and expertise in uncertain or challenging situations. One experienced social worker, whose career had started in work with older people before joining learning disability services, spoke of:

> '... [my] shock to come back [to work with older people]... to find...although social work practice with older people and the range of service provision [has] improved beyond recognition...when we hit the residential and nursing home sector, it's like nothing has changed, notwithstanding the Care Standards Act. ...They've not resolved the issue between "is this a home or a hospital ward?"' (Social worker)

This social worker compared being in hospital to some nursing homes:

> 'We all do go into hospital for a reason, we all suffer the institution because we've got a short-term medical need. We allow ourselves to be processed medically and you put up with all the indignities because the sole objective of you being there is...you'll get out. But that kind of clinical environment, it can't replace life. That can't be how your life is. A lot of nursing homes in particular are all very much modelled on that...' (Social worker)

This social worker was critical of the weekly rates paid for care home placements, as were others. Asked if awareness of the quality of some care homes was factored into decision-making and care planning, the social worker was equivocal: "I hope it wouldn't affect my judgment if I thought the consequence…was this person is going to end up in a care home, so (therefore) I won't do it."

## Dilemmas of resources

There could be little doubt that in this Department, as elsewhere, the provision of social services to older people was seen as one of managing supply and demand. In this, little has changed in policy and provision predating the introduction of the National Assistance Act and establishment of the NHS in the UK in 1948. In their social history of the development of the welfare state from the Poor Law to community care, Means and Smith (1998) identified the extended taproots of many current dilemmas in service provision for older people. These included rationing of domiciliary care (which only became mandatory for local authorities to provide in 1968), long standing cost-shunting between the NHS and local authorities about who pays for continuing health care needs, and an historical failure to establish older people as a priority for health or social care. Various dilemmas were described by social workers and their managers in The Department; healthcare quality dilemmas and resource shortfall dilemmas were particular challenges in work to support and safeguard older people from abuse.

### The healthcare quality dilemma

In this case study, social workers in The Department commented frequently on the absence of very basic care to older people in some healthcare settings, whether hospitals or care homes with nursing. Stories were told of casually dismissive treatment of older people in care homes, for example, where staff moved residents roughly, or where older people in wheelchairs were, as a social worker described, "trundled round corridors without foot rests". Securing a health check for an older person where there were abuse concerns could be difficult according to one social worker: "sometimes I find [NHS] people waver over things and don't consider (the older person) fully health-wise". Another spoke, presumably with irony, of waiting for the NHS to re-badge relatives as "partners in care", as relatives had to provide so much basic care, for example, helping a loved one to eat, or wash, when they were in hospital.

This social worker saw care homes as having become "the extension of the long stay geriatric wards", affected by the expectations professionals and families had of such services:

> 'I experienced a really good home in the Midlands recently. I was…waxing lyrical to myself about it and I thought about it again…why am I waxing lyrical about it? They're just providing the sort of care you'd expect to be provided for someone.' (Social worker)

Frontline social workers and team managers wondered about the extent to which they (with or without explicit awareness of what they were doing) factored the known poor quality of some services into their decision-making about care, support or safeguarding of an older person. One social worker described their own internal dialogue: "should this person be here? Or should they be somewhere else? At some level you're factoring that in, but I am aware it's a dangerous thought process." This social worker described a familiar dilemma of weighing up the quality of care an older person might have in their own home with that of a care home. Thinking about an older man who was cared for by relatives, the social worker commented that "whatever criticisms you might want to make of his care, and there are criticisms, it's probably significantly higher than your average nursing home".

That dilemma posed by the question – 'how far is known poor quality care influencing your care planning decisions with older people' – was an uneasy one to answer. A Department manager mused:

> 'I don't think for a minute social workers would actually walk away from a situation they thought was abusive but I do think if you said to social workers "are you content with where people are placed, is this the sort of quality of care you'd want," then probably the answer is no.'

That dilemma was not easily resolved:

> 'You've got somebody broken down at home, the carer can't possibly cope anymore, you're going to make a placement, it meets regulatory standards, it's acceptable, but well … That's a very real world for people.' (Departmental manager)

This manager continued:

'At what point can we say we're meeting our statutory duty
by being able to offer homes and at what point is the reality
becoming that if you haven't got a [financial] top-up you're
going to move further afield? Those are just horrible ethical
dilemmas that we live with and we keep saying, well are we
just about on the side of statutory compliance or not ...'

Financial limitations were not however regarded as the main reason
why the quality of care home provision sometimes sank so low:

'We tend to pay above inflationary increases because we
recognise that we're scraping the bottom of the realistic pay
scale...this year we're hoping to put [£] increase in. So the
homes often say you're not paying us enough to provide
high quality care and [while] there is an element of truth
to that, it's not quite that simple.' (Department manager)

These quotes point up the stark impact of these dilemmas on older
people: examples of poor quality care were recognised and known
about; there was an 'incremental' adjustment (but downwards) of
standards of acceptability; all counterposed with 'it's not quite that
simple' to suggest standards were low because of inadequate budgets. A
deeper questioning of the *context* of this dilemma – if quality of support
and services to older people is low and it's not all about money, why
do some older people have to live their final days like this? – was less
evident.

## The shortfall dilemma

Social workers and their managers were well aware of service shortfalls
in The Department, for example, in dementia care and extra care
housing services, or the dearth of some services, such as support to
older victims of domestic abuse. The amount of time people working
in The Department had to spend on adult protection work, generally,
or with older people, particularly, was also constrained. Department
managers spoke of their span of control as precluding long-term focus
on social services to older people, and of the dilemma this posed. As
one manager commented, "it feels a constraint in terms of the time
people like me and [colleague manager] can give to this work...we'd be
much more interested in creating the conditions in which people are
properly looked after". The same manager recognised the importance
of giving focus to older people's services and elder abuse: "I suppose

you can add all the usual money and things like that but I think… strategically it's about giving it attention."

For social workers, the care management process itself limited the time and nature of contact social workers had with an older person; as a manager commented: "they're [social workers] not with people long enough to necessarily get the full picture, but our process doesn't enable people to be in there for long enough". The pressure on time also extended to frontline staff being very aware of the financial implications of decision-making. A social worker in a focus group summed up the financial dilemmas some families faced when an older person lives in a care home:

> '[The Department] have about [£] as the base rate for residential care. Some costs [£ more] which means a top-up. Very few families can afford that, especially if you're talking about someone in their nineties. They could easily have pensioner children…top-ups are a very difficult subject. You say you're not supposed to use your mum's money for this but we know they do in cases, because what's the alternative? It does have a bearing doesn't it?' (Social worker)

## Dilemmas of care

The sub-title of Lipsky's *Street-Level Bureaucracy* was 'Dilemmas of the Individual in Public Services', meaning the individual public sector worker rather than user of the service. Experiences in The Department highlighted the diffused and complex nature of dilemmas social workers faced when dealing with concerns about older people.

### The capacity–choice dilemma

A 'capacity–choice' dilemma pervaded social worker and team manager accounts of the factors they would weigh up when dealing with potential abuse of an older person. As discussed earlier, if an older person had mental capacity, they were deemed able to make their own decisions about care, and about action that could be taken to safeguard them from abuse.

In the case of an older woman who continued to allow into her home an adult son who had physically and financially abused her, a team manager considered that:

'... critical here...is Mrs [X] herself and her capacity to make informed choices around the decision-making around access of her son...and therefore what should our response to that be in terms of fettering that discretion that she clearly has.'

Such dilemmas were portrayed as 'either/or' – either the person had the capacity to make a particular decision, in which case they do what they wanted, or, they lacked capacity and protection arrangements would be instigated. The decisions and 'choices' people made sometimes led to social workers expressing exasperation and bewilderment: "why would you *do* that?" was a weary refrain from one team manager. Nonetheless, considerations of mental capacity and choice featured large in decision-making: if people possessed the former, they were permitted the latter. There were no examples of proactive work with a service user on protecting their wellbeing in risky situations, of exploring the service user's appreciation of potential risks, or of ways to manage these. Similarly, the implications of either/or thinking for those who lacked capacity was equally unexplored. If a person with dementia lived in a care home of marginal quality, what 'choices' would be advocated for them to promote their presumed 'choice' – human right – to be cared for in a dignified and caring way?

## The family care dilemma

The quality of care given by family members to an older person was a source of many dilemmas social workers faced in safeguarding practice. The International Federation of Social Workers' definition of social work is:

> The social work profession promotes social change, problem solving in human relationships and the empowerment and liberation of people to enhance well-being. Utilising theories of human behaviour and social systems, social work intervenes at the points where people interact with their environments. Principles of human rights and social justice are fundamental to social work. (IFSW, 2000)

'Problem solving in human relationships' and intervention 'at the points where people meet their environments' posed particular dilemmas for social workers where there were known concerns about an older person. These 'family care dilemmas' were often located in family dynamics and family structures that had long pre-existed concerns about care, potential abuse or neglect.

Where one older person was caring for another with significant health and social care needs, sheer exhaustion and, not infrequently, a pre-existing poor relationship, could lead to fragile care situations reaching complete collapse. One partner may want the other admitted to a care home, one may refuse to have the other return home after a hospital admission. One team manager (quoted in Ash, 2010, p 206) described a referral concerning the unexplained bruising of an 85 year-old woman with severe rheumatoid arthritis cared for by her 93 year-old husband: "you go from 'this is abuse and is being done deliberately' to hang on a moment, to care for someone who's elderly is quite hard work".

### The protection dilemma

A key factor bearing on implementation of the adult protection procedures by frontline workers was, as noted earlier, their awareness of abuse. Taken up a level, as concerns about poor care or possible abuse came to light, social workers grappled with the 'protection dilemma' – at what point could or should they implement adult protection procedures (thus involving other agencies), in situations where an older person opposed this.

Alleged theft of money was one example. A social worker described a dilemma they had encountered more than once with different service users:

> 'The person said that money had gone missing, [taken] by a carer they liked very much. We held a strategy meeting, and decided the actions that people should take and I went down to speak to the person [service user] and basically he…denied it all even though he disclosed. But you couldn't take it any further then because he wouldn't take it any further. He said he found the money and he wanted the carer back, because the carer was suspended in the meantime, and he wasn't happy about that because he liked the carer.' (Social worker)

The failing physical health of an older person, and the need for high levels of care, could pose intractable protection dilemmas, particularly when concerns intersected with uncertainties about the older person's mental capacity. One social worker described the dilemma of a woman who was bedridden, had fluctuating mental capacity and deteriorating physical health, and who lived alone supported by carers for several hours a day. The woman developed pressure sores, her bed was often soiled, and it was difficult to secure a supply of appropriate incontinence pads for her. Professionals wanted to arrange hospital admission to build up her physical health, but she refused. Her son, who lived in another city, said he had promised his mother she would always be able to stay in her own home:

> 'We used to criticise the son but whenever you actually spoke to him, he was always extremely reasonable in what he said. His mother didn't like being in hospital, she was very unhappy, she screamed and she was very upset and tearful. ... It didn't appear to be what she wanted at the end of the day, but we weren't sure about the capacity. [When she was going to hospital] she would be screaming and crying and shouting and kicking at being led out of the house to the hospital ...so you could argue that she did know where she was and that she didn't want to leave her house.' (Social worker)

A countervailing factor for this practitioner was their concern about standards of hospital care and cleanliness, the risk to the older person of succumbing to a hospital-acquired infection such as MRSA, and whether the older person would be treated with respect, or adequately fed and hydrated while they were in hospital. It seemed that this, as well as the extremely strongly expressed feelings of the older person, resulted in the woman being cared for by paid carers until her death, at home. The reasons why 21st century UK health care could not provide suitable incontinence pads was not questioned by social workers though. Such 'dilemmas of care' were managed in a variety of ways, whether within or outside adult protection procedures.

## Power, discretion and procedures

As discussed in Chapter Five, there has been a long-running debate in UK social work about the loss of professional discretion to the technocratic box-ticking of care management. Accounts of adult protection work in The Department painted a subtle picture of how professional power and discretion in work to protect older people from abuse were exercised. Rather than another simplistic 'either/or' – either discretion is present or it is absent in professional decision-making –

social workers demonstrated a preference for both structured adult protection procedures, *and* for exercising discretion and professional power in *how*, *when* and *why* they used the adult protection framework.

## The value of procedures

Both managers and frontline staff were very positive about their regional adult protection procedures, which had been developed and implemented in the region shortly after national adult protection policy was agreed in 2000 (NAfW, 2000). First, people thought the procedures were clear and comprehensive, with one manager describing it as "a very, very good set of guidance" ... "very straightforward". A social worker found the guidance made "it clearer what you have to do".

Second, the clarity provided both a structure and an efficient process within which agencies such as the police, NHS and social services could jointly decide on action:

> 'To do the information sharing at the professional level [the procedures] actually speeds things up. You are able to find out a lot quite quickly that would be missed if you were doing it in your own little silo.' (Department manager)

This contrasted to case handling prior to agreement of the procedures, described by one Department manager as "…too mushy. You couldn't get hold of it. We used to think what shall we do? Now you can do something with it, and you can bring other people in to help you in that, whereas before you were on your own."

Social workers found the structured procedures their helped their practice and decision-making. The documented adult protection process, where decisions and reasons had to be recorded for actions taken or not taken, was seen as an aid to professional practice, rather than a threat to professional autonomy. *Not* proceeding to adult protection investigation, had to be signed off by a designated adult protection lead, "which is very good. If you're ending this [POVA process] here, why? What's the evidence?" (social worker).

Not being professionally isolated was another gain social workers identified in the adult protection framework. For example:

> 'You don't have to make a decision on your own about something that's quite serious sometimes. I don't think it hinders you really. It's reassuring to sit in a team of people

and make a big decision and not have that sitting on your
shoulders solely.' (Social worker)

Team managers agreed that collective multi-disciplinary decision-
making meant, as one said "you're less likely as a social worker (to be
in a situation) where you're on your own with a case". Timeframes for
discrete parts of the process were explicit. A strategy meeting had to be
held, for example, within a set number of days of an adult protection
alert being raised, if initial information gathering indicated adult
protection procedures should be instigated. Far from being viewed
as a bureaucratic impediment to professional autonomy, this was seen
to offer a basis for planning: "you know there's going to be action
within so many days. I find it really helpful" (social worker). Similarly,
the structure – a framework within which professional opinions were
offered and collective decisions reached – provided space for the
exercise of professional discretion: "I find that it does actually free you
up because it holds you. I find having a structure like that frees you
up" (social worker).

## Professional autonomy and the procedures

Professional autonomy was exercised in decision-making about
whether or not to use the adult protection procedures in the first
place. What was clear from managers and frontline staff was the cultural
'permission' to use, or not use, the procedures, rather than automatically
becoming enmeshed in a procedural process with a momentum of its
own. Frontline staff and managers spoke of the various ways in which
potentially risky situations of potential abuse would be managed, for
example, through risk management processes outside adult protection.

Similarly, cases were spoken of as 'going into and coming out of
POVA'; as one social worker commented "I'm very clear you don't
have to stay in POVA, you can come out as often as you want." The
message that procedures in and of themselves protected no one was
understood: "[e]ven if someone is being investigated under POVA...
it doesn't mean that person is actually going to be protected or the
situation will change, because there might not be the resources, it
doesn't create or magic extra resources" (social worker).

## Discretion in adult safeguarding

Under the adult protection procedures, the purpose of information gathering was for the designated adult protection lead to pool available information, and decide what action to take.

Managers were clear in the messages they said staff and team managers were given:

> 'We advise them (staff) not to use discretion in reporting to their line manager. We say..."it's your responsibility, it's your duty" quite clearly to report under these [procedures], so we don't ask them to use discretion. Then it's up to the line manager to decide whether they're going to take it into POVA or not. And I guess there's some leeway there because that's where that decision making is...is it [poor] practice, is it abuse?' (Department manager)

Other team managers felt The Department encouraged them to "undertake our designated adult protection lead duties with a certain amount of autonomy". Another manager commented:

> 'I think it's a culture in which discretion can be exercised. I know the procedures say you refer to a senior manager, that would be via a discussion so it's not that you refer to senior management for a decision. You'll discuss the decision-making with your manager and so long as that is sound – they will say have you considered this? – but it wouldn't be that they would make the decisions. [Designated adult protection leads] would be expected to be the decision makers, who would be using judgement.' (Department manager)

This expectation that professional judgement could and should be exercised in considering how to manage a case was recognised by others:

> 'As long as people are made to justify how they use their discretion...we all take responsibility for our own actions, so if I miss out [a stage of the procedures] and there's a total mess-up because of that, however good my rationalisation was for doing it, then I'm prepared to take responsibility.' (Social worker)

Discretion was also exercised – and recognised as such – in the way concerns or alerts were described, portrayed and presented in the discussion between the designated adult protection lead and social worker. The social worker quoted above remembered: "I had to generate pages and pages... in order to put the [designated adult protection lead] in a position where he wouldn't just be saying 'well I back your judgement', [but] so he could actually come to that decision himself." Presenting a case in this way was seen as a professional responsibility rather than power.

Despite many examples and descriptions of how professional autonomy and power were exercised within the adult protection procedural framework, these seemed all to be located in decision-making in relation to an individual older person. In other words, the exercise of professional power was individualised, both to the service user, or the social worker or team manager. The wider context to these individual situations, for example, poor care homes, poor treatment of some older people in hospital, was not debated. Systemic and contextual features that may themselves contribute to poor care, for example, perfunctory care plan reviews, fragmented regulation and service commissioning, were not considered or discussed by social workers.

Despite the lack of challenge by social workers in The Department to the poor care they encountered, it is the case that since 2004 in England and Wales that employers and registered social workers have had to comply with the codes of practice for social care workers and social care employers. Social workers are obliged to bring 'to the attention of your employer or the appropriate authority resource or operational difficulties that might get in the way of the delivery of safe care' (CCW, 2002). Social care employers are supposed to have systems in place for reporting poor care. NHS and local authorities have whistleblowing policies in place. Even so, the case study did not find examples where collective professional power had challenged those systemic constraints in the care, support and safeguarding of older people from abuse. Neither the resource shortfalls social workers and their managers identified, nor the constraints and dilemmas these placed on adult safeguarding practice, nor the obstacles and pitfalls of multi-agency work, were regarded as matters to be challenged, questioned or critiqued. The implications of this are described in Chapter Seven.

# SEVEN

# Discretion and dissonance in adult protection work

The case study described in the previous chapter threw light on the real, lived, sometimes messy and frequently contradictory world of adult safeguarding by social workers, with adult protection staff and their multi-agency partners. The influences on decision-making, the day-to-day constraints and the lived reality of this work bring into focus what otherwise remains in shadow: the financial, cultural and organisational context to work with older people. This contextual backcloth has a powerful, but usually invisible (certainly to performance monitoring and adult protection data collection systems and processes) impact on professional understanding of elder abuse.

This chapter reviews and reflects upon the findings of the case study presented in Chapter Six. This discussion utilises and evaluates Lipsky's (1980) concept of street-level bureaucracy; in particular in light of the discretion exercised and dissonance experienced by the social workers and their managers in The Department.

## Lipsky revisited

As noted, for Lipsky, what actually determined the public policy delivered to citizens were the day-to-day realities street-level bureaucrats grappled with: '[t]he decisions of street level bureaucrats, the routines they establish, and the devices they invent to cope with uncertainties and work pressures, effectively *become* the public policies they carry out' (Lipsky 1980, p xii. Emphasis in original). Chapter Five discussed four influences Lipsky identified that he said determined the actual (rather than intended) policy delivered to the public. These were, first, the exercise of *discretion* by street-level bureaucrats: discretion could not be removed as the nature of their work required its use. Second, street-level bureaucrats experienced *dissonance* as they struggled with amorphous or ambiguous policy goals, and developed *cognitive shields* to manage the tension inherent in trying to meet high public expectations, yet with inadequate resources. Third, Lipsky identified the significance of *workplace culture* in maintaining professional morale and, fourth, the paradox of *conflict* co-existing with *reciprocity* in relationships between street-level bureaucrats and managers.

## Discretion at work

For Lipsky, the structure of the street-level bureaucrat's work (whatever their role or profession) made the elimination of discretion impossible. A starting point for the case study had been speculation about why social workers did not always use adult protection procedures when there were safeguarding concerns about an older person. In fact, Department social workers and team managers used the procedures when safeguarding alerts were raised. In contrast to Lipsky's proposition, social workers and managers in The Department liked their regional adult protection procedures; as one social worker had remarked. "I'm very fond of them … I find the procedures great." Adult safeguarding procedures were not seen as limiting professional discretion. Social workers and their managers exercised discretion in their 'coming in and coming out of POVA', that is, case managing in or outside the adult protection framework. The formal adult safeguarding framework, with its flowcharts, time limits, guidance and signposts in and out of 'POVA', gave these social workers and their managers some professional 'cover' in what were often highly uncertain situations (as McCreadie *et al*, 2008 had found elsewhere). As the adult safeguarding procedures were signed up to by the police and NHS, social workers and their managers were provided with the 'protection' of multi-agency buy-in to adult protection decision-making.

To use one of Lipsky's images, this cover appeared to act like a *shield*, protecting one agency (in this case social services) from sole responsibility for decisions taken. In the case study, the structure and multi-agency nature of adult safeguarding work influenced *who* exercised *what* discretion, *where, when* and *how*. As discussed, the exercise of professional discretion in The Department was not an 'either/or' process, but was diffused across the adult safeguarding partnership. Discretion was exercised within Dworkin's 'doughnut', that is, within the procedural framework that represented, again in Dworkin's terms, the 'belt of restriction' that bounded the exercise of discretionary judgement (Dworkin, 1978, p 31).

Adult safeguarding decisions were made within a procedural framework that, by its very nature, structured decision-making (and hence the use of discretion) – but it did not replace it. The text of the procedures repeatedly told its users '*you must consider*', '*you should consult*' '*you must reach a decision and record it*'. These 'musts' and 'shoulds' were directions to consider, consult, reach a decision. None removed professional discretion; rather they directed that professional discretion *should be exercised* within the procedural framework (or within Dworkin's (1978) doughnut). The difference between the experiences of the social workers (street-level bureaucrats) in the case study, and Lipsky's analysis, was the *number* of agencies involved in this exercise of discretion. Rather than one social worker making a decision in a uni-agency bureaucratic hierarchy, decisions were reached by a number of people in a network of organisations, each with distinct yet overlapping remits, roles and responsibilities. In this way, the exercise of discretion was dispersed, but it was not removed.

There were many points in the case study where the identification (or 'seeing') of elder abuse and implementation of safeguarding policy were discretionary, that is not rule-bound but judgement-based activities. As noted in Chapter Three, a death certificate might state septicaemia as a cause of death, without reference (or indeed investigation) into the neglect that led to the condition underlying cause of death developing in the first place (AEA, 2007b). In this way, what was written on the death certificate was an exercise of discretion as well as a record of medical 'fact'. The 'naming' of 'septicaemia', and not neglect, as cause of death would, of course, foreclose further probing into reasons behind the death.

Hence there were many other points at which discretion, and its conjoined twin 'power', were exercised by social workers and by other agencies in this case study. Whether elder abuse was 'named' as such and action taken under adult protection procedures was, in a stark sense, discretionary. There seemed to be points where silent tolerance of a situation without assertive professional intervention, demonstrated an exercise of power and discretion by *inaction*. For example, the poor quality of one particular care home, as well as others, was known about by social workers and their adult safeguarding partners. They talked about it, they were concerned about it, but the adult safeguarding alert was eventually raised on this place by the care regulator. Neither social workers nor nurses used their professional power to name, challenge or confront the abuse, in that case at least.

Lukes (2005) has argued that power exists whether or it is not used; power is a dispositional concept, a *capacity*, not the actual exercise or vehicle of manifestation. In the case study Department, social workers, their managers and their adult safeguarding partners had to operate in the fragmented service and regulatory systems that surrounded provision and protection of vulnerable adults. This fragmentation appeared to *disempower* social workers. In a meeting observed as part of the case study research, one social worker had commented that "social workers are trained to assess, not to investigate". This may have been a reference to the police leading criminal investigations under adult protection procedures, but it said rather more than that. Core social work skills, in essence, comprise an ability to ask good questions; gather relevant information; consider the person in their individual and social context; work with uncertainty, complexity and conflict; to reason, challenge and, ultimately, to reach a professional judgment. These are also investigation skills.

The comment quoted here seemed to diminish the contribution social work skills could bring to adult protection investigations, most of which in any case would not involve a criminal investigation. In understanding this, Lukes again elucidates. Lukes suggested that power was the imposition of internal constraint, which those subject to come to see as natural (Lukes, 2005). In this Department, the apparent disempowerment illustrated above, manifested itself in other ways; for example, in a certain hopelessness, or sense of 'oh well, that's how it is'. There appeared to be a reluctant acceptance that, for example, police investigations into an adult protection alert where a crime was suspected took a long time because the police had other priorities (and there's not much health or social services could do about that); some care homes weren't very good (but they're a last resort anyway and we want to keep older people at home); vulnerable older people have the right to make bad choices (and if they've got mental capacity, they can 'choose' to stay in an abusive environment). Here, Lukes' third dimension of power seemed to play out, as 'the power to prevent people...from having grievances by shaping their perceptions, cognitions and preferences in such a way that they accept their role in the existing order of things' (Lukes 2005, p 11).

The acceptance by Department managers and street-level bureaucrats of their 'role in the existing order of things' was shaken up by the large-scale abuse investigation instigated during the time the research was being done. However, the pieces making up the jigsaw were unchallenged before the whistle was blown on that care home. As Bauman had observed, 'power is measured by the speed with which responsibilities can be escaped' (Fearn, 2006). Professional power to name and advocate and speak out seemed, on one hand, diluted by the complexity and fragmentation of accountability systems. On the other though, the overriding creeds of managerialism, partnership, marketisation and the like, guaranteed compliance – in the *not-questioning* – by persuading street-level bureaucrats that the constraints and realities were inevitable, that their power to do anything about them was limited. The dissonance implicit in this was something familiar to Lipsky (1980).

## Dissonance

As discussed, Lipsky regarded dissonance as a result of street-level bureaucrats struggling with dilemmas inherent in 'a corrupted world of service' (Lipsky, 1980, p xiii), where large caseloads and inadequate resources defeated any ideals and aspirations they brought to the work originally. Lipsky (1980, p 27) located dissonance in the *structure* of street-level bureaucrats' work, for example: chronically inadequate resources; an excess of demand for service over supply; conflicting agency expectations and goals; and involuntary clients.

As noted, Lipsky (1980, p 153) suggested street-level bureaucrats developed 'cognitive shields' to manage this dissonance and survive in the workplace. He suggested cognitive shields might involve street-level bureaucrats' blaming clients for their predicament, in that way lessening the responsibility of the street-level bureaucrat to achieve anything with the client. In the case study Department, dilemmas of resources (usually inadequacy) and dilemmas of care (including its quality) peppered the stories and accounts social workers and their managers gave. But unlike a 'client blaming' cognitive shield of the sort Lipsky had envisaged, these accounts did not suggest a cognitive *shield* (implying some sort of solid, protective barrier), but into a *cognitive mask* that blocked any view of the *context* to those dilemmas (see Ash, 2013 for a fuller discussion of this). Cognitive masks served to silence any questioning about *why* dilemmas existed. They rendered the context surrounding those professional dilemmas invisible, thus closing off assertive, persistent questioning of why there were few if any services to older people abused by their spouses or close family members, why the quality of care in some care homes was so miserable, and why registered and regulated professionals apparently tolerated all this without demur. The cognitive masks limited the capacity of social workers, their managers and adult safeguarding partners to see through, and beyond, contractual and regulatory compliance requirements and systems that, in and of themselves, could not prevent abusive cultures and practices developing like a malignancy in some care homes.

Metaphorically, cognitive masks are formed in a particular time, place and history. They originate from the interpenetration of wider social, cultural and economic influences into organisations, professions and into individual professional practice. At the same time they also – paradoxically – screen off any view of how those ageist social, political and cultural influences impact on the care and support older people may receive, and on the way adult safeguarding partnerships go about their business. Cognitive masks hide the dissonance that can arise when professionals 'know' some care homes and healthcare services are poor, and 'know' the cash put into services and support to older people is inadequate. By not questioning why some care homes are run like old-style geriatric hospitals, or why resources are so limited, cognitive masks obscure the unstated, wordless acceptance of all the dilemmas the street-level bureaucrats in the case study described.

## Workplace culture

For Lipsky (1980), workplace culture was critical in maintaining morale in the face of the dilemmas, ambiguities and pressures street-level bureaucrats faced. In The Department, the adult safeguarding 'workplace' was not one place, team or profession, but many. Multi-agency policy and the fragmented nature of a marketised service system have shifted the 'workplace' to partnerships and inter-agency decision-making.

The 'culture' of this multi-agency workplace was made up both of *instrumental* duties and responsibilities, as well as *expressive* working relationships, shared histories and experiences of working together (Dalley, 1991). In the case study, 'understanding' mutual workload pressures and a tolerance of delays in adult protection work were part of this culture. Professionals from different agencies had to work together, and they accepted the operational and resource pressures their partners faced, as they were under pressure too. Conflict, expressed as holding other agencies to account, or challenging the actions or inactions of partners, was rare in The Department. NHS partners rarely attended adult protection multi-agency meetings, and in any case could not be required to show up. Without a statutory requirement on named agencies to cooperate, the workplace culture of the wider adult protection system was one that accommodated the contradictions inherent within those arrangements (under-resourcing, the differential engagement of partners, and so on). This cultural accommodation –'we're all in the same boat'– seemed, as Lipsky had suggested, to be important in keeping the system going. How far it met the needs of abused older people was less certain. For those older people likely to die in a care home contaminated by institutionalised abusive practices, the professional accommodations of a multi-agency workplace culture would probably hold little interest.

## Conflict between Department managers and street-level bureaucrats

Lipsky (1980) said that the relationship between managers and street-level bureaucrats was inherently conflictual and reciprocal. Conflict arose, he suggested because street-level bureaucrats may not accept organisational rules or had different priorities from managers, whereas managers wanted consistency and compliance. Reciprocity came about as the result of managers accepting informal work processing by street-level bureaucrats to protect the organisation.

The findings of the case study did not support Lipsky's points about conflict in three particular ways. First, at the interpersonal or presentational level, social workers and Department managers spoke of their subordinates and superiors as valued professional colleagues, and the organisational culture as supportive. The exercise of discretion and judgement was encouraged. The 'us and them' conflicted relationships Satyamurti (1981) had described (writing contemporaneously with Lipsky, 1980) between social workers and their managers were not in evidence: the culture appeared unified and mutually supportive. Department managers were social work trained and had come up through the operational ranks (senior practitioner, team manager, operational and strategic management in social services) to the post they held.

Second, cost control, awareness of scarce resources, the need to manage limited cash to best effect – the lifeblood of managerialism – were talked up more by the street-level bureaucrats than by their managers. Social workers spoke, for example, of the costs to a service when a carer was suspended during an adult protection investigation. One team manager in particular was concerned to establish facts by interviewing an alert-raiser (more than once if necessary) before calling a strategy meeting, so as to avoid the costs of unnecessarily bringing professionals together. Managers spoke of making small amounts of cash go further by finding creative ways to deliver services (although few examples were provided in relation to work with abused older people). Like mother's milk, managerialism had been absorbed by social workers and their managers. These street-level bureaucrats did not undermine the system, they operated it. They were incorporated into it.

Third, the rules the adult protection procedures laid down were not resented by street-level bureaucrats. Like managerialism, they were immersed in these: "I like a process to follow, I like 'stages 1, 2, 3, 4'" as one social worker (quoted in Ash, 2013, p 109) said. It is the case that social workers often seek more structured guidance on their work, not less (Preston-Shoot and Wigley, 2002; Evans and Harris, 2004). Street-level bureaucrats in The Department may not have raised many safeguarding alerts to protect vulnerable older people, but they were glad they had the adult safeguarding procedures.

## Lipsky 'then' and 'now'

Lipsky's depiction of life in the US street-level bureaucracies he studied in the 1960s and 1970s has continuing resonance. It is inevitable though, decades on, that differences can be seen between then and early 21st century work to safeguard older people from abuse. The political, organisational and social contexts have fundamentally shifted. Nonetheless the findings of the case study illustrate how the past can play out in the present.

Means and Smith (1998) counselled against summoning up some golden past age –'it was better when' (hardly, if ever, the case where the care and support of older people are concerned) – or cooking up something 'new' that merely recycles old thinking. As discussed in Chapter Four, the political drive in contemporary social care in early 21st century UK has been personalisation in one shape or another (DH, 2006; HM Government, 2007; Leadbeater et al, 2008). In the 1990s, the conceptual buzz was for community, not residential, care. The ideological inheritance of this was evident in The Department, summed up by one manager as "residential and nursing care bad, community good". The primacy of community over residential provision in service planning had led this Department, as elsewhere, to reduce that part of the residential care sector used by older people unable to finance their own care. A 'barely acceptable' care home is not generally a destination of choice for an older person with any real choice about the matter. This is something more than a simple distaste for communal living. The luxury care home market has typically been spared any stigma that can attach to care home living: Lloyd (2006), for example, reported waiting lists for top-end care homes.

Looking back to the inception of the UK NHS in 1948, policy aspirations had been high for post-Poor Law residential care. The old master and servant relationship of the workhouse was to be replaced 'by one more approaching that of a hotel manager and her guests' (Ministry of Health 1950, cited in Means and Smith, 1998, p 155), with the workhouse replaced by 'attractive hostels or hotels… (accommodating people)…who will live there as guests not inmates' (Garland, 1945, cited in Means and Smith, 1998, p 155). The level of investment, though, never matched the aspiration. Whatever ideological *motif* finds approval in public policy, support to older people is seldom a favoured focus. As Phillipson commented decades ago, 'the elderly are an ongoing problem in society where institutions are geared primarily around issues of production and reproduction' (Phillipson, 1977, cited in Means and Smith, 1998, p 8).

In the case study Department, social workers implemented procedures to protect an older person with inadequate resources *and* within the considerably intensified inspectorial and audit regime that regulated increasingly fragmented service and commissioning systems. The extent, nature and complexity of fragmentation, regulatory policing and proceduralisation generate their own pressures on street-level bureaucrats. The place at which those 'regime requirements' met pressure on resources was where dissonance took shape and cognitive masks were created (Ash, 2013). As one manager mused "I suspect what happens really…is that incrementally you know people adjust their standards…and you have to make sure their standards stay above what's acceptable."

Lipsky's 'blaming the client for their predicament' cognitive shield has thus shifted into something less overt. The metaphorical 'cognitive mask' excludes peripheral vision of social, political and cultural factors that bear on how older people are 'seen', supported and treated. A lack of NHS engagement in adult protection structures, or care homes of marginal quality for older people, are facts of professional life for many of those working in health and social care services. They are a commonplace part of a familiar landscape. Add to that a unified *esprit de corps* and a professional distaste for challenge of poor care, and the cognitive mask clouds up even more. The 'commonplace' features, pooled with those generally considered 'a good thing' (supportive colleagues, cooperating with other agencies) can result in inertia (Ash, 2013). Here, Lipsky's observations still resonate:

> Organizational patterns of practice in street level bureaucracies are the policies of the organization. Thus, workers' private redefinition of agency ends result directly in accepting the means as ends…
>
> Accepting limitations as fixed rather than problematic… discourages innovation and encourages mediocrity. It is one thing to say that resources are limited, another to say that the practices arising from trying to cope with limited resources are optimal. (Lipsky 1980, p 144)

A difference between UK social care in the first part of the 21st century and Lipsky's 20th-century urban America, is a regulatory framework that sets national minimum standards for care that, inevitably, become aspirational targets rather than basic requirements. An individual practitioner care planning with an older person may face the dilemma – the trade-off – of, say, a 'collapsed domestic care situation' versus 'risk of hospital-acquired infection here' or 'poor care home there'. That dilemma is bounded by another (which, of course, the practitioner can do nothing about) – 'minimum' care standards that may not be met. Surround that with the miasma of ageism, increasing levels of dependency, a lack of professional challenge to poor care or colleagues – all of this within a complex, diffused and fragmented service and regulatory system – and a toxic fog can descend on street-level implementation of policy to protect older people from abuse. Thresholds for intervention go up as a matter of organisational survival: as Russell (2008) commented, if all concerns raised about vulnerable adults and children led to intervention, social services would collapse. Contradictory pressures of high public expectations and resource shortfalls remain as potent as Lipsky depicted. In this, Lipsky's observations about the significance of the system and structure of street-level bureaucracies on the actual policy and practice at the local level were as relevant for social workers and managers in The Department as they had been for Lipsky's street-level bureaucrats many decades before, although the context within which street-level bureaucrats operate has changed significantly from that Lipsky described.

# EIGHT

# Cultures and contexts of complicity

The case study Department, described in Chapters Six and Seven, had a unified *esprit de corps*. The practice of its street-level bureaucrats (to use Lipsky's language) was not poor; its management was considerate and professional; staff and managers operated as best they could in the adult safeguarding system they were part of. But social workers did not challenge the poor practice they knew about in the care and protection of some older people. They often juggled the least worst options when planning care to meet an older person's needs. Social workers and their managers tolerated delays in police investigations into adult protection allegations, and their NHS partners' infrequent attendance at adult protection meetings held to protect and older person from abuse. Why the silence? Why the unspoken tolerance?

To discuss these conundrums, this chapter looks at the apparent complicity that 'turning a blind eye' to poor or inadequate care, support and protection of older, and other vulnerable, people, illustrates. The case study, and Chapter Five which discussed Lipsky's street-level bureaucracy, identified the influence that social, cultural and institutional contexts have on decisions taken to safeguard older people from abuse. In this chapter, that contextual influence is examined by, firstly, looking at some of the findings of two reports published over 45 years apart: *Sans Everything* (Robb, 1967) and the 2013 Francis Report (2013a) on Mid Staffordshire Foundation NHS Trust. The findings of the Francis Report are considered at length as they illustrate and bear upon a number of the themes identified in the case study. Second, that context is examined a little more deeply, by drawing on the work by Adams and Balfour (1998) on 'administrative evil'. It will be argued that the wider target-driven, standards-based regulatory and management context street-level bureaucrats like nurses, doctors and social workers operate in, powerfully influences the way they do their work in adult safeguarding and with older people more generally. It is a context that can itself create circumstances where institutional neglect and abuse of older people can take root.

While this context was not that of the mid-1960s when *Sans Everything* (Robb, 1967) was published, historic underfunding of health and social support to older people with its entrenched ageism, assumptions of policy and practice as to what 'older people' need have, as noted previously, a long provenance. The argument is not that poor practice and institutional mistreatment of vulnerable people sprouted up only after the introduction of the 1990 NHSCC Act, following some mythic golden age. It is not to say that all professionals are hapless victims of a malevolent system, nor that they should be excused any duty to raise concerns or challenge poor practice. Rather it is to suggest that the chopped-up, rule-bound, target-driven context to health and care itself, the system that street-level bureaucrats and their managers work within, masks the harm vulnerable people using it may suffer.

## Long tail, long tale

Examples of institutional harm and abuse of those whom we would now call 'adults at risk' have a long tail with an extended backward reach. They tell a long tale. *Sans Everything* (Robb, 1967) contained the accounts of family members, nurses, social workers and other professionals, some of them sworn on affidavit, of treatment they had witnessed in hospitals in which older people lived out their last days. One account, by a nurse working in the English Midlands, could have been written of Winterbourne View, a private hospital for people with learning disabilities in England (SGASB, 2012). (This place was closed down in 2011 less than five years after it had opened because of the neglect and ill treatment of service users by nurses and support workers who were paid to provide assessment and treatment.) The account in *Sans Everything* read as follows:

> I have nursed for the last seven years in a well-known geriatric hospital here. It has a growing reputation, largely due to self-advertisement, for the humanitarian and 'new approach' conditions under which the aged patients live. The actual treatment of these helpless old men and women is such that I have taken out an expensive insurance policy in order than I may never find myself a patient there. (A nurse quoted in Robb, 1967, p 5)

In what can now be recognised as a pattern of institutional deafness as well as blindness to concerns raised by professionals, the nurse's accounts, passed by her to the hospital matron, the hospital administrator (twice) and the local press, were rejected.

The person raising concerns finding themselves isolated, disbelieved or victimised are also experiences with a long tail. Another nurse reported in *Sans Everything* that:

> [w]hen you are a student nurse at the beginning of your career, you want to tell your family and friends about the exploitation and brutality that you witness every day. But you soon learn that they don't want to hear about such things. ...You find yourself isolated with your problems. ... once you are qualified you find that to attempt to bring about changes raises problems. It will lead to investigations which may be unwelcome to colleagues whom they involve; to your being blamed for people losing their jobs, and – no matter how legitimate your complaint – to your being penalized. ...it becomes a case of 'Give in – or get out.' And it is always easier, in all professions, to accept the *status quo*. (Robb, 1967, p 16)

In the Foreword to *Sans Everything* (Robb, 1967), consultant psychiatrist Russell Barton pulled no punches:

> Institutions develop powerful instruments of defence for their protection and perpetuation. Sometimes their officers or governing bodies lose sight of the primary purpose for which they were planned and their energies become deployed in rituals or personality conflicts. The purpose becomes subordinated to the personnel. (Barton, 1967, p ix)

Barton identified characteristic protective responses to poor care, including 'no comment', 'denial', and discrediting the person raising concerns, whom we would now call a whistle-blower. He commented:

> Discrediting the person giving evidence is a more subtle defensive mechanism. It may be done implicitly by informal gossip. ...Imputation that a person is motivated by malice or pathological zeal is a variation of this *ad hominem* approach... (Barton, 1967, p ix)

The process involved, using psychiatric language of the time, was described as this:

> [s]taff of institutions develop neurotic self-propagating
> traditions such as misplaced loyalty of one staff member
> to another. Only a deviant will shop a colleague. ...To
> criticise forcibly rather than to cover up is to rock the
> boat. Victimization of anyone who is critical, whether
> justifiably or not, may be automatic. Poor references, bad
> ward assignation, night duty, permission for holidays at
> inconvenient times, no promotion, are some of the more
> obvious 'punishments' that may be meted out without fear
> of criticism. (Barton, 1967, p x)

Over 45 years later, in 2013, the Francis Report was published in England. This was the product of a public inquiry that had followed an independent inquiry (also chaired by Robert Francis, QC) into the NHS care and treatment people received from Stafford hospital (and some neighbouring NHS facilities) in England between 2005 and 2009. Before this, the Healthcare Commission (HCC) in England had published a highly critical report in March 2009 of its investigation into concerns about mortality and the standard of care provided at the Mid Staffordshire NHS Foundation Trust. The Independent Inquiry had observed that 'it was striking how many accounts related to basic nursing care as opposed to clinical errors leading to injury or death' (Mid Staffordshire NHS Foundation Trust Inquiry, 2010, p 9). About half the patients and their families, who gave oral evidence, spoke of problems patients had obtaining appropriate food and drink. This failure to ensure basic needs such eating and drinking were met featured recurrently in other reports on published contemporaneously with the inquiries into Mid Staffordshire NHS Foundation Trust (for example, OPCW, 2010; EHRC, 2011; CQC, 2012).

In his press statement made on 6 February 2013, the day the Public Inquiry report was published, Robert Francis QC, the Inquiry Chairman, spoke of the:

> appalling and unnecessary suffering of hundreds of people.
> They were failed by a system which ignored the warning
> signs and put corporate self interest and cost control ahead
> of patients and their safety. ...There was a lack of care,
> compassion, humanity and leadership. The most basic
> standards of care were not observed, and fundamental
> rights to dignity were not respected. Elderly and vulnerable
> patients were left unwashed, unfed and without fluids. They
> were deprived of dignity and respect. Some patients had

to relieve themselves in their beds when they offered no help to get to the bathroom. Some were left in excrement stained sheets and beds. They had to endure filthy conditions in their wards. There were incidents of callous treatment by ward staff. Patients who could not eat or drink without help did not receive it. Medicines were prescribed but not given. The accident and emergency department as well as some wards had insufficient staff to deliver safe and effective care. Patients were discharged without proper regard for their welfare. (Francis, 2013c, p 1)

The 2013 Francis Report (2013b) described the culture of the Mid Staffordshire Foundation NHS Trust as one of self promotion, devoid of self-critical analysis and openness; one that took false assurance from good news, yet tolerated or explained away bad news. Business was conducted in private. Reports raising concerns were denied or discounted as unfair: it was believed that there was much good practice, as though good practice in one area mitigated the harm and suffering of patients elsewhere. The Board and managers relied passively on external assessments rather than unfavourable internal ones (Mid Staffordshire NHS Foundation Trust Inquiry, 2010, p 16), and took false comfort from reports that appeared not to have been read or understood, for example, mortality rate data (Francis Report, 2013a). On 15 April 2013, Mid Staffordshire NHS Foundation Trust was placed in administration as it was neither clinically nor financially sustainable. On 29 August 2013, the UK Health and Safety Executive announced its first criminal prosecution of Mid Staffordshire NHS Foundation Trust over the death of a diabetic patient admitted to Stafford hospital after a fall in 2007 who was not given insulin (*The Guardian*, 2013).

## Treating targets, not patients

Mid Staffordshire NHS Foundation Trust's focus on targets rather than the patient experience, and indeed patient survival of care and treatment, saw concerns responded to by reference to generic data or star ratings of one sort or another, rather than the experiences of patients. Hence targets were 'treated', that is, received attention, but patients were often not provided with very basic nursing care. Target-driven priorities, for example the wait time to be seen and receive care in the Accident & Emergency (A&E) department in Stafford Hospital, 'generated a fear, whether justified or not, that failure to meet the target could lead to the sack' (Mid Staffordshire NHS Foundation Trust

Inquiry, 2010, para 43, p 16). The experience of a staff nurse who blew the whistle on fabricated records is discussed further below.

The Independent Inquiry came to the view that while benchmarks and star ratings might be useful tools, they may not always bring to light serious systemic failings (Mid Staffordshire NHS Foundation Trust Inquiry, 2010). The Primary Care Trusts (PCTs, the local commissioners of healthcare at the time, who were charged with monitoring and improving the quality of services they procured from the public purse) had the tools that, on paper, would have allowed them to require safety and quality standards, monitor performance, and pursue remedies on behalf of patients, individually and collectively, when standards were not met. However, at the wider system level, PCTs worked to national (DH) guidance that did not lend itself to more than relatively crude measures, with the focus on financial control and a handful of access targets. The Francis Report did not consider it surprising that this slow development of sophisticated tools, against this backcloth of political and policy obsession with targets and financial control, had the result that, despite the quality industry and its seductive rhetoric, 'one of the worst examples of bad quality service delivery imaginable was not detected by this system' (Francis Report, 2013b, p 48).

## Someone else's job

The Independent Inquiry found the Trust Board relied on the distinction between strategic and operational issues, and disclaimed its responsibility for the latter. The Independent Inquiry did not consider this distinction justified: directors should not fail to interest themselves in operational matters when governance systems were either not in place, or were untested (Mid Staffordshire NHS Foundation Trust Inquiry, 2010). Three years later, the Public Inquiry noted the 'constant refrain from those charged with managing, leading, overseeing or regulating the Trust's provision of services that no cause for concern was drawn to their attention, or that no one spoke up about concerns' (Francis Report, 2013b, p 41). Local GPs only expressed concern about the quality of care provided after the Healthcare Commission had launched its investigation and they were asked about concerns they had (Francis Report, 2013b, p 47). The HCC investigation into this Trust was embarked upon only because there was serious cause for concern. Yet the reaction of other bodies responsible for oversight and regulation was to await the outcome of the investigation and to rely on the HCC to inform them of matters requiring the urgent attention, rather than to consider for themselves what was wrong and what if anything, needed to be done for the protection of patients in the here and now, not in some post-report future (Francis Report, 2013b, p 43).

Professor Sir Bruce Keogh, the NHS medical director of the DH at the time, described some generally prevalent, instinctive reactions to healthcare performance data such as the Hospital Standardised Mortality Ratios, or HSMRs. Causes for concern that HSMR data in Mid Staffordshire NHS Foundation Trust highlighted had been claimed by the Trust to be simply artefacts of coding. A first response was to dispute the data as wrong, a second to say data analysis was wrong and then, Professor Sir Bruce Keogh said, '… you get a bunch of academics to argue about it. …I think it would be fair to say that at the same time as allowing that argument to happen, it would be sensible to go in and look and see if there's a fire where there's some smoke' (Francis Report 2013a, p 1362).

In considering concerns raised in connection with the Trust, the strategic health authority often concluded there was nothing of concern that required exceptional action:

> It took false comfort from the notion that some potential causes for concern were not exceptional in trusts under its oversight. This was due to an overall culture which was too ready to place trust in provider boards, was readier to defend providers than to consider the implications of criticisms and concerns being expressed, and was prepared to assume that others would share information showing concern and requiring action without being asked. (Francis Report, 2013b, p 50)

The overlapping functions of the then health regulators in England had the result that regulators tended to assume that the identification and resolution of non-compliance was the responsibility of another entity (Francis Report, 2013b, p 67–8). The Francis Report found the system operated on the basis of misplaced trust; that other parts of the regulatory and policy system should be trusted to do their bit, irrespective of evidence that indicated systemic and operational concerns.

The Public Inquiry found many examples of misplaced trust, including the assumption by one regulator (Monitor, set up in 2004 to authorise and regulate NHS foundation trusts) that another regulator (the HCC) knew of the Trust's application for Foundation Trust status and that the HCC would tell it of any concerns; and a general reliance by the DH and HCC on the accuracy of self-assessments of compliance and on exception reporting (where no news is deemed to be good news). (Francis Report, 2013a), On 'misplaced trust' and 'mistaken assumptions', the Francis Report (2013a, p 1365) concluded:

> No organisation charged with a responsibility of supervision, oversight or regulation was entitled to assume others were fulfilling theirs. Were such a position to be considered valid it is open to question whether there was any purpose in having such a responsibility at all. It would be one devoid of any accountability, as, except in extreme circumstances, it could always be met by reliance on the assumption.

In his press statement to launch the Public Inquiry Report, Robert Frances said he hoped his recommendations marked the beginning of a journey towards a healthier culture, 'where personal responsibility is not thought to be satisfied by a belief that someone else is taking care of it; where protecting and serving patients is the conscious purpose of everything everyone thinks about day in day out' (Francis Report, 2013c, p 9).

## Boiling the frog

The gradual erosion of standards of patient care in parts of the Mid Staffordshire NHS Foundation Trust, and indeed the cessation of any questioning about the quality of care provided, and what registered professionals like doctors and nurses should do about it, illustrated the corrosive, subtle effects of a silent acceptance of the unacceptable. Like boiling a frog, the effect is slow, initially not painful, but is ultimately, and inevitably, tragic. With one or two exceptions, registered doctors and nurses stopped raising concerns. One A&E consultant said the corrosion was so gradual that he ceased to recognise it (Francis Report, 2013a). It seems indeed, that for evil to thrive, it is enough that good people do nothing.

The Francis Report called for a cultural change, where honesty, transparency and candour were upheld, and where personal interests were not allowed to outweigh the duty to be honest, open and truthful; a culture that did not mislead by not telling the whole story, and one where directors of healthcare organisations were under a statutory obligation to be truthful in any information they gave to outside bodies such as the healthcare regulator and healthcare commissioners. As an illustration of a 'culture of withholding', thirteen pages of the Francis Report were devoted to the case of John Moore-Robinson, a previously fit young man, who had been examined by a junior doctor in A&E at Stafford Hospital after an accident on his mountain bike. He was discharged, in a wheelchair as he could not walk and was being sick, and advised to take pain killers. Mr Moore-Robinson died the following day at another hospital; he had a ruptured spleen. The Trust withheld from the Coroner three reports of an A&E consultant who had grave concerns, and was of the opinion that care of Mr Moore-Robinson in A&E had been negligent. The Public Inquiry concluded that the reports of the A&E consultant should have been disclosed to the Coroner.

## Whistleblowing: an acid test of a healthy organisational culture

The Francis Report illustrated the far-reaching impacts of organisational culture on individual and team professional practice and behaviour. Examples of bullying, feeling bullied, of raising concerns and then giving up when they were ignored; of blaming and scapegoating the person raising concerns or of finding fault with the way they raised the concern, rather than dealing with the concern itself, were repetitive themes in the way in which the Trust responded. The failure to speak out of the majority was not related to a pay-grade or profession. Doctors and consultants who gave evidence to the Public inquiry fared little better than nurses; they spoke of the Trust's bullying culture, the dictatorial style of the Trust chief executive whose departure from consultants' meetings would be followed by a torrent of complaints and criticisms, none of which had been raised when he was in the room (Francis Report, 2013a). A few doctors took action to pursue concerns; no clinician appeared to have taken their concerns outside the Trust to a regulator, the PCT or the strategic health authority. Some registered medical practitioners had not heard of the then healthcare regulator, the HCC. One consultant, asked why he had not done more to voice his concerns about patient care said 'you're always watching your back. At the end of the day, I'm a human being. I might make a mistake and that could be the end of my career, because it will be used against me.' Another doctor, not a consultant at the time but with 25 years' NHS experience, raised his concerns about the Trust's A&E department, and reported these to the HCC. He did not regard himself as a whistleblower: 'I regarded myself as a professional who was attempting to understand if it was just me that felt that this was an unacceptable state of affairs, and whether or not other people were saying "No, actually, this is – this is okay and you can do this, this and this, and this will help to change the direction'" (Francis Report, 2013a, pp 238–40).

As noted earlier, the falsification of patient wait times in A&E had been raised by a whistleblower: this staff nurse's report, making a serious and substantial allegation about the leadership of A&E department in Stafford Hospital, was at the centre of the Public Inquiry (Francis Report, 2013a, pp 107–11). In October 2007 the staff nurse alleged said she had been asked to fabricate the times recorded in the notes of a number of patients whose length of stay in A&E exceeded the four-hour waiting time target, that is, to make it look as though the patient care had not been in breach. The staff nurse understood the sisters in charge of A&E were put under pressure not to report target breaches. One month later the staff nurse made a second complaint and reported she had been threatened by colleagues of the nurses referred to in her first report. She alleged that there was bullying of staff and junior doctors, a fear of speaking out and an extremely violent response when concerns were raised. After she had made her complaint, the staff nurse was warned by others to watch out as 'people knew where she lived'. She approached her professional body, the Royal College of Nursing (RCN), for assistance. Unknown to her, the RCN officer she saw was also advising and representing the nurses who were the subject of the complaint. The staff nurse described the RCN officer as 'dismissive', telling her to 'keep her head down' (Francis Report, 2013a, p 109). In June 2008, nine months after raising concerns, the staff nurse found a job elsewhere. Ex-colleagues subsequently told her they felt deterred from raising concerns because of what happened to her.

The Francis Report (2013a) was of the view that a department in which performance information was or alleged to be fabricated, and in which staff felt bullied into so doing, was not one that could be relied upon to provide a safe service to patients. It was more likely that the general conduct of management, driven by the perceived importance of targets, sent out the message that jobs would be lost if targets were missed, and that no complaints about the means to reach these targets would be welcomed (Francis Report, 2013a, pp 235–8). In other words, without the words being spoken or a direction being issued, the inviolable cultural message was transmitted, understood and actioned, in those small, everyday actions and accommodations the healthcare staff – the street-level bureaucrats to return to Lipsky's term – in Stafford Hospital made.

What caused such this widespread system failure? The Francis Report found an unhealthy and dangerous culture pervaded not only the Trust but also the system of oversight and regulation as a whole, and at every level. It did not conclude that this could be blamed simplistically on this or that policy. It did not consider the dysfunctional aspects of the culture it uncovered, including bullying, low staff morale, high sickness absence rates, acceptance of low standards and poor behaviour, were confined to Stafford; it said these could be found throughout the NHS. The Francis Report found an institutional culture that elevated the business of the system over the priority of the protection of patients and maintaining public trust. It was a culture that did not consider properly the impact on patients of actions taken, or the implications for patients of concerns that were raised. Its focus was on hitting targets, but it missed the point – patient care.

To probe the origins of this more deeply, the next section examines the concept of 'administrative evil' (Adams and Balfour, 1998), and considers the validity and utility of this concept in understanding how decent people, such as registered professionals working in a national health service, become implicated in the circumstances described in the 2013 Francis Report. The final section of this chapter returns once more to the impact of the context that doctors, nurses and social workers (Lipsky's street-level bureaucrats) and their managers work in, on what they do and how they do their work to support older people and those vulnerable due to illness, disability and poor health.

## 'Administrative evil'?

The very word 'evil' is not one that sits easily in contemporary life or thought. Social science may describe and evaluate, but not make ethical judgements (Adams, 2011). Evil is a concept that struggles to free itself from, say, the war-rhetoric of past US President George W Bush ('axis of evil') or a fire and brimstone religiosity. Emotionally incontinent talk of 'evil' can undermine the serious thinking and insight that may be found in a dispassionate scrutiny of its dynamics (Bernstein, 2002). Adams and Balfour's (1998) book *Unmasking Administrative Evil* started from the premise that evil, while defying easy definition and understanding, is inherent in the human condition. The book's Foreword referred to the trial of Adolph Eichmann. At the end of his trial in Israel, Eichmann had thanked his homeland Austria, his employer Germany and Argentina for hiding him. He did not speak of millions of people he had rationally administered to their death. This evil was administrative, driven by rules, systems, structures.

Hannah Arendt, who sat through Eichmann's trial, coined the phrase 'the banality of evil' to describe him. Arendt argued that Eichmann failed to think about the crime he was committing. He implemented policy, but lacked 'intentions' because, for Arendt, having intentions required reflective thought about actions and their impact on, and inter-connectedness to, other human beings. Arendt feared that what was 'banal' was the *non-thinking* about actions that were egregiously wrong. If a crime against humanity had become in some sense 'banal' it was committed routinely, systematically, without being adequately named, challenged or opposed. Infused with a technical rationality, it became accepted, and was implemented without moral revulsion or political indignation and resistance (Arendt, 1963; Butler, 2011).

If we are to use the word 'evil' devoid of political rhetoric or hellfire connotations, a definition that encompasses its *behavioural* dimensions is needed. Katz (1993, p 4) used 'evil' 'to mean behaviour that deliberately deprives innocent people of their humanity, from small scale assaults on a person's dignity to outright murder…It focuses on how people behave towards one another – where the behaviour of one person, or an aggregate of persons, is destructive to others.' This suggests a spectrum of evil, from 'small scale assaults' to inhumanity. Evil is what people do. It is not to suggest a false equivalence between, say, sexual assault of an older person with dementia, with the unwelcome, patronising 'pleasantries' such as 'love' and 'duck' directed at them. But regarded as a continuum, then small, insignificant acts are at one end of a spectrum that has the systematic, unnoticed mistreatment of older people at the other. Administrative evil falls on a continuum where people do not recognise that they are doing anything 'wrong'. An administrator may act, perfectly appropriately, within role, not breaking rules or policy expectations, yet nonetheless perpetrate harm on others, usually very vulnerable people (Adams and Balfour, 2008).

Adams and Balfour (1998, p xx, p xxi) said that evil had become 'un-named' in what they called a 'scientific-analytic mind-set'. 'Administrative evil' is hard to see at the time it is being committed, because all the parts of the process are not in view. To achieve efficiency, large and complex modern organisations chop up responsibilities across individual tasks and roles. The whole is greater than the sum of the parts. Administrative evil can be done without knowledge or deliberation; unlike evil, which involves knowing pain and suffering are inflicted. 'Evil, in many cases, is enmeshed in cunning and seductive processes that can lead ordinary people in ordinary times down the proverbial slippery slope' (Adams and Balfour, 1998, p 3).

Adams and Balfour considered 'administrative evil' as distinct from evil perpetrated through history. They held that administrative evil was *masked*, observing that '… no one has to accept an overt invitation to commit an evil act, because overt invitations are rarely issued'

(Adams and Balfour, 1998, p 4). Much of the business of modern large organisations takes place without awareness of the connectedness of all or other parts of work. Patterns and processes may culminate in administrative evil without people noticing the wider impact (as discussion above about 'boiling the frog' suggested).

As Reed (2012 p 189) noted, it is appropriate to question a florid, emotive use of the word 'evil', but 'to get to evil we have to come to terms with some culturally imbedded and relative foundational concepts like right and wrong'. The concept of a spectrum, or continuum, of evil has utility for a policy-maker, practitioner or manager to grasp its potential in the perpetration of harm (if the power of the word 'evil' is unpalatable). For Reed (2012, p 190) the masking of evil is exacerbated when accountability for individual actions is diffused. Chopping up work processes that serve systems not people increases the likelihood of harm to those who are the reason the system exists; such service and regulatory systems have enormous situational power over individual dispositions (Zimbardo, 2007).

Public policy is rooted in a scientific–analytical tradition where problem-solving implies an agreed-upon end-point, say the elimination of a particular social problem (Adams and Balfour, 1998). Saul (1992) argued that the 'dictatorship of reason', technical-rationality by another name – was not best placed to solve social problems. Technical-rationality is deracinated from history, complexity and social processes. It does not recognise the implicit and unavoidable messiness of human endeavour. Bauman (1989) saw this in the faith imbued in experts who claim social problems can be solved with different policies. This search for the 'right' policy is disconnected from deeper understandings of history, language and culture. An uncritical embrace of technical-rationality alongside an ignorance of history and social formation leads inexorably to fix-it solutions. The 2013 Francis Report discussed above urged government not to re-organise and re-structure the NHS; a cursory reading of its findings indicates not just the futility of structural change, but the administrative evil that results from an obsession with structures and target-chasing.

Public policy that involves a technical or instrumental goal 'drives out ethics', resulting in a 'moral inversion' unseen by people pursuing the policy. (Moral inversion can be differentiated form Bandura's (1999) concept of 'moral disengagement', which is discussed below). 'Moral inversion' occurs when something evil is defined as worthy or right: '…ordinary people can all too easily engage in acts of administrative evil while believing that what they are doing is not only correct but, in fact, good' (Adams and Balfour (1998, p xx). As a result of this, professional ethics become anchored in a technical–rational approach, and in the professions, both of which Adams and Balfour considered:

> ...effectively useless in the face of administrative evil. Because administrative evil wears many masks, it is entirely possible to adhere to the tenets of public service ethics and participate in great evil, and not be aware of it until it is too late (or perhaps not at all). (Adams and Balfour, 1998, p 4)

People can be doing their job, following the rules, doing what others around them are doing, but carrying out what, to a critical, reasonable observer, would be recognised as evil. 'Doublethink', or the holding, and acceptance, of two contradictory beliefs simultaneously, may result (Orwell, 2008). The implication here is not that committed professionals and managers set out to do administrative evil or to personify 'doublethink', but to illuminate a propensity for administrative evil inherent within 'rational' public policy.

The street-level bureaucracies described in Chapter Five, such as the NHS, police or local authorities, draw up rules for professionals to follow. The underpinning assumption is that following the rules – doing things right – secures ethical behaviour. However, rule-following does not mean the right things have been done from the point of view of the person on the receiving end of the action. Rules won't much help the street-level bureaucrat grappling with a moral dilemma. As Adams and Balfour observed (1998, p 170) 'norms of legality, efficiency, and effectiveness – however "professional" they may be – do not necessarily promote or protect the well-being of individuals, especially of society's most vulnerable members'. At the other end of a spectrum of 'administrative evil', most of those involved in perpetrating the Holocaust were never brought to justice, but secured good jobs in Germany and the US. No laws against genocide were broken (Rubenstein, 1975, cited in Adams and Balfour, 1998, p 167); the administrative excellence of the execution of their work was consistent with technical-rationality efficiency. Obedience to rules set down by authority, without questioning, can lead to catastrophic outcomes.

Milgram's (1974) highly controversial social experiments provided piercing insight into the power of authority to comply obedience. In obedience to authority – obeying orders – an individual can abdicate personal responsibility for actions. Milgram described the process of 'the agentic shift', where the person moves from exercising autonomy (the autonomous state') to the 'agentic state'. A person may abdicate personal responsibility and follow instructions, without considering the consequences or whether the request is legitimate. This 'agentic shift' and diffusion of responsibility mean that the person no longer regulates their own behaviour. In Milgram's experiments (where volunteer subjects administered what they believed were increasingly harsh electric shocks to 'learners', who were actors feigning pain) participants who obeyed the instructions to administer electric shocks either justified themselves as following orders, or blamed themselves, again for following orders. Those who rebelled, a minority, questioned the authority of the experimenter, arguing that there was a greater ethical imperative at stake to protect the learner from the experimenter. Rather than making 'the agentic shift', they remained autonomous. Milgram (1974) held that people in the agentic state behaved without thinking about what was expected of them, and without conscience, as long as the order came from a legitimate authority. As Bandura (1999, p 197) put it, the higher the level of authority issuing destructive commands, the higher the level of 'obedient aggression'.

The cherished elevation of individualism in public policy and social discourse blocks – or masks to return to the image of the cognitive mask developed in Chapter Seven – understanding of how administrative evil can be perpetrated. Believing that people choose to obey or not, or to do right not wrong, misunderstands how harmful behaviour is socially constructed. It can mean a vapid trumpeting of the 'individual choice' mantra that is oblivious to the social context within which that choice is exercised. What Zanetti and Adams (2000, p 542) called the 'moral vacuity of technical–rational professionalism' drives out moral reasoning. The assumptions of new public management – individualism, consumer choice and their like – reduce society and the social contract to little more than the means to an end. In discussing Milgram's work, Katz (1993, pp 5–6) suggested a person could be 'beguiled' in a social setting where immediate circumstances dominate 'the entire field of moral vision'. Katz said that beguilement into committing evil acts could involve: a packaging of evil (making it acceptable to those who would not be predisposed to it); small, incremental steps towards it (as in boiling the frog); a bureaucratisation of evil producing a morally bankrupt orderliness; and creation of a culture of cruelty where the cruelty is itself rewarding. Evil was not produced by so-called crazy people, but by the ordinary or banal. It is not to suggest perpetrators of, say, the abuses of people with learning disabilities at the English private hospital Winterbourne View (SGASB, 2012) have equivalence with lesser injustices, or indeed with atrocities like the Holocaust. Rather it is to suggest that understanding the extraordinary, for example, the institutional abuse of older people or other 'adults at risk', requires we look, dispassionately, at the 'ordinary'.

To understand how decent ('ordinary') people can become implicated in the generation of 'evil', Bandura described a process of 'moral disengagement'. He argued that many inhumanities were carried out through what were intended to be supportive networks of legitimate endeavour, run by otherwise considerate people who nonetheless contribute to destructive activities by disconnected subdivision of functions and diffusion of responsibility (Bandura 1999, p 193). Bandura suggested moral agency is exercised both inhibitively – the power to refrain from behaving inhumanely – and proactively, or the power to act humanely. As noted in Chapter Two, euphemistic language is used to make harmful conduct respectable and reduce personal responsibility for it. For Bandura (1999, p 195), 'euphemising is an injurious weapon. People behave much more cruelly when assaultive actions are verbally sanitized than when they are called aggression.' He argued that a cognitive restructuring of harmful conduct through moral justification and sanitizing language, are powerful psychological mechanisms for disengaging moral control. Authorities, by keeping themselves intentionally uninformed, maintain oblivion to wrongdoing; they do not look for it, and obvious questions that might reveal wrongdoing are not asked. When harmful practices are publicised they are dismissed as only isolated incidents arising from misunderstandings of what was authorised. Investigators who look for incriminating evidence authorisation are naïve about the insidious ways pernicious practices become tacitly sanctioned. Thus what Bandura (1999, p 197) called 'decisional arrangements of foggy nonresponsibility rather than incriminating traces of smoking guns' are common outcomes of reports into system or organisational failure. As long as harmful consequences of actions are ignored, minimised, distorted or disbelieved there is little reason for self censure to arise; moral disengagement is complete (Bandura, 1999 p 199).

Katz (1993) identified paradoxes involved in the social construction of evil. First, ordinary people may make extraordinary contributions to evil. However, ordinary people can also turn away from it. As we saw above, a trainee doctor and a staff nurse spoke out about what they saw happening in A&E department at Stafford Hospital (Francis Report, 2013a). However, harm and suffering were heaped upon patients and their families who used A&E. Evil – (using Katz's 1993, p4, definition above) that is, the behaviour of one person, or group of people, destructive to others – was perpetrated. A second paradox is an erroneous emphasis on the uniqueness of systemic and systematic harm, rather than on its universal nature. Inquiries and reports of serious policy failure in the UK, where innocent, vulnerable, dependent people have suffered gross harm, are usually greeted by those with power (such as a secretary of state or chief executive) with bewilderment, head-shaking, and promises that 'lessons have been learned', promises that may well have been made before.

The use of the word 'evil' is a tricky call, as it will repel those operating in a technical–rational paradigm mind-set. However, its use to describe behaviour that is destructive to others and that 'deliberately deprives innocent people of their humanity, from small scale assaults on a person's dignity to outright murder' (Katz, 1993, p 4) is not misplaced when considering the unintended outcome of the dysfunctional pursuit of targets and the failure of the paraphernalia of regulation to come anywhere near knowing what was going on in places such as Stafford Hospital. None of that offers any protection against future health or care abuses. More of the same is proposed, the same that did not assist after the last time the predecessors of those people stood up saying lessons had been learned.

## Doing more of the same misguided things better

Rather than trying to doing the same wrong things better (see Seddon 2008; 2013), a dispassionate, critical, detached knowledge and awareness is required, one that refuses to exceptionalise harm and evil, but tries instead to understand how it came about, how it is masked, and how the context to harm itself is implicated in the perpetration of harm. Like the street-level bureaucrats in the case study, with their cognitive masks, blinkers need to be removed.

The 2013 Francis Report described some shocking aspects of 21st century UK healthcare. Nonetheless, its precursor Independent Inquiry (Mid Staffordshire NHS Foundation Trust Inquiry, 2010) had concluded that benchmarks and star ratings might be useful tools, while at the same time acknowledging these had failed to bring to light the serious systemic failings reported. The Francis Report described the backcloth of political and policy obsession with targets and financial control. It concluded that 'one of the worst examples of bad quality service delivery imaginable was not detected by this system' (Francis Report, 2013b, p 48). It cautioned against further structural reform of the NHS as a response to the systemic, rooted, everyday examples of poor patient care it reported. However, it did not present a deeper critique of the part the targets, compliance and the inspection apparatus had played in distorting the behaviour of registered medical and nursing professionals, paid healthcare staff and managers who operated the compliance system in the tragedy that was Stafford Hospital.

Instead, the headline recommendation of the 2013 Francis Report was a call for 'an integrated hierarchy' of evidence-informed, measurable standards of service, to promote safe and effective delivery of the service. It exhorted a plea for 'zero tolerance' of a service or professional who failed to comply with these fundamental standards. It was as though the impact all this had had on the patients and their families using Stafford Hospital the Francis Report was so careful to describe, had not occurred. It suggested that doing the same wrong things harder and better would mean an end to scandals such as Stafford Hospital (Seddon, 2013).

This is, of course, a technical–rational response to system failure. It involves more of the same – inspections, compliance checks and targets for street-level bureaucrats to meet (to use Lipsky's term again), and more reports for their managers to make on targets. It repeats past technical–rational responses that have followed previous inquiries into child deaths such as those of Victoria Climbié and Peter Connolly (Laming Report, 2003; HLSCB, 2009). It fails to grasp how top-down, system-driven demands produce unintended consequences, the treating of targets, not patients. It ignores the ethical vacuum that exists in technical–rational responses to the complexities and messiness health and social care systems face in providing care and support to people who need it.

None of the 'do more of the same and try harder this time' package is based on evidence that it works, as targets and standards are not developed from evidence of effectiveness. On the contrary, the findings of the 2013 Francis Report highlight a heart-breaking futility of once more going down the technical–rational route. The bullying culture the Report described, where highly trained professionals had been reduced to fearful silence in the face of threats from those desperately seeking targets, illustrates the futility of doing more of the same, when the same has produced – unintentionally and in the hands of largely well-intentioned people – such appalling administrative evil. 'Zero tolerance', a meaningless management sound-bite, is likely to generate more witch-hunts of street-level bureaucrats, devoid of attention to the context that frames their behaviour, or to the evidence the Francis Report graphically laid out – that fear-based, number-chasing target cultures grotesquely distort care and treatment and produce hideously perverse consequences. In this, Lipsky's (1980) observation that the problem of the street-level bureaucrat lies in the system and structure of their work is again resonant.

# NINE

# Ethics, policy and practice

This chapter is in three sections. The first opens up discussion on the ethical dimensions of care and abuse of older people highlighted in the case study in Chapters Six and Seven, and, more generally, in work to safeguard older people from abuse. The second, more abstract, section considers the moral dimensions of 'recognition', and, in particular, the work of Axel Honneth (1995) on the struggle for recognition. The individual and social construction of compassion in care, support and protection of older people from abuse are examined, and the case is made for the contexts to care to emanate and support the giving and receiving of compassionate care to older people, and those at risk of abuse. The final section develops a concrete application of the more abstract discussion that precedes it. It considers Tronto's (1993) elucidation of four elements of an ethic of care, and suggests that this offers a practical application of how compassionate and ethical care, support and protection can be provided to older people at risk of abuse, within the social and cultural contexts that frame that provision.

## A question of ethics

The Parliamentary and Health Service Ombudsman for England commented that the cases she reported, some of which opened Chapter One:

> ...illuminate the gulf between the principles and values of the NHS Constitution and the felt reality of being an older person in the care of the NHS in England. The investigations reveal an attitude – both personal and institutional – which fails to recognise the humanity and individuality of the people concerned and to respond to them with sensitivity, compassion and professionalism. (Parliamentary and Health Service Ombudsman, 2011, p 7)

The case study, presented and discussed in Chapters Six and Seven, described a number of dilemmas managers and social workers in The Department (Lipsky's street-level bureaucrats) encountered in their work to protect older people from abuse. None of dilemmas described, such as juggling, balancing or calibrating least worst alternatives when care planning with an older person, was regarded as an ethical matter. Overcoming the professional reluctance to challenge poor quality care an older person may receive was not viewed as an ethical imperative (see Ash, 2010, for an account of this).

The findings of the case study were not unique to the Department concerned. Wilson's (2002) research interviews with 24 social workers and their first line managers in an English local authority explored the understandings respondents had of elder abuse. She found little attention paid to the impacts of gender, race and power dynamics on the particular elder abuse cases. Wilson reported a case of an older woman admitted to hospital after falling, and who was found to be dehydrated. Her house had been stripped of its contents and its ownership passed to her son and daughter, the perpetrators of the abuse. Following the woman's hospital discharge, the perpetrators found their mother once more, and continued the abuse. The social worker accounted for her input in this case as identifying the abuse, but not in influencing the outcome for the woman. This was seen as the woman's 'choice' (Wilson, 2002, p 86).

Echoing the findings of The Department in the case study, Wilson reported dilemmas that social workers encountered. Dilemmas were described as a problem, situation or set of choices present in a professional or personal context where there was no possibility of a good outcome or resolution. Wilson gave an instance of a social worker's dilemma about whether to suggest an abused older person moved from an abusive domestic situation to institutional care of one sort or another 'where it was highly likely they would be victims of institutional abuse, and possibly of physical or financial abuse, by residential care staff' (Wilson, 2002, p 88). As described in Chapter Six, this trade-off, the weighing-up of least worst options, was one social workers in The Department grappled with.

Wilson (2002) found that disclosure of abuse did not usually bring much improvement for the older person; it was rare for a case to have a good outcome from the older person's point of view. In procedural terms, where discretion could be exercised, some adult safeguarding dilemmas (and ethical decisions) could be avoided, for example, by not investigating cases and thus not acknowledging the abuse as such. Instead, social work practice gave way to avoidance of ethical issues and thence to reliance on guidelines and management directions. Multi-agency adult protection case conferences could be helpful to social workers in that responsibility for decisions was shared; and committee-made decisions could sidestep uncomfortable ethical issues. Again, the case study described in Chapter Six had examples of social workers liking adult protection procedures as their use meant the decision-making was not theirs alone, but was taken with partner agencies.

Contextually, the work of Wilson's (2002) social workers (like their counterparts elsewhere) was managed primarily by performance indicators (PIs). In fact, these indicate nothing about the practical and ethical aspects of elder abuse. PIs emphasise throughput (getting in, on and out of a case within specified time periods); they implicitly 'biased staff against complex cases'; resource constraints meant securing organisational agreement for complex (that is, costly) care packages was hard as PIs took no account of complexity (Wilson, 2002, p 90). None of this encouraged or valorised any exploration of the impact of, say, race, poverty or gender on the risk, incidence or nature of elder abuse or on how to tackle that.

As in the case study reported in Chapters Six and Seven, Wilson's respondents did not conceptualise their dilemmas in terms of ethical failings:

> ...discourses on ethical practice had been silenced by the dilemmas faced by staff in the service under review. The dilemmas created were not part of the dominant professional discourse but appeared in interviews as hidden areas of disquiet and stress. ... Staff reacted to the dilemmas with which they were faced mainly by avoiding ethical issues. They evaluated their practice in terms of the relationships they had with service users rather than ethical terms. (Wilson, 2002, p 92)

Despite the intention that 'ethical awareness is a fundamental part of the professional practice of social workers' (IFSW, 2012), Wilson's respondents, like their counterparts in the case study reported in Chapters Six and Seven, seemed to operate in an 'ethics-lite' context. Recognition of the lived reality of abuse in older age, and compassion for the human dimensions of the situations the older people were in, were muted.

## Understandings of 'ethics'

In public policy and adult safeguarding practice, the grand statements about 'valuing people', 'zero tolerance' of abuse or 'safeguarding is everyone's business' that are often sprinkled about policy and political discourse don't seem to have much to say about 'ethics'. And yet, ethics are at the heart of what it is to be valued, to be human and, certainly, what it is to be safe from harm.

For Held (2006), developing ethics of care was a normative pursuit; an attempt to identify what is wrong and make it better, and one centring on personal relationships, ties and connections to others. A defining feature of ethics of care for Held was the focus upon the moral significance of attending to and meeting the needs of others. In this, Held regarded care ethics as respecting, and not being removed from particular others; she saw it as a relational conception of interconnections between people, rather than individualistic or atomised.

Holstein (2010) regarded ethical considerations as taking in a process of disciplined reflection, along with a means of testing moral values, judgements, responsibilities, aims and actions. Holstein considered there were many gaps in the questions asked by ethicists considering old age. Holstein and Minkler (2003) had earlier identified some, including: are emerging cultural constructs about old age morally significant, and if so how?; how do ageing bodies influence moral standing?; and what are ethical meanings of class, poverty, race? Holstein argued for a contextual view of ethics as enacted in everyday lives, practices and relationships. Context, in social and political terms, can be regarded as a constraint on individual agency: 'awareness of context, like power, is critical if ethics is to be a force for social change' (Holstein, 2010, p 638).

For Banks (2008), the way in which professionals such as social workers perceive the ethical dimensions of their work influences how they understand situations they are confronted with, as well as the actions they may take. In social work, for example, 'ethical issues' are often discussed as 'no-win' situations that can paralyse particularly obdurate cases, often the ones involving lawyers and the courts. Alternatively, they may be something for a profession's code of practice, and not much considered unless a breach of the Code is alleged. Except they are not: neither Codes of Practice for Social Care Workers in England or Wales, nor that of the Nursing & Midwifery Council mentions ethics or morality (CCW, 2002; NMC, 2008; GSCC, 2010). In professional practice, the context framing 'ethical choices' is often viewed as 'policy' or 'politics' (with all the associated baggage of 'hard choices', 'winners and losers' and the like), something happening outside immediate practical decision-making in the here and now (Sevenhuijsen, 1998; Lloyd, 2004).

Banks (2008) was clear that individual decision-making in social work could not be abstracted from its political and policy context. Neither can it be uprooted from its *social* context of course. The social nature of being human means the autonomy exercised by a person is often focused on small, everyday aspects of life, matters that reflect an individual's identity in their relationship with others (Kittay, 1999; Holstein, 2010). For example, the way in which an older person is helped to wash by a carer is riddled with ethical considerations, such as how privacy is respected, how the older person may feel about exposing their ageing body to a young, seemingly perfectly formed paid carer who has a 15-minute care slot to bathe and dress them, write down what they've done and then rush off to the next call. Holstein (2010, p 637) viewed this type of everyday occurrence as raising care-giving to a deeply moral relationship: 'long term care involves relationships, gratitude, reciprocity, love, and fairness, and so it is, above all, about morality'. Care-giving occurs in psychological and social contexts that shape and are shaped by caring practice. As Kittay (2005) pointed out, caring-giving and receiving are intensely personal, and inextricably symbolic and meaningful. Care-giving can be done well, badly, and in ways that variously dignify, mistreat, abuse or honour the cared-for person. Caring affects those giving and receiving it. Caring brings into being or rests upon a relationship with significant cultural and ethical meanings.

Holstein (2010) regarded debates about ethical matters in old age as often constellating around autonomy or confidentiality. In the US, she noted *Principles of Biomedical Ethics* (by Beauchamp and Childress and first published in 1979) set out four principles that permeated decision-making in intensive care or clinical settings, and that were later transferred to care homes: autonomy, beneficence, non-maleficence and justice. The outcome of this has been the location of 'ethics' to situations where values were conflicted and the possibility of a solution was present. Placing ethics 'out there' (back to hard choices) results in everyday issues of care falling outside an ethical purview. Further, the elevation of autonomy and the individual over the collective drives a pursuit of individualised strategies for betterment, with little – or no – focus on the context of care and support, and the changing of it. This doesn't really get near the older person who may be infirm, reliant on others, and in need support and protection from abuse.

## Contexts to ethical practice

Bauman (1994, p 182) remarked that 'the context of life...is messy. It is not easy to be a moral person'. The institutional arrangements of health and social care in late modernity have expanded inspectorial surveillance, instrumental decision-making, bureaucratised care arrangements, as well as increasing the drive to centralise consumer empowerment (Harrison and Smith, 2004). One upshot of this was discussed in Chapter Eight's consideration of the findings of the 2013 Francis Report on the Mid Staffordshire NHS Foundation Trust. This surveillance edifice in different parts of the UK has included the Care and Social Services Inspectorate Wales, the Care Quality Commission, various social services inspectorates, regulatory care councils such as the Scottish Social Services Council and Northern Ireland Social Care Council, as well as the Audit Commission. The tools deployed by this apparatus include performance targets and data, standards and regulation. Systemic failures of care are usually responded to with more measures of this sort to improve 'public confidence', again as considered in Chapter Eight.

Harrison and Smith (2004) argued that this emphasis on public confidence neglects the significance for service users of professional qualities like trust, tact, kindness, compassion, humility; the public 'confidence' focus fails to acknowledge the role of uncertainty, morality and discretion in the provision of care. For Nussbaum (2001, p 395), the outcomes of rule-based human contact can be stark: 'relationships between people that are mediated only by rule and not by empathy frequently prove more fragile in times of hostility, more prone to a dehumanizing type of brutality'.

Exploring the nature of professional integrity, Banks (2010) considered how social welfare practitioners performed as people of integrity in the course of their work. Banks identified three versions of professional integrity: first, morally right conduct; second, commitment to a set of deeply held values; and third, the capacity for reflexive sense-making and accountability. Banks considered some reported professional misconduct cases accounts of practitioners, and argued that the concept of professional integrity was weakened when conduct was measured only according to minimum standards of good practice. Banks called for the ideals and core purposes of social welfare work to be reinvigorated by the second version of integrity as a moral quality or virtue – commitment to values, a focus on the moral motivations of practitioners based on the idea of professional integrity. Banks (2010) regarded her second and third versions of integrity as important moral qualities and attitudes. Bisman similarly argued that social work had to re-engage with its moral core, that is, respond to a moral imperative of work with social justice and disadvantage, and 'place knowledge development within the context of the profession's larger aims' (Bisman, 2004, p 120).

## Recognition and compassion

Social workers' 'not seeing' potential abuse of an older person was described in the case study presented in Chapters Six and Seven. This failure to 'bear witness', as it were, can be understood as a failure of recognition. The concept of recognition, developed particularly by Honneth (1995), is valuable because it makes it possible to distinguish between forms of social interaction and patterns of respect for another person that that entails.

Honneth (1995) argued that the need for recognition is a human need; denying people the recognition they deserve is injustice. People in marginalised groups or who are deemed marginal – we may include very old, frail, dependent beings here – may be denied recognition of their worth, culture, way of life, dignity or status as people. Honneth considered struggles for the establishment of relations of mutual recognition, and stressed the importance of social relationships in the development and maintenance of a person's identity. He proposed an account that situated a critical perception of injustice more generally within individuals' negative experiences of having their moral expectations violated. After Hegel, Honneth suggested the idea that fully human flourishing is dependent on 'ethical relations' including relations of love, law and 'ethical life' that can only established through a struggle for recognition.

For Honneth (1995), the potential or possibility to sense, interpret and realise needs as an autonomous person depended on the development of self-confidence, self-respect and self-esteem. These are not pure states but are socially derived from a dynamic process where a person comes to experience, through the recognition of others, the self as having certain status, whether as a focus of social concern or disparagement, or of worth. One's relationship to oneself is therefore an intersubjective process; it is an attitude that emerges in the encounter of a person with another. Self-realisation is thus dependent on the establishment of relationships of mutual recognition. For Honneth (1995), such relationships go beyond friendships; they include legally institutionalised relations of universal respect for the autonomy and dignity of the person, as well as networks of solidarity and shared values within which the worth of individuals is acknowledged. The prevailing values of a culture and its social conditions determine the development of self-esteem. Honneth used the term 'solidarity' to represent the cultural climate where developing self-esteem becomes possible, where a shared interest, concern or value is present. He claimed that a good society is one where each individual has a real opportunity for self-realisation.

Hence, to conceive of an ethical life from a theory of recognition, can only fully succeed to the degree it is supported by cultural customs (how we relate to each other reciprocally) and by all parts of society (Honneth, 1995). The denial of recognition of the older person that can characterise abuse and mistreatment is arguably a prevailing feature of cultural customs that do not derive from ethical, or compassionate, bases.

## Compassionate contexts

Like 'evil', the word 'compassion' does not sit comfortably in western modernity; its conceptual association with suffering is not always palatable. Collins et al (2012, pp 252–3) set out a conception of compassion as a virtuous act that expresses regret for the existence of suffering: virtues 'are acquired, stable dispositions. They are applied morals; they require behaviours.' Considered in this way, virtue is characterised by habit, rather than sporadic exercise.

Nussbaum (2001, p 301) differentiated compassion – 'a painful emotion occasioned by the awareness of another person's undeserved misfortune' – from empathy, sympathy or pity. Compassion was the recognition that the 'basic worth of a person remains even when the world has done its worse' (Nussbaum, 2001, p 406). She regarded compassion as connected to justice, and distinct from empathy, which involved an 'imaginative reconstruction of the experience of the sufferer' (Nussbaum, 2001, p 327). Empathy that might lead to compassion could be 'blocked in several ways' (Nussbaum, 2001, p 342); social hierarchies, racism, for example, make it hard for people to see their own possibilities in the sufferings of another. Nussbaum (2001, p 343) considered that 'social institutions, then, construct the shape compassion will take'; in other words context influences the expression of compassion.

As compassion is thus individually and socially constructed, it can be partial and unreliable. Nussbaum suggested compassion should be considered at both the level of individual psychology and institutional design, as '…a political conception that tries to win *overlapping consensus* among citizens of many different kinds, respecting the spaces within which they each elaborate and pursue their different reasonable conceptions of the good' (Nussbaum, 2001, p 401. Emphasis in the original). Institutional design includes basic structures of society, such as relations between rich and poor people, rich and poor nations, and distributional principles of tax systems and welfare transfers: 'compassionate individuals construct institutions that embody what they imagine; and institutions, in turn, influence the development of individuals' (Nussbaum, 2001, p 405). Nussbaum argued that:

> [c]ompassion requires the judgement that there are serious bad things that can happen to others through no fault of their own. …Even though good institutions cannot prevent old age and death, they can address the needs of the elderly, those who care for the elderly, and the bereaved relatives. But this will not happen if we do not cultivate in citizens a compassionate understanding of the weight and meaning of these predicaments… (Nussbaum, 2001, p 405)

If institutions shape, and are shaped by citizens' conceptions of basic public goods, then they influence also the social responsibility and compassion for others that develops. Nussbaum called for social education for compassionate citizenship, arguing that neither empathy nor compassion was partial. The social lip-service paid to respect for older people cannot sit compassionately alongside institutional mistreatment, ageism, or a loathing of frailty or dependency throughout life, not just in old age. Manifesting compassion in work to safeguard older people from abuse depends, critically, on social institutions and infrastructures that themselves emanate those qualities. Kittay (2001b, p 560) remarked:

> [t]he [caring] labor can be done without an appropriate attitude. Yet without the attitude of care, the open responsiveness to another that is so essential to understanding what another requires is not possible. That is, the labor unaccompanied by the attitude of care cannot be good care.

At the wider social, cultural and institutional level, that must still hold true. Those delivering safeguarding or other services to an older person who has been mistreated operate within institutional systems and frameworks that influence their actions and behaviour. For social workers, nurses or doctors, those institutions *regulate* their conduct. The resource base of those institutions – *contra* political deceit that passes off public expenditure cuts as 'efficiency savings' (see, for example, HM Treasury, 2013) – is an ethical matter.

## The universality of dependency

A social and cultural distaste for 'dependency', discussed in previous chapters, is a significant feature of contexts to safeguarding older people from abuse. Dependency cannot be air-brushed out of life in some spoof magical thinking. Although dependency is universal and inevitable, it nonetheless remains 'the elephant in the room of discourse around many ethical, social and political issues' (Kittay et al, 2005, p 445). The universalist nature of interdependence, and the reciprocity of giving and receiving care (Shakespeare, 2000; F. Williams, 2001; Lloyd, 2004; Kröger 2009) are features of being human. Rather than denying this, and in so doing eclipsing both the person giving as well as receiving care, Kittay suggested (2005, p 467) ' ...we acknowledge our own dependency and vulnerability instead of demanding an illusory independence, one that can only be maintained by denying our connection to and reliance on others, then we not need to make the care giver invisible'.

On this universality of caring and being cared for, Kittay (2005, p 443) noted, graphically, that:

> [p]eople do not spring from the ground like mushrooms. People produce people. People need to be cared for and nurtured throughout their lives by other people, at some times more urgently and more completely than at other times.

This need for care and nurturance throughout life is surrounded by a context, which:

> ...while dictated in part by the nature of human need, is also conditioned by cultural and ethical understandings and by economic and political circumstances. ...Care and dependency, particularly in the form of dependency care have been, are, or are likely to be features of all our lives. (Kittay, 2005, p 443)

As care and dependency are features of human life, the economic and political circumstances Kittay (2005) spoke of would today include the choice agenda of public policy. 'Choice', as argued elsewhere in this book, is a slippery concept. It features strongly in the various manifestations of personalisation. The ethical dimensions of a personalised budget for its user (whether an older person or other adult at risk) are not often explored. As Hughes et al (2005) observed, transforming care into personal assistance may leave any ethical imperative of recognition of the other out of the moral equation.

In a study that examined the governance context of personalisation in six European countries and the US, Rummery (2011) identified the risks of under-governance that can characterise these personalised care arrangements. Rummery said the rolling back of the state involved can lead to a proliferation of unregulated and unprotected care-giving, both from the point of view of those cared-for and those providing care. Cost containment means the risks of these schemes are devolved onto their users and their kin. Personalisation introduces money into relationships that are, potentially, characterised by disempowering obligations, 'being a burden' feelings and inflexible care services. Rummery found that different schemes for personalisation internationally varied on dimensions of empowerment, emancipation and the protection of both those in need of care, and those paid to provide it. Paid carers are generally low-wage and non-unionised, and sometimes illegal workers. Schemes providing better protection for care workers (for example, unionised work with decent pay) had better outcomes for those receiving care. Hence, rather than reducing state governance of personalisation schemes, Rummery (2011) concluded that a benign but powerful welfare state was needed to ensure an ethic of care was upheld in practice, and the rights and empowerment of both people using and working on those schemes were protected.

## Joan Tronto's four elements of an ethic of care

At a practical level, if ethics cannot be separated out of decision-making around elder care or safeguarding older people from abuse, then the features of an ethic of care in practice need to be delineated. In her work on moral boundaries, Tronto (1993) suggested care involved taking the needs of the other as a basis for action. Tronto defined care very widely as a 'species activity that includes everything that we do to maintain, continue and repair our 'world' so we can live in it as well as possible' (Tronto (1993, p 103). Tronto said that the 'everything that we do' involved four phases, that is, caring about, taking care of, care-giving, and care-receiving; and she set out four elements of an ethic of care, each of which resonates closely with the day-to-day reality of caring for another, and being cared for.

The first element of Tronto's ethic of care was that of *attentiveness*. For Tronto, noticing needs is a primary human task. Within an ethical framework, *not* to notice, *not* to see, *not* to attend, are moral failings.

In Honneth's (1995) schema, this might be regarded as a failure of recognition. The second element of Tronto's ethic of care was *responsibility*. A problematic concept in some ways, responsibility has come to be viewed as duty and obligations, the 'oughts', 'shoulds' and 'musts' of life. Rather, Tronto (1993, p 133) suggested that responsibility was located in cultural practices, and not in rules about those 'oughts' and 'shoulds':

> Responsibility has different meanings depending on one's perceived gender roles, and issues that arise out of class, family status, and culture, including cultural differences based on racial groupings. ...I am suggesting we are better served by focussing on a flexible notion of responsibility than we are by continuing to use obligation as the basis of understanding what people should do for each other.

In this, such a 'flexible notion' might embrace, or cultivate, the *ability* to *respond* to the other.

*Competence* was the third element of Tronto's ethic of care. Tronto argued that competence counterbalanced 'taking care of' with 'care-giving', and said that 'intending to provide care...but then failing to provide good care, means that in the end the need for care is not met' (Tronto, 1993, p 133). While inadequate resourcing could compromise the delivery of competent care, care had to be competently provided: 'how could it not be necessary that the caring work be competently performed in order to demonstrate one cares?' (Tronto, 1993, p 133).

The fourth moral element of an ethic of care Tronto proposed was *responsiveness*: that of the care-giver to the care-receiver. Anyone needing care is placed in a position of relative vulnerability. The response made by the care-giver to that real and perceived vulnerability is a moral matter, with moral consequences; hence the need to stay alert to 'the possibilities for abuse that arise with vulnerability' (Tronto, 1993, p 133).

The four phases of care (caring about, taking care of, care-giving, and care-receiving) Tronto set out, and her four elements of an ethic of care (attentiveness, responsibility, competence and responsiveness) were not options or alternatives. All were necessary to realise an ethic of care. In work to safeguard older people from abuse, utilising this moral perspective would suggest reigning in the rush to more rules, standards, or numerical targets. As argued in Chapter Eight, targets are typically divorced from the context to the human transaction and interaction, which is giving and receiving care. Rather, an ethic of care makes the care, support and protection of an older person profoundly expressive, affective and personal. For Tronto, caring practice required 'a deep and thoughtful knowledge of the situation, of all the actors' situations, needs and competencies' (Tronto, 1993, p 136). That 'thoughtful knowledge' is framed by the social, cultural and political contexts that surround that exchange of care. It was 'privileged irresponsibility', Tronto (1993, p 120) suggested, to ignore, set aside or deny the essential nature of care to every human being. Attentiveness to the circumstances and contexts of care-giving and care-receiving demands awareness of the social, economic and cultural components of those contexts. Rules, standards and codes may be necessary but they are not sufficient to secure, that is, to *safeguard* that attention, that 'thoughtful knowledge'. The danger is, as Chapter Eight's discussion of the 2013 Francis Report argued, the rule or target gets the attention, not the person.

In an application of Tronto's (1993) work, Brannelly (2006) used Tronto's four elements of ethic of care as the analytical framework to her study of dementia care. This considered the practice of professionals such as social workers and community psychiatric nurses in their work with older people living with dementia. Brannelly (2006) found that adoption in practice of an ethic of care increased the participation and inclusion of older people in their care. Each of the four elements was apparent in professional practice. Brannelly (2006) argued that incorporation of the four elements into current cultures of care would enable practitioners to acknowledge the interdependency of care-givers and care-receivers, to collaborate in care, and consider care quality from point of view of person. The study suggested how Tronto's (1993) ethic of care could embrace both the perspectives of both the care-receiver and care-giver. Brannelly (2006, p 198) concluded that 'an ethic of care has, as one of its strengths, the ability to accommodate not only the different disciplines of care, but also the actors involved, notably lay carers as well as people with dementia'.

Finally to return to the significance of social, cultural and political contexts of caring and safeguarding older people from abuse, as Barnes (2012) observed, Tronto's (1993) four phases of an ethic of care – caring about, taking care of, care-giving and care-receiving – don't imply each is practised by the same person. To provide attentive, responsive, competent and responsible care directly to an older person, and to safeguard them from mistreatment, requires that the context surrounding that care-giving, or safeguarding, supports their efforts (see Ash, 2014, for discussion on ethical contexts to care). This might include, but is not limited to, respite care for the carer and cared-for, or primary care support that itself manifests Tronto's (1993) four elements of an ethic of care (attentiveness, responsibility, competence, responsiveness).

At a wider social, economic and cultural level, ethical care calls for a social recognition of and collective solidarity with the pain, drudgery, joy, anxiety, exhaustion and humour – the infinity of experience that care-giving and care-receiving can encompass. Compassionate, ethically driven contexts to care are vigilant to the administrative evil (to draw upon the discussion in Chapter Eight) that can result from chopped-up, profit-driven, target-riven systems masquerading as 'care', but which can result in the dehumanisation, abuse or death of older citizens at their most vulnerable.

# TEN

# Safeguarding older people from abuse: ethical futures

This book opened with cases reported by the Parliamentary and Health Service Ombudsman (2011). These were not isolated or exceptional cases. Almost one fifth (18%) of the complaints about the NHS made to the Ombudsman's office in 2009 concerned the care older people received. In the language of adult safeguarding, many involved neglect, emotional and physical abuse. The Ombudsman found it 'incomprehensible' that she needed 'to hold the NHS to account for the most fundamental aspects of care: clean, comfortable surroundings, assistance with eating if needed, drinking water available and the ability to call someone who will respond'. The Parliamentary and Health Service Ombudsman was of the view that '[u]nderlying such acts of carelessness and neglect is a casual indifference to the dignity and welfare of older patients' (Parliamentary and Health Service Ombudsman, 2011, p 10).

This volume set out to understand at a deeper level how and why the systems, processes and practices involved the care, support and protection of older people from harm, and the professionals and paid staff that work in them, can sometimes appear blind to elder mistreatment or, worse, or can perpetrate shockingly poor care. The critical significance of context to safeguarding policy and practice, be that social, political, cultural or organisational and professional, has been identified. Acknowledging a role for standards, regulations, rules and procedures in safeguarding older people from abuse, the argument has been made that heightened regulation and rule-making in adult safeguarding will not *ipso facto* wake policy-makers, social workers, healthcare and criminal justice professionals up to the reality of abuse in old age, nor will they improve the quality of services and the response to elder abuse. Instead, the book has made a case for theory-informed, critically aware and ethically-driven policy and practice in work to safeguard older people from abuse. It has argued a need for ethical 'right action' in that work, as well as in the wider care and support systems some older people rely upon.

The book has considered the potential of Michael Lipsky's (1980) concept of street-level bureaucracy has to understanding the dilemmas and trade-offs street-level bureaucrats, such as social workers and nurses, make when dealing with suspected abuse of an older person. The regulatory regimes of marketised, privatised welfare bureaucracies were not part of the world occupied by Lipsky's US street-level bureaucracies. The case study presented in this volume identified the powerful impact these have on factors influencing safeguarding policy implementation. In addition, it showed how social and cultural factors, like ageism and a cultural disgust of dependency, can permeate public policy and safeguarding practice. While Lipsky's fundamental narrative remains valid – that the 'problem' of street-level bureaucrats lies in the structure, system or organisation of their work – the case study has enlarged understanding of that structure, and the impacts it has on street-level implementation of policy to protect older people.

As Evans (2011; 2012) found elsewhere, the case study showed that discretion cannot be removed from street-level decision-making. It illustrated how the exercise of discretion and power in safeguarding older people from abuse is now diffused and spread across the adult safeguarding system. Chapter Eight discussed the experiences documented in *Sans Everything* in 1967 (Robb, 1967), and the failings at Stafford Hospital reported over 45 years later (Francis Report, 2013a). Like these, the case study findings confirmed that workplace culture – how people work and go about their business together – is a significantly powerful shaper of professional behaviour. In adult safeguarding work now, however, the 'workplace' is communication between a plethora of agencies expected to coordinate their efforts to implement adult protection policy. Challenge of poor practice, and critique of opinions offered by other professionals, may be sacrificed in the spirit of partnership and getting the safeguarding job done. Fault lines in the fragmented, regulated service and care world of the 21st century UK street-level bureaucrat are exposed: service commissioners contract on quality standards with a care home for example, regulators inspect it, nurses and social workers review the care plans of those people they place there; yet low level abusive cultures and practices may develop. Like boiling a frog, initially insignificant vicissitudes can have profoundly negative consequences. In the case study, as in Lipsky's street-level bureaucracies decades earlier, street-level bureaucrats like social workers, nurses and their adult safeguarding colleagues, made adjustments and accommodations to this 'real world'. The dissonance arising at the point where professional aspirations meet Lipsky's 'corrupted world of service' would be as familiar to one of Lipsky's street-level bureaucrats as to a social worker in the Welsh authority that was the case study. The metaphor of the 'cognitive masks' described how contextual factors are woven into the stories and accounts of the dilemmas of street-level bureaucrats; like a fencing mask that both protects and partially obscures, these cognitive masks shut off any questioning of *why* those dilemmas existed (Ash, 2013).

Elder abuse may not be 'seen' – it may be cognitively masked – by ageism (domestic abuse services that are not age-aware, for example), by low expectations of services for dependent, frail older people, or by the people-processing practices of volume delivery (Prottas, 1979). 'Either/or' thinking cognitively masks 'seeing' what may be a painfully real (but obscured) situation of, say, a severely disabled 80-year-old woman, intentionally, coldly and violently emotionally abused by her spouse and sole carer, for protracted periods characterised by angry, intense, silent, misogynist contempt. This research suggested domestic abuse like this is unlikely to be noticed or, if it is, may be construed as a long-standing relationship feature, and thus a matter of 'choice'. The multiple oppressions and their consequences for this woman are likely to be masked by ageism, a lack of age-appropriate services for older abused woman, and the ideological policy preferences of the day.

Contextual social constructions of growing old are internalised by people, irrespective of age, who live in unconsciously ageist societies. The 'burden burden' is an example. There cannot be many carers, paid or unpaid, who have not heard variations on the theme of an older person worrying about 'not wanting to be a burden', or of being an 'old codger', and thus somehow marked down on a social scale of worthiness. This internalisation of pervasive, subtle (but usually unsubtle) ageist put-downs can mean that an older person desperately in need of care, support and help disparages that need and in the process of so-doing, themselves. The social fear and loathing of dependency has remarkably pervasive and dysfunctional unintended consequences. The innocence and good intention of not wanting the otherwise able-bodied, who encounter illness or accident, to slide into a slough of despond becomes itself 'the burden of burden' for an older person in need of care.

As the case study highlighted, older people experiencing poor care in a barely regulatory compliant care home are likely to die in that environment. Without understanding what life is like for that older person, public policy, law and adult safeguarding structures are likely to develop ever more refined bureaucratic systems that may hit various targets but *miss the point*, which is that policy implementation and adult protection structures are a means, not an end. In this, a better understanding is needed of how to elevate ethics and morality to a point beyond mere rhetoric. Tronto's (1993) delineation of four elements of an ethic of care – attentiveness, responsibility, competence and responsiveness, discussed in Chapter Nine – offers a practical yet potent means to establish those features in public policy, as well as adult safeguarding practice and the care and support of older people more generally.

Significantly, the dilemmas street-level bureaucrats and managers described in the case study were not generally framed as matters of ethics, rights or justice. In the concluding chapters of *Street-Level Bureaucracy*, Lipsky (1980) deliberated about the potential for reform of street-level bureaucracies, and considered various organisational responses to the dilemmas and ambiguities that permeated the work structure, and hence the work of, the street-level bureaucrat. In none of this discussion, were the ethical dimensions of human transactions within street-level bureaucracies directly mentioned. In other words, Lipsky's powerful and enduring analysis of street-level bureaucracies returned, in the end, to considering strategies to make them 'work better'. To be fair, Lipsky was under no illusion that organisational 'solutions' such as more training, opportunities for deliberation in the workplace and so on, would be more than palliative in effect, as street-level bureaucracies were part of 'organisational relations in the society as a whole' (Lipsky, 1980, p 192). The case study reported in Chapters Six and Seven has added to Lipsky's analysis, by locating an absence of ethical discourse in street-level policy implementation and wider service planning, delivery and systems. It has identified, after Lukes, how street-level decision-making is imprinted with imposed internalised constraints, such as cost control and a distaste for challenge, redolent of acceptance by street-level bureaucrats of their 'role in the existing order of things' (Lukes, 2005, p 11).

If morality and an ethic of care are not foregrounded in the design and implementation of policy to protect elders (as well as in the care, support and protection older people at risk of abuse), then when things go wrong we are likely to continue the futile search for a holy grail of more standards and targets, and see professional and safeguarding responsibilities become more rule-based, and not ethically driven. This endless search, doing the 'same-old, same-old', is what Grint (2010) called the 'cuckoo clock syndrome', or the way in which we repeatedly configure and pattern the world in certain fixed ways. If the messy problems of human services and adult safeguarding are regarded as crises or moral panics, then the fixed political and policy responses are increased top-down direction, more standards, increased regulation. The evidence that the 'same-old, same-old' may not have fixed a similar problem the last time it was rolled out is seldom noticed or questioned.

Perceptively, Tronto (1993) situated 'responsibility' in cultural practices, not rules. Lipsky also concluded that rustling up more rules was likely to be futile. Instead he called for a response that would 'secure or restore the importance of human interactions in services that require discretionary intervention or involvement' (Lipsky, 1980, p xv). As this book has argued, those human interactions take place within the complex, congested policy and political environment within which street-level bureaucrats work. The metaphorical 'cognitive mask' obscures the impacts this environment has on the decisions and actions street-level bureaucrats such as doctors, nurses, social workers, police officers take, in their work to care, support and protect older people from abuse.

From an ethical vantage point, cognitive masks occlude seeing moral inadequacy when professional power and discretion are not exercised in favour of an older person. Ethically, cognitive masks hinder seeing *competence* as having a moral dimension. When 'competence' is measured by minimum standards or compliance with rules, processes documenting compliance or measurement become emphasised, not people. The drive to meet four-hour wait times at in A&E Stafford Hospital England, between 2005 and 2009 (discussed in Chapter Eight) exemplified this. There, it could be said that cognitive masks closed down any ethical challenge and critique to the moral need to provide competent care, and to resource its provision adequately. Masks obscured the administrative evil perpetrated when the imperative of meeting numerical targets resulted in the hideous parody of care reported in cases presented to the Inquiry (Francis Report, 2013a). As Green (2009) commented, institutions should not deform practices that lead to right action with the proliferation of paperwork that elevates the measurable and not the valuable. Human services have had long enough to observe what the audit society and its 'rituals of verification' (Power, 1997) have visited upon health and social services.

Implementing policy, regulation and practice in adult safeguarding with an ethic of care at the centre, offers up the possibility that administrative evil will be seen, exposed and stopped before it takes root to contaminate a workplace culture. People providing care, support and protection older people that is driven by an ethic of care, as well as regulators of health and social care (Preston-Shoot, 2011), might expose administrative evil before it becomes the cultural norm. As the Francis Report (2013a, p 1367) on the Mid Staffordshire NHS Foundation Trust observed, the more common, that is, unremarkable or everyday, is a problem, the less likely it is that energy and resources are expended doing something about it. Without ethically driven critical scrutiny, without understanding the consequences of these practices – in other words, removing the cognitive masks – learning from failure to safeguard adults at risk will be continue to outsourced *post hoc* to judicial inquiries, large investigations, inspections, serious case reviews and the like after things have gone badly wrong (Butler and Drakeford, 2005). This results, often, in the narrative (usually of failure) being constructed by external 'experts' who will judge failings against standards, not as an ethic of care. More rules and structural reform often result, as was seen in England following inquiry and review, respectively, into the circumstances surrounding the deaths of Victoria Climbié and Peter Connolly (Laming Report, 2003; HLSCB, 2009). The wider systemic contexts remain unquestioned; the cognitive masks stay firmly in place. Instead of 'after the fact' inquiries (with all the associated expense, inordinate delays, and protracted stress for those involved), learning in real time, in the here and now, might stand more chance of preventing the sort of cultures taking hold that were seen in Stafford Hospital and one care home discussed in the case study.

Removing the cognitive masks requires the development and nurturance of organisational cultures that not only encourage professionals and staff to challenge and question practices but also make it a cultural *sine qua non* – a defining feature of the way they do what they do. These cultures would valorise theory-informed critical thinking and questioning. They would be led by those who recognised their role as more than budget management, political fire-fighting, and performance managing others to meet targets; and by managers who modelled reflexivity and humility, and who developed and rewarded those traits in their staff. These leaders would want to have reports of 'near misses' (poor or risky practice) as well as five-star work. In this sort of organisational culture, managers would ask, routinely, why there were no or few whistle-blowers (or people 'raising concerns' if the term whistle-blowing was too loaded). They would model self-challenge and encourage professional debate as a matter of course. Staff would demonstrate professional confidence, competence and sensitivity in questioning, challenging and critiquing practices and thinking.

Developing organisational cultures of challenge and critique would require the acquisition and use of theory-informed critical thinking. Gambrill (2007) identified skills required, which include asking well-constructed (and sometimes awkward) questions, critically appraising information, looking out for propaganda (untested conventional wisdoms, meaningless mantras), and challenging agencies and practices that are obstacles to ethical practice. Ethically driven critical thinking is the response to Green's question (2009, p 116), 'can it be that all there is to being a "professional" is proving one can deliver someone else's targets or else demonstrate that one has met one's own pre-specified objectives?'

Put starkly, rational, rule-based policy-making, may be necessary but it is not sufficient to safeguard vulnerable elders, if policy, practice and resourcing are institutionally ageist, dependency-averse or uncritically propelled by the *zeitgeist* of the day. As an alternative, ethically driven policy-making should favour, and resource, structures and systems built upon the premise of an ethical and socially just, duty of care to the older person at risk of abuse. Street-level bureaucrats such as doctors, nurses, social workers and police officers, have a professional duty of care to an abused older person; the social and policy context within which they operate has similarly to support their discharging this duty.

In the end, as Barnes (2012) observed, if people don't care enough to care, if systems don't care enough to care, then care is not given or received. If the state avoids responsibilities for care needs of older people (beyond exhorting citizens to take individual responsibility and exercise 'choice'), then to use Tronto's elements of an ethic of care, the state's competence, responsiveness and attentiveness to those care needs is diminished. It fails, therefore, to meet the moral, physical and emotional precepts of an ethic of care. Safeguarding older people from mistreatment is not segmented or set apart from this. Abuse at its most unadorned, is an abuse of care, love and trust. Robbing, raping, neglecting or treating an older person with loathing or contempt, are acts bereft of compassion. That abuse does not occur in a vacuum, it has a context. That context, if devoid of compassion, ethics and morality at the state, policy, organisational and individual level, will not safeguard an older person from small or gross acts of cruelty. Hugman (2005) said ethics could not be *taught*, but had to be learned. If that is the case, then ethical policy and practice in adult safeguarding have to be learned and imprinted throughout the social, economic and cultural contexts that surround the protection of older people from abuse.

# References

Adams, G.B. (2011). 'The Problem of Administrative Evil in a Culture of Technical Rationality'. *Public Integrity*, *13*(3), 275–84.

Adams, G.B., & Balfour, D.L. (1998). *Unmasking Administrative Evil.* Thousand Oaks, CA: Sage Publications.

AEA (Action on Elder Abuse). (2007a). *Consultation Paper on the Potential for Adult Protection Legislation in England, Wales and Northern Ireland.* London: Action on Elder Abuse.

AEA (Action on Elder Abuse). (2007b). *Submission by Action on Elder Abuse to the Joint Commission on Human Rights April 2007.* London: Action on Elder Abuse.

Alley, D.E., Putney, N.M., Rice, M., & Bengtson, V.L. (2010). 'The Increasing Use of Theory in Social Gerontology'. *Journal of Gerontology: Social Sciences*, *65B*(5), 583–90.

Anetzberger, G. (2005). 'The Reality of Elder Abuse'. *Clinical Gerontologist*, *28*(1–2), 1–25.

Anetzberger, G., Korbin, J.E., & Austin, C. (1994). 'Alcoholism and Elder Abuse'. *Journal of Interpersonal Violence*, *9*(2), 184–93.

Arendt, H. (1963). *Eichmann in Jerusalem: The Banality of Evil.* New York: Viking.

Arksey, H., & Kemp, P.A. (2008). *Dimensions of Choice: A Narrative Review of Cash-for-care Schemes.* York: Social Policy Research Unit, University of York.

Arntz, M., & Thomsen, S. (2011). 'Crowding out Informal Care? Evidence from a Field Experiment in Germany'. *Oxford Bulletin of Economics and Statistics*, *73*(3), 398–427. Cited in N. Moran et al, 2011, p 15.

Ash, A. (2010). 'Ethics and the Street Level Bureaucrat: Implementing Policy to Protect Elders from Abuse'. *Ethics & Social Welfare*, *4*(2), 201–9.

Ash, A. (2011a). 'Personalisation and Safeguarding: What Can We Learn from Serious Case Reviews?' Paper given to 'Practical Safeguarding', 16th National Conference of Action on Elder Abuse. Manchester Conference Centre. 28–29 March.

Ash, A. (2011b). 'A Culture of Complicity'. *Community Care*, 31 March.

Ash, A. (2013). 'A Cognitive Mask? Camouflaging Dilemmas in Street Level Policy Implementation to Safeguard Older People from Abuse'. *British Journal of Social Work*, *43*(1), 99–115.

Ash, A. (2014). 'Safeguarding Older People from Mistreatment: Social Work's Ethical Dilemmas and an Ethic of Care'. In Sven Hessle (Ed.), *Human Rights and Social Equality: Challenges for Social Work Volume 1*, 59–63.

Atkinson, R. (2000). 'Narratives of Policy: The Construction of Urban Problems and Urban Policy in the Official Discourse of British Government 1968–1998'. *Critical Social Policy*, 20(2), 211–32.

Baker, A. (1975). 'Granny Battering'. *Modern Geriatrics*, 5(8), 20–4.

Baker, M.W., LaCroix, A.Z., Wu, C., Cochrane, B.B., Wallace, R., & Woods, N.F. (2009a). 'Mortality Risk Associated with Physical and Verbal Abuse in Women aged 50 to 79'. *Journal of the American Geriatrics Society*, 57(10), 1799–809.

Baker, M.W., Sugar, N.F., & Eckert, L.O. (2009b). 'Sexual Assault of Older Women: Risk and Vulnerability by Living Arrangement'. *Sexuality Research & Social Policy*, 6(4), 79–87.

Baldwin, M. (2000). *Care Management and Community Care: Social Work Discretion and the Construction of Policy*. Aldershot: Ashgate.

Band-Winterstein, T., & Eisikovits, Z. (2009). '"Aging Out" of Violence: The Multiple Faces of Intimate Violence Over the Life Span'. *Qualitative Health Research*, 2, 164–80.

Band-Winterstein, T., & Eisikovits, Z. (2010). 'Towards Phenomenological Theorizing About Old Women'. *Ageing International*, 35, 201–14.

Bandura, A. (1999). 'Moral Disengagement in the Perpetuation of Humanities'. *Personality and Social Psychology Review*, 3(3), 193–209.

Banks, S. (2008). 'Critical Commentary: Social Work Ethics'. *British Journal of Social Work*, 38, 1238–49.

Banks, S. (2010). 'Integrity in Professional Life: Issues of Conduct, Commitment and Capacity'. *British Journal of Social Work*, 40(7), 2168–84.

Barnes, M. (2011). 'Abandoning Care? A Critical Perspective on Personalisation from an Ethic of Care'. *Ethics & Social Welfare*, 5(2), 153–67.

Barnes, M. (2012). *Care in Everyday Life: An Ethic of Care in Practice*. Bristol: The Policy Press.

Barrett, S.M. (2004). 'Implementation Studies: Time for a Revival? Personal Reflections on 20 Years of Implementation Studies'. *Public Administration*, 82(2), 249–62.

Barton, R. (1967). 'Foreword' In B. Robb (Ed.), *Sans Everything. A Case to Answer* (pp ix-x). London: Thomas Nelson and Sons Ltd.

Bauman, Z. (1989). *Modernity and The Holocaust*. Ithaca, New York: Cornell University Press.

Bauman, Z. (1994). *Postmodern Ethics*. Oxford: Blackwell.

Bauman, Z. (2000). 'Am I My Brother's Keeper?' *European Journal of Social Work*, *3*(1), 5–11.

Beach, S.R., Schulz, R., Williamson, G., Miller, L.S., Weiner, M., & Lance, C.E. (2005). 'Risk Factors for Potentially Harmful Informal Caregiver Behavior'. *Journal of the American Geriatrics Society*, *53*(2), 254–261.

Bengtson, V.L., & Schaie, K.W. (Eds). (1999). *Handbook of Theories of Aging*. New York: Springer Publishing Company.

Bengtson, V.L., Burgess, E.O., & Parrott, T.M. (1997). 'Theory, Explanation and a Third Generation of Theoretical Development in Social Gerontology'. *Journal of Gerontology: Social Sciences*, *52B*(2), 572–88.

Bengtson, V.L., Parrott, T.M., & Burgess, E.O. (1996). 'Progress and Pitfalls in Gerontological Theorizing'. *The Gerontologist*, *36*(6), 768–72.

Bengtson, V.L., Putney, N.M., & Johnson, M.L. (2005). 'The Problem of Theory in Gerontology'. In M.L. Johnson (Ed.), *The Cambridge Handbook of Age and Ageing* (pp 3–20). Cambridge: Cambridge University Press.

Bengtson, V.L., Rice, C.J., & Johnson, M.L. (1999). 'Are Theories of Aging Important? Models and Explanations in Gerontology at the Turn of the Century'. In V.L. Bengtson & K.W. Schaie (Eds), *Handbook of Theories of Aging* (pp 3–20). New York: Springer Publishing Company.

Bergeron, R. (2006). 'Self-Determination and Elder Abuse: Do We Know Enough?' *Journal of Gerontological Social Work*, *46*(3/4), 81–102.

Bernstein, R.J. (2002). *Radical Evil: A Philosophical Investigation*. Cambridge: Polity Press.

BGS (British Geriatrics Society). (2005). *Aims and Functions of the Society (Revised 2005)*. BGS Compendium document 1.1. http://www.bgs.org.uk/

Biggs, S. (2001). 'Towards a Critical Narrativity. Stories of Aging in Contemporary Social Policy'. *Journal of Aging Studies*, *15*, 303–16.

Biggs, S., & Haapala, I. (2013). 'Elder Mistreatment, Ageism and Human Rights'. *International Psychogeriatrics*, *25*(8), doi:10.1017/S1041610212002372.

Biggs, S., Hendricks, J., & Lowenstein, A. (2003a). 'The Need for Theory in Gerontology'. In S. Biggs, A. Lowenstein & J. Hendricks (Eds), *The Need for Theory: Critical Approaches to Social Gerontology* (pp 1–12). New York: Baywood Publishing Company, Inc.

Biggs, S., Hendricks, J., & Lowenstein, A. (2003b). 'Where is Theory Headed? In S. Biggs, A. Lowenstein & J. Hendricks (Eds), *The Need for Theory: Critical Approaches to Social Gerontology* (pp. 245–8). New York: Baywood Publishing Company, Inc.

Biggs, S., Lowenstein, A., & Hendricks, J., (Eds). (2003c). *The Need for Theory: Critical Approaches to Social Gerontology*. New York: Baywood Publishing Company Inc.

Birrell, D. (2012). *Comparing Devolved Governance*. Basingstoke: Palgrave Macmillan.

Birren, J.E., & Bengtson, V.L. (Eds). (1988). *Emergent Theories of Aging*. New York: Springer.

Bisman, C. (2004). 'Social Work Values: The Moral Core of the Profession'. *British Journal of Social Work*, *34*, 109–23.

Blumer, H. (1971). 'Social Problems as Collective Behaviour'. *Social Problems*, *18*(3), 298–306.

Bonomi, A.E., Anderson, M.L., Reid, R.J., Carrell, D., Fishman, P.A., Rivara, F.P. & Thompson, R.S. (2007). 'Intimate Partner Violence'. *The Gerontologist*, *47*(1), 34–41.

Bourdieu, P. (1977). *Outline of a Theory of Practice* (Trans. R. Nice). Cambridge: Cambridge University Press.

Bourdieu, P. (1990). *The Logic of Practice*. Cambridge: Polity Press.

Bourdieu, P. (2000). *Pascalian Meditations*. Cambridge: Polity Press.

Bowes, A., Avan, G., & Macintosh, S.B. (2012). 'Cultural Diversity and the Mistreatment of Older People in Black and Minority Ethnic Communities: Some Implications for Service Provision'. *Journal of Elder Abuse & Neglect*, *24*(3), 251–75.

Boxall, K., Dowson, S., & Beresford, P. (2009). 'Selling Individual Budgets, Choice and Control: Local and Global Influences on Social Care Policy for People with Learning Difficulties'. *Policy & Politics*, *37*(4), 499–515.

Brammer, A., & Biggs, S. (1998). 'Defining Elder Abuse'. *Journal of Social Welfare and Family Law*, *20*(3), 285–304.

Brandl, B., & Cook-Daniels, L. (2002). *Domestic Abuse in Later Life*. National Center on Elder Abuse. http://www.elderabusecenter.org/pdf/research/abusers.pdf.

Brannelly, T. (2006). 'Negotiating Ethics in Dementia Care: An Analysis of an Ethic of Care in Practice'. *Dementia*, *5*(2), 197–212.

Broadhurst, K., Wastell, D., White, S., Hall, C., Peckover, S., Thompson, K., Pithouse, A., & Davey, D. (2010). 'Performing "Initial Assessment": Identifying the Latent Conditions for Error at the Front-Door of Local Authority Children's Services'. *British Journal of Social Work*, *40*, 352–70.

Brodkin, E.Z. (1997). 'Inside the Welfare Contract: Discretion and Accountability in State Welfare Administration'. *Social Service Review*, *71*(1), 1–33.

Brodkin, E.Z. (2008). 'Accountability in Street-Level Organizations'. *International Journal of Public Administration, 31*, 317–36.

Brodkin, E.Z. (2011). 'Policy Work: Street-Level Organizations Under New Managerialism'. *Journal of Public Administration Research and Theory*, doi:10.1093/jopart/muq1093.

Brogden, M., & Nijhar, P. (2000). *Crime, Abuse and the Elderly.* Devon: Willan.

Buchbinder, E., & Winterstein, T. (2003). '"Like a Wounded Bird": Older Women's Life Experiences with Intimate Violence'. *Journal of Elder Abuse & Neglect, 15*(2), 23–44.

Burstow, P. (2013). *Care and Corporate Neglect. Corporate Responsibility and Adult Safeguarding.* http://paulburstow.org.uk.

Butler, I., & Drakeford, M. (2005). *Scandal, Social Policy and Social Welfare* (Second edn). Bristol: Policy Press.

Butler, J. (2011). 'Hannah Arendt's Challenge to Adolph Eichmann'. *The Guardian.* 29 August. http://www.guardian.co.uk.

Butler, R. (1975). *Why Survive? Being Old in America.* New York: Harper and Row.

Bytheway, B. (1995). *Ageism.* Buckingham: Open University Press.

Bytheway, B., & Johnson, J. (1990). 'On Defining Ageism'. *Critical Social Policy, 10*(29), 27–39.

Calnan, M., Tadd, W., Hillman, A., Read, S., & Bayer, A. (2013). '"I Often Worry About the Older Person Being in that System": Exploring the Key Influences on the Provision of Dignified Care for Older People in Acute Hospitals'. *Ageing & Society, 33*(3), 465–85.

CCW (Care Council for Wales). (2002). *Code of Practice for Social Care Workers.* www.ccwales.org.uk.

Challis, D., & Davies, B. (1986). *Case Management and Community Care.* Aldershot: Gower.

Clark-Daniels, C.L., & Daniels, R.S. (1995). 'Street-Level Decision Making in Elder Mistreatment Policy: An Empirical Study of Service Rationing'. *Social Science Quarterly, 76*(2), 460–73.

Clarke, J. (2005). 'New Labour's Citizens: Activated, Empowered, Responsibilized, Abandoned? *Critical Social Policy, 25*(4), 447–63.

Cohen, M., Halevy-Levin, S., Gagin, R., Priltuzky, D., & Friedman, G. (2010). 'Elder Abuse in Long-term Care Residences and the Risk Indicators'. *Ageing & Society, 30*, 1027–40.

Collins, M.E., Cooney, K., & Garlington, S. (2012). 'Compassion in Contemporary Social Policy: Applications of Virtue Theory'. *Journal of Social Policy, 41*(2), 251–69.

Cooper, C, Huzzey, L., & Livingston, G. (2012). 'The Effect of an Educational Intervention on Junior Doctors' Knowledge and Practice in Detecting and Managing Elder Abuse'. *International Psychogeriatrics, 24*(9), 1447–53.

Cooper, C. (2013). 'Detecting Elder Abuse'. Paper given to World Elder Abuse Awareness Day Conference, University College Dublin, 13 June.

Cooper, C. (2009). 'Abuse of People with Dementia by Family Carers: Representative Cross Sectional Survey'. *BMJ, 338*(b155), doi:10.1136/bmj.b155.

Cooper, C., Dow, B., Hay, S., Livingston, D., & Livingston, G. (2013). 'Care Workers' Abusive Behavior to Residents in Care Homes: A Qualitative Study of Types of Abuse, Barriers, and Facilitators to Good Care and Development of an Instrument for Reporting of Abuse Anonymously'. *International Psychogeriatrics*, doi:10.1017/S104161021200227X.

Cooper, C., Selwood, A., & Livingston, G. (2008). 'The Prevalence of Elder Abuse and Neglect: A Systematic Review'. *Age and Ageing, 37*, 151–60.

Cornwall Adult Protection Committee. (2007). *The Murder of Steven Hoskin: A Serious Case Review.* Executive Summary. Report prepared by Margaret C. Flynn. http://www.elderabuse.org.uk.

Coyne, A.C., Reichman, W.E., & Berbig, L.J. (1993). 'The Relationship Between Dementia and Elder Abuse'. *American Journal of Psychiatry, 150*(4), 643–6.

CPS (Crime Prosecution Service). (2008). *Crimes Against Older People – CPS Prosecution Policy.* London: CPS, July.

CQC (Care Quality Commission). (2012). *The State of Health Care and Adult Social Care in England.* London: The Stationery Office. HC 763.

Crawford, M. (1971). 'Retirement and Disengagement'. *Human Relations, 24*, 255–78. Cited in C. Estes, S. Biggs & C. Phillipson, 2003, p 9.

CSSIW (Care and Social Services Inspectorate). (2013). *Adult Protection Monitoring Report 2010–2012.* http://wales.gov.uk/docs/cssiw/report/130320adulten.pdf.

Cutler, T., Waine, B., & Brehony, K. (2007). 'A New Epoch of Individualization? Problems with 'Personalisation' of Public Services'. *Public Administration, 85*(2), 847–55.

Dalley, G. (1991). 'Beliefs and Behaviour: Professionals and the Policy Process'. *Journal of Aging Studies*, 5(2), 163–80.

Daly, J., Merchant, M.L., & Jogerst, G.J. (2011). 'Elder Abuse Research: A Systematic Review'. *Journal of Elder Abuse & Neglect*, 23, 348–65.

Dannefer, D., & Phillipson, C., (Eds). (2010). *The Sage Book of Social Gerontology*. London: Sage Publications.

Davey V., Snell T., Fernandez J-L., Knapp M., Tobin R., Jolly D., Perkins, M., Kendal J., Pearson C., Vick, N., Swift, P., Mercer, M., & Priestley, M. (2007). *Schemes Providing Support to People Using Direct Payments: A UK Survey*. London: Personal Social Services Research Unit, LSE.

Davis, R.E. (2002). '"The Strongest Women": Exploration of the Inner Resources of Abused Women'. *Qualitative Health Research*, 12(9), 1248–63.

de Souza, V. (2011). 'The Adult Support and Protection Act (Scotland) 2007 – initial impact and emerging themes. *Action Points*(43), 25–8, January–February.

Decalmer, P., & Glendinning, F. (1993). *The Mistreatment of Elderly People*. London: Sage.

DH (Department of Health) Social Services Inspectorate. (1992). *Care Management and Assessment. Managers' Guide*. London: HMSO.

DH (Department of Health). (1989). *Caring for People: Community Care in the Next Decade and Beyond*. London: HMSO. Cm 849.

DH (Department of Health). (1998). *Modernising Social Services: Promoting Independence. Improving Protection. Raising Standards*. London: The Stationery Office. November. Cm 4169.

DH (Department of Health). (2000). *No Secrets: Guidance on Developing and Implementing Multi-Agency Policies and Procedures to Protect Vulnerable Adults from Abuse.* London: Department of Health.

DH (Department of Health). (2006). *Our Health, Our Care, Our Say: A New Direction for Community Services*. London: DH.

DH (Department of Health). (2010). *A Vision for Adult Social Care: Capable Communities and Active Citizens*. London: DH, 16 November.

Dow, B., & Joosten, M. (2012). 'Understanding Elder Abuse: A Social Rights Perspective'. *International Psychogeriatrics*, 24(6), 853–5.

Duffy, S. (2010). 'The Citizenship Theory of Social Justice: Exploring the Meaning of Personalisation for Social Workers'. *Journal of Social Work Practice*, 24(3), 253–67.

Du Gay, P. (2003). 'The Tyranny of the Epochal: Change, Epochalism and Organizational Reform'. *Organization*, 10(4), 663-84.

Dunér, A., & Nordström, M. (2006). 'The Discretion and Power of Street-level Bureaucrats: An Example from Swedish Municipal Eldercare'. *European Journal of Social Work*, 9(4), 425–44.

Dworkin, R. (1978). *Taking Rights Seriously. New Impression with a Reply to Critics*. London: Duckworth.

EHRC (Equality and Human Rights Commission). (2011). *Close to Home: An Inquiry into Older People and Human Rights in Home Care*: www.equalityhumanrights.com/homecareinquiry, November.

Eisikovits, Z., Koren, C., & Band-Winterstein, T. (2013). 'The Social Construction of Social Problems: The Case of Elder Abuse and Neglect'. *International Psychogeriatrics, 25*(8), 1291–98.

Eisikovits, Z., Winterstein, T., & Lowenstein, A. (2004). *The National Survey on Elder Abuse and Neglect in Israel*. Haifa: Haifa University, and JDC-ESHEL, Center for Research and Study on Ageing, December.

Eldridge, J.E.T., & Crombie, A.D. (1974). *A Sociology of Organisations*. London: George Allen and Unwin.

Ellis, K. (2004). 'Promoting Rights or Avoiding Litigation? The Introduction of the Human Rights Act 1998 into Adult Social Care in England'. *European Journal of Social Work, 7*(3), 321–40.

Ellis, K. (2007). 'Direct Payments and Social Work Practice: The Significance of "Street-Level Bureaucracy" in Determining Eligibility. *British Journal of Social Work, 37*, 405–22.

Ellis, K. (2011). '"Street-level Bureaucracy" Revisited: The Changing Face of Frontline Discretion in Adult Social Care in England'. *Social Policy & Administration, 45*(3), 221–44.

Ellis, K. (2013). 'Professional Discretion and Adult Social Work: Exploring Its Nature and Scope on the Front Line of Personalisation'. *British Journal of Social Work*, Advance access published 21 April, doi:10.1093/bjsw/bct1076.

Ellis, K., Davis, A., & Rummery, K. (1999). 'Needs Assessment, Street-level Bureaucracy and the New Community Care'. *Social Policy & Administration, 33*(3), 262–80.

Estes, C. (1979). *The Aging Enterprise*. San Francisco: Jossey Bass.

Estes, C., Biggs, S., & Phillipson, C. (2003). *Social Theory, Social Policy and Ageing: A Critical Introduction*. Maidenhead: Open University Press.

Evans, T. (2011). 'Professionals, Managers and Discretion: Critiquing Street-Level Bureaucracy'. *British Journal of Social Work, 41*, 368–86.

Evans, T. (2012). 'Organisational Rules and Discretion in Adult Social Work'. *British Journal of Social Work*, doi:10.1093/bjsw/bcs1008.

Evans, T., & Harris, J. (2004). 'Street-level Bureaucracy, Social Work and the (Exaggerated) Death of Discretion'. *British Journal of Social Work, 34*, 871–95.

Fearn, N. (2006). 'His Concerns are Consumerism, Modernity and Power. To Some He is the Greatest Living Sociologist. And He Lives Quietly in Leeds'. *New Statesman* (16 January), 30–2.

Ferguson, I. (2007). 'Increasing User Choice or Privatizing Risk? The Antimonies of Personalization'. *British Journal of Social Work*, *37*, 387–403.

Filinson, R. (2006). '"No Secrets" and Beyond: Recent Elder Abuse Policy in England'. *Journal of Elder Abuse & Neglect*, *18*(1).

Fine, M., & Glendinning, C. (2005). 'Dependence, Independence or Inter-dependence? Revisiting the Concepts of "Care" and "Dependency"'. *Ageing & Society*, *25*, 601–21.

Fisher, B., Zink, T., & Regan, S.L. (2011). 'Abuses Against Older Women: Prevalence and Health Effects'. *Journal of Interpersonal Violence*, *26*(2), 254–68.

Forder, J. (2008). *The Costs of Addressing Age Discrimination in Social Care*. Canterbury: PSSRU Discussion Paper 2538, April.

Foucault, M. (1980). *Power/Knowledge: Selected Interviews and Other Writings 1972–1977*. Hemel Hempstead: The Harvester Press.

Francis Report. (2013a). *Report of the Mid Staffordshire NHS Foundation Trust Public Inquiry. Volumes 1–3*. London: The Stationery Office. HC 898-I. 6 February.

Francis Report. (2013b). *Report of the Mid Staffordshire NHS Foundation Trust Public Inquiry. Executive Summary*. London: The Stationery Office. HC 947. 6 February.

Francis, R. (2013c). *Chairman's Press Statement. Mid Staffordshire NHS Foundation Trust Inquiry*: http://www.midstaffspublicinquiry.com/. 6 February

Fyson, R., & Kitson, D. (2007). 'Independence or Protection – Does it Have to be a Choice? Reflections on the Abuse of People with Learning Disabilities in Cornwall'. *Critical Social Policy*, *27*, 426–36.

Gambrill, E. (2007). 'Views of Evidence-Based Practice: Social Workers' Code of Ethics and Accreditation Standards as Guides for Choice'. *Journal of Social Work Education*, *43*(3), 447–62.

Gambrill, E. (2012). *Critical Thinking in Clinical Practice: Improving the Quality of Judgments and Decisions* (Third edn). New Jersey: John Wiley & Sons Inc.

Garland, R. (1945). 'End of the Poor Laws – and a New Era Dawns on British Social Welfare'. *Social Welfare*, *11*(2), 36. Cited in R. Means & R. Smith, 1998, p 155.

Giddens, A. (1984). *The Constitution of Society – Outline of the Theory of Structuration*. Cambridge: Polity Press.

Glasby, J. (2012). 'The Controversies of Choice and Control: Why Some People Might Be Hostile to English Social Care Reforms'. *British Journal of Social Work*. doi:10.1093/bjsw/bcs125.

Glendinning, C., Challis, D., Fernandez, J.-L., Jacobs, S., Jones, K., Knapp, M., Manthorpe, J., Moran, N., Netten, A., Stevens, M., & Wilberforce, M. (2008). *Evaluation of the Individual Budgets Programme. Final Report.* York: Social Policy Research Unit, October.

Goergen, T., & Beaulieu, M. (2013). 'Critical Concepts in Elder Abuse'. *International Psychogeriatrics*, 25(8), 1217–28.

Green, J. (2009). 'The Deformation of Professional Formation: Managerial Targets and the Undermining of Professional Judgement'. *Ethics & Social Welfare*, 3(2), 115–30.

Grenier, A. (2012). *Transitions and the Lifecourse.* Bristol: The Policy Press.

Grint, K. (2010). *The Cuckoo Clock Syndrome: Addicted to Command, Allergic to Leadership*: University of Warwick, institutional repository, http://go.warwick.ac.uk/wrap.

GSCC (General Social Care Council). (2010). *Code of Practice for Social Care Workers.* www.skillsforcare.org.uk.

Hagestad, G.O., & Dannefer, D. (2001). 'Concepts and Theories of Aging: Beyond Microfication in Social Science Approaches'. In R.H. Binstock & L.K. George (Eds), *Handbook of Aging and the Social Sciences* (Fifth edn, pp 3–21). San Diego, California: Academic Press.

Harbison, J. (2008). 'Stoic Heroines or Collaborators: Ageism, Feminism and the Provision of Assistance to Abused Old Women'. *Journal of Social Work Practice*, 22(2), 221–34.

Harrison, S., & Smith, C. (2004). 'Trust and Moral Motivation: Redundant Resources in Health and Social Care'. *Policy & Politics*, 32(3), 371–86.

Hatton, C., Waters, J., Duffy, S., Senker, J., Crosby, N., Poll, C., Tyson, A., O'Brien, J., and Towell, D. (2008). *A Report on in Control's Second Phase. Evaluation and Learning 2005–2007.* London: In Control Publications.

Held, V. (2006). *The Ethics of Care: Personal, Political, Global.* Oxford: Oxford University Press.

Hendricks, J., & Powell, J.L. (2009). 'Theorizing in Social Gerontology: The *raison d'être*'. *International Journal of Sociology and Social Policy*, 29(1/2), 5–14.

Hendricks, J., Applebaum, R., & Kunkel, S. (2010). 'A World Apart? Bridging the Gap Between Theory and Applied Gerontology'. *The Gerontologist*, 50(3), 284–93.

Henwood, M., & Hudson, B. (2008). Individual Budgets and Personalisation: A New Model for Integration? *Journal of Integrated Care*, 16(3), 8–16.

Hester, M., Williamson, E., Regan, L., Coulter, M., Chantler, K., Gangoli, G., Davenport, R., & Green, L. (2012). *Exploring the Service and Support Needs of Male, Lesbian, Gay, Bi-sexual and Transgendered and Black and Other Minority Ethnic Victims of Domestic and Sexual Violence*. Report prepared for Home Office SRG/06/017. Bristol: University of Bristol.

Hill, M. (1987). 'Street Level Bureaucracy in Social Work and Social Services Departments'. In J. Lishman (Ed.), *Social Work Departments as Organisations* (pp 69–81). London: Jessica Kingsley Publishers, Research Highlights 4.

Hill, M. (2012). *The Public Policy Process* (Sixth edn). Harlow: Pearson Education Limited.

Hill, M., & Hupe, P. (2009). *Implementing Public Policy: An Introduction to the Study of Operational Governance* (Second edn). London: Sage Publications.

HLSCB (Haringey Local Safeguarding Children Board). (2009). *Serious Case Review 'Child A'. March 2009*. Published by the Department for Education, 26 October. http://www.education.gov.uk.

HM Government. (2007). *Putting People First: A Shared Vision and Commitment to the Transformation of Adult Social Care*. London: HM Government, 10 December.

HM Government. (2012). *Caring for Our Future: Reforming Care and Support*. Norwich: The Stationery Office, July. Cm 8378.

HM Treasury. (2013). *Spending Round 2013*. Norwich: The Stationery Office. Cm 8639.

Holstein, M. (2010). 'Ethics and Old Age: The Second Generation'. In D. Dannefer & C. Phillipson (Eds), *The Sage Handbook of Social Gerontology* (pp 630–40). London: Sage Publications.

Holstein, M.B., & Minkler, M. (2003). 'Self, Society, and the "New Gerontology"'. *The Gerontologist*, *43*(6), 787–96.

Holstein, M.B., Parks, J.A., & Waymack, M.H. (2010). *Ethics, Aging, and Society: The Critical Turn*. New York: Springer Publishing Company.

Homer, A., & Gilleard, C. (1990). 'Abuse of Elderly People by Their Carers'. *Br Med J*, *301*, 1359–62.

Honneth, A. (1995). *The Struggle for Recognition: The Moral Grammar of Social Conflicts*. Cambridge: Polity Press.

Hooyman, N.R., & Kiyak, H.A. (2008). *Social Gerontology: A Multidisciplinary Perspective* (eighth ed.). Boston: Pearson/Allyn & Bacon.

Howe, D. (1991). 'Knowledge, Power, and the Shape of Social Work Practice'. In M. Davies (Ed.), *The Sociology of Social Work* (pp 202–20). London: Routledge.

HSC (Health and Social Care Board). (2012). *Commissioning Plan 2012/13*. http://www.hscboard.hscni.net/. 13 September.

Hudson, B. (1997). 'Michael Lipsky and Street Level Bureaucracy'. In M. Hill (Ed.), *The Policy Process. A Reader* (Second edn, pp 393–403). Hemel Hempstead: Prentice Hall/Wheatsheaf.

Hughes, B., McKie, L., Hopkins, D., & Watson, N. (2005). 'Love's Labour Lost? Feminism, the Disabled People's Movement and an Ethic of Care'. *Sociology 39*(2), 259–75.

Hugman, R. (2005). 'Exploring the Paradox of Teaching Ethics for Social Work Practice'. *Social Work Education, 24*, 535–45.

Hunter, S., Manthorpe, J., Ridley, J., Cornes, M., & Rosengard, A. (2012). 'When Self-directed Support Meets Adult Support and Protection: Findings from the Evaluation of the SDS Test Sites in Scotland'. *The Journal of Adult Protection, 14*(4), 206–15.

Hupe, P. (2011). 'The Thesis of Incongruent Implementation: Revisiting Pressman and Wildavsky'. *Public Policy and Administration, 26*(1), 63–80.

Hupe, P., & Hill, M. (2007). 'Street-level Bureaucracy and Public Accountability'. *Public Administration, 85*(2), 279–99.

Hussein, S., Manthorpe, J., & Penhale, B. (2007). 'Public Perceptions of the Neglect and Mistreatment of Older People: Findings of a United Kingdom Survey'. *Ageing & Society, 27*, 919–40.

Iborra, I. (2008). *Elder Abuse in the Family in Spain.* Valencia: Queen Sofía Center.

ICSS (Independent Commission on Social Services in Wales). (2010). *From Vision to Action. The Report of the Independent Commission on Social Services in Wales.* http://www.icssw.org/.

IFSW (International Federation of Social Workers). (2000). *Definition of Social Work.* Adopted by the IFSW General Meeting in Montréal, Canada, July. http://www.ifsw.org/.

IFSW (International Federation of Social Workers). (2012). *Statement of Ethical Principles.* http://ifsw.org/policies/statement-of-ethical-principles/.

James, A.N. (2008). 'A Critical Consideration of the Cash for Care Agenda and Its Implications for Social Services in Wales'. *The Journal of Adult Protection, 10*(3), 23–34.

Janis, I.L. (1982). *Groupthink: Psychological Studies of Policy Decisions and Fiascoes.* Boston: Houghton Mifflin.

JCHR (Joint Committee on Human Rights). (2007). *The Human Rights of Older People in Healthcare. Eighteenth Report of Session 2006–07. Volume 1 – Report and Formal Minutes.* London: The Stationery Office, HL Paper 156-1, HC 378-1.

Jeary, K. (2004). 'Sexual Abuse of Elderly People: Would We Rather Not Know the Details?' *Journal of Adult Protection*, *6*(2), 21–30.

Katz, F. (1993). *Ordinary People and Extraordinary Evil. A Report on the Beguilings of Evil*. Albany: State University of New York Press.

Katz, S. (2003). 'Critical Gerontological Theory: Intellectual Fieldwork and the Nomadic Life of Ideas'. In S. Biggs, A. Lowenstein & J. Hendricks (Eds), *The Need for Theory: Critical Approaches to Social Gerontology* (pp 15–31). New York: Baywood Publishing Company Inc.

Katz, S., & Marshall, B. (2003). 'New Sex for Old: Lifestyle, Consumerism, and the Ethics of Aging Well'. *Journal of Aging Studies*, *17*, 3–16.

Kilbane, T., & Spira, M. (2010). 'Domestic Violence or Elder Abuse? Why It Matters for Older Women'. *Families in Society*, *91*(2), 165–170.

Kittay, E.F. (1999). *Love's Labor: Essays on Women, Equality and Dependency*. London: Routledge.

Kittay, E.F. (2001a). 'A Feminist Public Ethic of Care Meets the New Communitarian Family Policy'. *Ethics*, *111*(3), 523–47.

Kittay, E.F. (2001b). 'When Caring is Just and Justice is Caring: Justice and Mental Retardation'. *Public Culture*, *13*(3), 557–79.

Kittay, E.F. (2005). 'At the Margins of Moral Personhood'. *Ethics*, *116*(1), 100–31.

Kittay, E.F., Jennings, B., & Wasunna, A.A. (2005). 'Dependency, Difference and the Global Ethic of Longterm Care'. *Journal of Political Philosophy*, *13*(4), 443–69.

Kosberg, J.I. (2005). 'Meeting the Needs of Older Men: Challenges for Those in Helping Professions'. *Journal of Sociology and Social Welfare*, *XXXII* (1), 9–31.

Kosberg, J.I. (2007). 'Introduction'. *Journal of Elder Abuse & Neglect*, *19*(1/2), 1–5.

Kröger, T. (2009). 'Care Research and Disability Studies: Nothing in Common?' *Critical Social Policy*, *29*(3), 398–420.

Kuhn, T.S. (1970). *The Structure of Scientific Revolutions*. Chicago: University of Chicago Press.

LAC (DH) (2008). 1. *Transforming Social Care*. London: Department of Health.

Lachs, M., & Pillemer, K. (2004). 'Elder Abuse'. *Lancet*, *364*, 1263–72.

Lachs, M.S., & Berman, J. (2011). *'Under the Radar: New York State Elder Abuse Prevalence Study'*. Rochester, NY: Lifespan, May.

Lachs, M.S., Berkman, L., Fulmer, T., & Horwitz, R.I. (1994). 'A Prospective Community-based Pilot Study of Risk Factors for the Investigation of Elder Mistreatment'. *Journal of the American Geriatrics Society*, *42*(2), 169-73.

Lachs, M.S., Williams, C., O'Brien, S., Hurst, L., & Horwitz, R. (1997). 'Risk Factors for Reported Elder Abuse and Neglect: A Nine-Year Observational Cohort Study'. *The Gerontologist, 37*(4), 469–74.

Lachs, M.S., Williams, C., O'Brien, S., Pillemer, K.A., & Charlson, M.E. (1998). 'The Mortality of Elder Mistreatment'. *Journal of the American Medical Association, 280*(5), 428–32.

Lachs, M.S., Williams, C.S., O'Brien, S., & Pillemer, K. (2002). 'Adult Protective Service Use and Nursing Home Placement'. *The Gerontologist, 42*(6), 734–39.

Lafferty, A., Treacy, M.P., Fealy, G., Drennan, J., & Lyons, I. (2012). *Older People's Experiences of Mistreatment and Abuse*. Dublin: NCPOP, University College Dublin.

Laming Report. (2003). *The Victoria Climbié Inquiry Report. Report of an Inquiry*. Norwich: The Stationery Office. Cmnd 5730.

Laumann, E.O., Leitsch, S.A., & Waite, L.J. (2008). 'Elder Mistreatment in the United States: Prevalence Estimates From a Nationally Representative Study'. *Journal of Gerontology Social Sciences, 63B*(4), S248–S254.

Law Commission. (2011). *Adult Social Care*. London: The Stationery Office, HC 941.

Leadbeater, C., Bartlett, J., & Gallagher, N. (2008). *Making It Personal*. London: Demos.

Leisey, M., Kupstas, P.K., & Cooper, A. (2009). 'Domestic Violence in the Second Half of Life'. *Journal of Elder Abuse & Neglect, 21*, 141–55.

Lewin, K. (1952). *Field Theory in Social Science: Selected Theoretical Papers*. London: Tavistock.

Lewis, J., & Glennerster, H. (1996). *Implementing the New Community Care*. Buckingham: Open University Press.

Lipsky, M. (1980). *Street-level Bureaucracy: Dilemmas of the Individual in Public Services*. New York: Russell Sage Foundation.

Lipsky, M. (2010). *Street-level Bureaucracy: Dilemmas of the Individual in Public Services* (Updated edn.). New York: Russell Sage Foundation.

Lloyd, L. (2004). 'Mortality and Morality: Ageing and the Ethics of Care'. *Ageing & Society, 24*(2), 235–56.

Lloyd, L. (2006). 'A Caring Profession? The Ethics of Care and Social Work with Older People'. *British Journal of Social Work, 36*, 1171–85.

Lloyd, L. (2012). *Health and Care in Ageing Societies: A New International Approach*. Bristol: The Policy Press.

Lloyd-Sherlock, P., McKee, M., Ebrahim, S., Gorman, M., Greengross, S., Prince, M., Pruchno, R., Gutman, G., Kirkwood, T., O'Neill, D., Ferrucci, L., Kritchevsky, S.B., & Vellas, B. (2012). 'Population Ageing and Health'. *The Lancet, 379*(9823), 1295–6.

Lord Chancellor's Department. (1997). *Who Decides? Making Decisions on Behalf of Mentally Incapacitated Adults. A Consultation Paper Issued by the Lord Chancellor's Department*. London: Lord Chancellor's Department.

Lukes, S. (2005). *Power: A Radical View* (Second edn). Basingstoke: Palgrave Macmillan.

Lundy, M., & Grossman, S.F. (2004). 'Elder Abuse: Spouse/Intimate Partner Abuse and Family Violence Among Elders'. *Journal of Elder Abuse & Neglect, 16*(1), 85–102.

Luoma, M-L., Koivusilta, M., Lang, G., Enzenhofer, E., De Donder, L., Verté, D., Reingarde, J., Tamutiene, I., Ferreira-Alves, J., Santos, A.J., & Penhale, B. (2011). *Prevalence Study of Abuse and Violence Against Older Women in Austria, Belgium, Finland, Lithuania, and Portugal (European Report of the AVOW Project)*. Finland: National Institute for Health and Welfare (THL).

Lymbery, M. (1998). 'Care Management and Professional Autonomy: The Impact of Community Care Legislation on Social Work with Older People'. *British Journal of Social Work, 28*, 863–78.

Lymbery, M. (2001). 'Social Work at the Crossroads'. *British Journal of Social Work, 31*, 369–84.

Lymbery, M. (2010). 'A New Vision for Adult Social Care? Continuities and Change in the Care of Older People'. *Critical Social Policy, 30*(5), 5–26.

Lynott, R.J., & Lynott, P.P. (1996). 'Tracing the Course of Theoretical Development in the Sociology of Aging'. *The Gerontologist, 36*, 749–60.

Manthorpe, J., & Samsi, K. (2013). '"Inherently Risky?" Personal Budgets for People with Dementia and the Risks of Financial Abuse: Findings from an Interview-Based Study with Adult Safeguarding Coordinators'. *British Journal of Social Work, 43*(5), 889–903.

Manthorpe, J., Hindes, J., Martineau, S., Cornes, M., Ridley, J., Spandler, H., Rosengard, A., Hunter, S., Little, S., & Gray, B. (2011). *Self-directed Support: A Review of the Barriers and Facilitators*. Edinburgh: Scottish Government Research. www.scotland.gov.uk/socialresearch.

Manthorpe, J., Stevens, M., Rapaport, J., Challis, D., Jacobs, S., Netten, A., Jones, K., Knapp, M., Wilberforce, M., & Glendinning, C. (2010). 'Individual Budgets and Adult Safeguarding: Parallel or Converging Tracks? Further Findings from the Evaluation of Individual Budget Pilots'. *Journal of Social Work*, doi: 2010.1177/1468017310379452.

Maynard-Moody, S., & Musheno, M. (2000). 'State Agent of Citizen Agent: Two Narratives of Discretion'. *Journal of Public Administration and Research and Theory, 10*(2), 329–58.

Maynard-Moody, S., & Portillo, S. (2011). 'Street-level Bureaucracy Theory'. In R.F. Durant (Ed.), *The Oxford Handbook of American Bureaucracy*: Oxford Handbooks Online, doi:10.1093/oxfordhb/9780199238958.003.0011.

McCreadie, C. (1991). *Elder Abuse: An Exploratory Study.* London: Age Concern Institute of Gerontology, King's College.

McCreadie, C. (1996). *Elder Abuse: An Update on Research.* London: Age Concern Institute of Gerontology, King's College.

McCreadie, C., Bennett, G., Gilthorpe, M.S., Houghton, G., & Tinker, A. (2000). 'Elder Abuse: Do General Practitioners Know or Care?' *Journal of the Royal Society of Medicine*, *93*, 67–71.

McCreadie, C., Mathew, D., Filinson, R., & Askham, J. (2008). 'Ambiguity and Cooperation in the Implementation of Adult Protection Policy'. *Social Policy & Administration*, *42*(3), 248–66.

McDonald, L., & Thomas, C. (2013). 'Elder Abuse Through a Lifecourse Lens'. *International Psychogeriatrics*, *25*(8), 1235–43.

McDonald, L., Beaulieu, M., Harbinson, J., Hirst, S., Lowenstein, A., Podnieks, E., & Wahl, J. (2012). 'Institutional Abuse of Older Adults: What We Know, What We Need to Know'. *Journal of Elder Abuse & Neglect*, *24*, 138–60.

Means, R. (2012). 'A Brave New World of Personalized Care? Historical Perspectives on Social Care and Older People in England'. *Social Policy & Administration*, *46*(3), 302–20.

Means, R., & Smith, R. (1998). *From Poor Law to Community Care* (Second edn). Bristol: Policy Press.

Mid Staffordshire NHS Foundation Trust Inquiry. (2010). *Independent Inquiry into Care Provided by Mid Staffordshire NHS Foundation Trust. January 2005–March 2009.* (Vol. 1). London: The Stationery Office. HC375-I Session 2009/10.

Milgram, S. (1974). *Obedience to Authority: An Experimental View.* New York: Harper and Row.

Minichiello, V., Browne, J., & Kendig, H. (2000). 'Perceptions and Consequences of Ageism: Views of Older People'. *Ageing and Society*, *20*, 253–78.

Ministry of Health. (1950). *Report of the Ministry of Health for the Year Ended 31st March 1949 including the Report of the Chief Medical Officer on the State of the Public Health for the Year ended December 31st, 1948.* London: HMSO. Cmnd 7910. Cited in R. Means & R. Smith, 1998, p 155.

Ministry of Health. (1955). *Report of the Ministry of Health for Year Ended 31st December 1954.* London: HMSO. Cmnd 9566. Cited in R. Means and R. Smith, 1998, p 319.

Minkler, M. (1996). 'Critical Perspectives on Ageing: New Challenges for Gerontology'. *Ageing & Society*, *16*, 467–87.

Montminy, L. (2005). 'Older Women's Experiences of Psychological Violence in Their Marital Relationships'. *Journal of Gerontological Social Work*, *46*(2), 3–22.

Moran, N., Glendinning, C., Wilberforce, M., Stevens, M., Netten, A., Jones, K., Manthorpe J., Knapp M., Fernandez J-L., Challis, D., & Jacobs, S. (2013). 'Older People's Experiences of Cash-for-care Schemes: Evidence from the English Individual Budget Pilot Projects'. *Ageing & Society*, *33*(5), 826–51.

Morgan, G. (1997). *Images of Organization*. Thousand Oaks, CA: Sage.

Morgan, P. (2013). 'What Social Workers Should Do When Care Arranged by a User is Unsafe'. *Community Care*, 4 April. http://www.communitycare.co.uk/.

Mowlam, A., Tennant, R., Dixon, J., & McCreadie, C. (2007). *UK Study of Abuse and Neglect of Older People: Qualitative Findings*. London: Comic Relief.

NAfW (National Assembly for Wales). (2000). *In Safe Hands: Implementing Adult Protection Procedures in Wales*: Cardiff: National Assembly for Wales.

NAfW (National Assembly for Wales). (2011). *Welsh Liberal Democrats Debate*. The Record of Proceedings, 9 March. http://www.assemblywales.org/.

Naughton, C., Drennan, J., Treacy, M.P., Lafferty, A., Lyons, I., Phelan, A., Quin, S., O'Loughlin, A., & Delaney, L. (2010). *Abuse and Neglect of Older People in Ireland. Report on the National Study of Elder Abuse and Neglect*. Dublin: University College Dublin, November.

Needham, C. (2011a). *Personalising Public Services: Understanding the Personalisation Narrative*. Bristol: The Policy Press.

Needham, C. (2011b). 'Personalization: From Story-line to Practice'. *Social Policy & Administration*, *45*(1), 54–68.

Nelson, T. (2005). 'Ageism: Prejudice Against Our Feared Future Self'. *Journal of Social Issues*, *61*(2), 207–21.

Netten, A., Jones, K., Knapp, M., Fernandez, J-L., Challis, D., Glendinning, C., Jacobs, S., Manthorpe, J., Moran, N., Stevens, M., & Wilberforce, M. (2011). 'Personalisation Through Individual Budgets: Does It Work and for Whom?' *British Journal of Social Work*, doi: 2010.1093/bjsw/bcr2159.

NHSSB (Northern Health and Social Services Board). (2006). *Safeguarding Vulnerable Adults: Regional Adult Protection Policy & Procedural Guidance*. Ballymena: Social Services Directorate, Northern Health and Social Services Board, September.

NIASP (Northern Ireland Adult Safeguarding Partnership). (2012). *Annual Report 1st April 2011 to 31st March 2012*. http://www. hscboard.hscni.net.

Nickerson, R.S. (1986). *Reflections on Reasoning*. Hillsdale, NJ: Erlbaum. Cited in E. Gambrill, 2012, p 210.

NMC (Nursing & Midwifery Council) (2008). *The Code: Standards of Conduct, Performance and Ethics for Nurses and Midwives*. London: NMC, May.

Northern Ireland Office. (2010). *Adult Safeguarding in Northern Ireland. Regional and Local Partnership Arrangements*: http://www.dhsspsni.gov. uk/asva-_march_2010.pdf.

Nussbaum, M. (2001). *Upheavals of Thought: The Intelligence of Emotions*. Cambridge: Cambridge University Press.

O'Keeffe, M., Hills, A., Doyle, M., McCreadie, C., Scholes, S., Constantine, R., Tinker, A., Manthorpe, J., Biggs, S. & Erens, B. (2007). *UK Study of Abuse and Neglect of Older People: Prevalence Survey Report*. Prepared for Comic Relief and the Department of Health. London: Comic Relief, June.

Ockleford, E., Barnes-Holmes, Y., Morichelli, R., Morjaria, A., Scocchera, F., Furniss, F., Sdogati, C., & Barnes-Holmes, D. (2003). 'Mistreatment of Older Women in Three European Countries. Estimated Prevalence and Service Responses'. *Violence Against Women*, *9*(12), 1453–64.

OPCW (Older People's Commissioner for Wales). (2010). *Dignified Care? The Experiences of Older People in Hospital in Wales*. Cardiff: OPCW.

Orwell, G. (2008). *Nineteen Eighty-Four*. Harmondsworth: Penguin.

Parliamentary and Health Service Ombudsman. (2011). *Care and Compassion? Report of the Health Service Ombudsman on Ten Investigations into NHS Care of Older People*. London: The Stationery Office, HC778.

Penhale, B. (1999). 'Bruises on the Soul: Older Women, Domestic Violence, and Elder Abuse'. *Journal of Elder Abuse & Neglect*, *11*(1), 1–22.

Penhale, B. (2003). 'Older Women, Domestic Violence, and Elder Abuse: A Review of Commonalities, Differences, and Shared Approaches'. *Journal of Elder Abuse & Neglect*, *15*(3/4), 163–83.

Penhale, B., & Kingston, P. (1997). 'Elder Abuse, Mental Health and Later Life: Steps Towards an Understanding'. *Aging & Mental Health*, *1*(4), 296–304.

Phillipson, C. (1977). 'The Emergence of Retirement'. Working paper in sociology, no 14, Durham University. Cited in R. Means and R. Smith, 1998, p 8.

Pillemer, K.A., & Finkelhor, D. (1988). 'The Prevalence of Elder Abuse: A Random Sample Survey'. *The Gerontologist*, *28*(1), 51–7.

Pillemer, K., & Finkelhor, D. (1989). 'Causes of Elder Abuse: Caregiver Stress Versus Problem Relatives'. *American Journal of Orthopsychiatry*, *59*, 179–87.

Pillemer, K., Mueller-Johnson, K., Mock, S., Suitor, J.J., & Lachs, M.S. (2006). 'Prevention of Elder Mistreatment'. In L. Doll, J. Mercy, S. Bonzo & D.A. Sleet (Eds), *Handbook on Injury and Violence Prevention* (pp 241–54). Secausus, NJ: Springer.

Ploeg, J., Fear, J., Hutchison, B., MacMillan, H., & Bolan, G. (2009). 'A Systemic Review of Interventions for Elder Abuse'. *Journal of Elder Abuse & Neglect*, *21*, 187–210.

Podnieks, E. (1992). 'National Survey on Abuse of the Elderly in Canada'. *Journal of Elder Abuse & Neglect*, *4*, 5–58.

Podnieks, E., Penhale, B., Goergen, T., Biggs, S., & Han, D. (2010). 'Elder Mistreatment: An International Narrative'. *Journal of Elder Abuse & Neglect*, *22*, 131–63.

Polanyi, M. (1967). *The Tacit Dimension*. London: Routledge & Kegan Paul.

Poll, C., Duffy, S., Hatton, C., Sanderson, H., & Routledge, M. (2006). *A Report on In Control's first phase 2003–2005*. London: In Control Publications.

Poole, C., & Rietschlin, J. (2012). 'Intimate Partner Victimization among Adults Aged 60 and Over: An Analysis of the 1999 and 2004 General Social Survey'. *Journal of Elder Abuse & Neglect*, *24*(2), 120–37.

Power, M. (1997). *The Audit Society. Rituals of Verification*. Oxford: Oxford University Press.

Pressman, J., & Wildavsky, A. (1984). *Implementation: How Great Expectations in Washington Are Dashed in Oakland; Or, Why It's Amazing that Federal Programs Work at All, This Being a Saga of the Economic Development Administration as Told by Two Sympathetic Observers Who Seek to Build Morals on a Foundation of Ruined Hopes* (Third edn). Berkeley: University of California Press.

Preston-Shoot, M. (2001). 'Regulating the Road of Good Intentions: Observations on the Relationship Between Policy, Regulations and Practice in Social Work'. *Practice*, *13*(4), 5–20.

Preston-Shoot, M. (2010). 'On the Evidence for Viruses in Social Work Systems: Law, Ethics and Practice'. *European Journal of Social Work*, *13*(4), 465–82.

Preston-Shoot, M. (2011). 'On Administrative Evil-doing Within Social Work Policy and Services: Law, Ethics and Practice'. *European Journal of Social Work*, *14*(2), 177–94.

Preston-Shoot, M., & Wigley, V. (2002). 'Closing the Circle: Social Workers' Responses to Multi-Agency Procedures on Older Age Abuse'. *British Journal of Social Work*, *32*, 299–320.

Pritchard, J. (2001). 'Neglect. Not Grasping the Nettle and Hiding Behind Choice'. In J. Pritchard (Ed.), *Good Practice with Vulnerable Adults* (pp 225–44). London: Jessica Kingsley Publishers.

Pritchard, J. (2002). 'Male Victims of Elder Abuse: Their Experiences and Need'. *Joseph Rowntree Foundation Findings*, *362*. http://www.jrf.org.uk/knowledge/findings/socialcare/pdf/362.pdf.

Pritchard, J. (2007). 'Identifying and Working with Older Male Victims of Abuse in England'. *Journal of Elder Abuse & Neglect*, *19*(1/2), 109–27.

Prottas, J.M. (1979). *People-processing: The Street-level Bureaucrat in Public Service Bureaucracies*. Lexington, Massachusetts: Lexington Books.

Rabiee, P., Moran, N., & Glendinning, C. (2009). 'Individual Budgets: Lessons from Early Users' Experiences'. *British Journal of Social Work*, *39*, 918–35.

Ray, R.E. (2003). 'The Perils and Possibilities of Theory'. In S. Biggs, A. Lowenstein & J. Hendricks (Eds), *The Need for Theory: Critical Approaches to Social Gerontology* (pp 33–44). New York: Baywood Publishing Company Inc.

Reed, G.E. (2012). 'Leading Questions: Leadership, Ethics, and Administrative Evil'. *Leadership*, *8*(2), 187–98.

Robb, B. (1967). *Sans Everything: A Case to Answer*. London: Thomas Nelson and Sons Ltd.

Roulstone, A., & Morgan, H. (2009). 'Neo-liberal Individualism or Self-directed Support: Are We All Speaking the Same Language on Modernising Adult Social Care?' *Social Policy & Society*, *8*(3), 333–46.

Rubenstein, R.L. (1975). *The Cunning of History: The Holocaust and the American Future*. New York: Harper and Row. Cited in G. Adams and D. Balfour, 1998, p 167.

Rummery, K. (2011). 'A Comparative Analysis of Personalisation: Balancing an Ethic of Care with User Empowerment'. *Ethics & Social Welfare*, *5*(2), 138–52.

Russell, J. (2008). 'Children No Longer at Risk'. *The Guardian*, 8 December 2008. http://www.guardian.co.uk/.

Salman, S. (2007). '"Playing the game"'. *Society Guardian*, 1 August.

Sandfort, J.R. (2000). 'Moving Beyond Discretion and Outcomes: Examining Public Management from the Front Lines of the Welfare State'. *Journal of Public Administration and Research and Theory*, *10*(4), 729–56.

Satyamurti, C. (1981). *Occupational Survival:. The Case of the Local Authority Social Worker*. Oxford: Basil Blackwell.

Saul, J.R. (1992). *Voltaire's Bastards: The Dictatorship of Reason in the West*. New York: Random House.

SCIE (Social Care Institute for Excellence). (2010). *Personalisation: A Rough Guide*. London: SCIE. Adults' Services Report 20.

Scottish Government. (2009). *Adult Support and Protection (Scotland) Act 2007. Code of Practice*. www.scotland.gov.uk.

Scottish Government. (2010). *Self-Directed Support: A National Strategy for Scotland*. Edinburgh: Scottish Government, October.

Scourfield, P. (2005). 'Implementing the Community Care (Direct Payments) Act: Will the Supply of Personal Assistants meet the Demand and at what Price?' *Journal of Social Policy*, *34*(3), 469–88.

Seddon, J. (2008). *Systems Thinking in the Public Sector. The Failure of the Reform Regime ... and a Manifesto for a Better Way*. Axminster: Triarchy Press.

Seddon, J. (2013). 'Ask a Legal'. *Vanguard News*, March 2013, www. systemsthinking.co.uk.

Sevenhuijsen, S. (1998). *Citizenship and the Ethics of Care*. London: Routledge.

SGASB (South Gloucestershire Safeguarding Adults Board). (2012). *Winterbourne View Hospital. A Serious Case Review*. www.southglos. gov.uk/wv/report.pdf.

Shakespeare, T. (2000). 'The Social Relations of Care'. In G. Lewis, S. Gewirtz & J. Clarke (Eds), *Rethinking Social Policy* (pp 52–65). London: Sage.

Slater, P. (2002). 'Training for *No Secrets*: A Strategic Initiative'. *Social Work Education*, *21*(4), 437–48.

Smyth, L., Stewart, A., Gelling, J., Campbell, J., Baker, S., Stevens, S., Lee H., Clayton, A., Erskine, C., Tidder, L., & Sprakes, H. (2006). 'Voices of Experience'. In J. Leece & J. Bornat (Eds), *Developments in Direct Payments* (pp 123–42). Bristol: The Policy Press.

SSI (Social Services Inspectorate). (1992). *Confronting Elder Abuse: An SSI London Region Survey*. London: HMSO.

SSI (Social Services Inspectorate). (1993). *No Longer Afraid: The Safeguard of Older People in Domestic Settings*. London: HMSO.

Stanley, N., & Manthorpe, J. (Eds). (2004). *The Age of the Inquiry: Learning and Blaming in Health and Social Care*. Abingdon: Routledge.

Stevens, M., Glendinning, C., Jacobs, S., Moran, N., Challis, D., Manthorpe, J., Fernández, J-L., Jones, K., Knapp, M., Netten, A. and Wilberforce, M. (2011). 'Assessing the Role of Increasing Choice in English Social Care Services'. *Journal of Social Policy*, 40(2), 257–74.

Stöckl, H., Watts, C., & Penhale, B. (2012). 'Intimate Partner Violence Against Older Women in Germany: Prevalence and Associated Factors'. *Journal of Interpersonal Violence*, *27*(13), 2545–64.

Stolee, P., Hiller, L.M., Etkin, M., & McLeod, J. (2012). '"Flying by the Seat of Our Pants": Current Processes to Share Best Practices to Deal with Elder Abuse'. *Journal of Elder Abuse & Neglect*, *24*, 179–94.

Tadd, W., Hillman, A., Calnan, S., Calnan, M., Bayer, T., & Read, S. (2011). *Dignity in Practice: An Exploration of the Care of Older Adults in Acute NHS Trusts*. London: Department of Health and Comic Relief, June.

Taylor, I., & Kelly, J. (2006). 'Professionals, Discretion and Public Sector Reform in the UK: Re-visiting Lipsky'. *International Journal of Public Sector Management*, *19*(7), 629–42.

*The Guardian*. (2012). 'NHS Hospital Trust Apologises for "Appalling" Neglect: Health Secretary Jeremy Hunt "Disgusted" as Worcestershire NHS Trust Apologises to Families for Mistreatment of Patients'. http://www.theguardian.com. 23 December.

*The Guardian*. (2013). 'Mid Staffordshire NHS Trust to be Prosecuted Over Death of Patient'. http://www.theguardian.com. 29 August.

Thompson, E.H., Buxton, W., Gough, P.C., & Wahle, C. (2007). 'Gendered Policies and Practices that Increase Older Men's Risk of Elder Mistreatment'. *Journal of Elder Abuse & Neglect*, *19*(1/2), 129–51.

Titmuss, R. (1976). *Commitment to Welfare* (Second edn). London: George Allen & Unwin.

Townsend, P. (1981). 'The Structured Dependency of the Elderly: A Creation of Social Policy in the Twentieth Century'. *Ageing & Society*, *1*(1), 5–28.

Tronto, J.C. (1993). *Moral Boundaries. A Political Argument for an Ethic of Care*. New York: Routledge.

Tyson, A., Brewis, R., Crosby, N., Hatton, C., Stansfield, J., Tomlinson, C., Waters, J. and Wood, A. (2010). *A Report on In Control's Third Phase. Evaluation and Learning 2008–2009*. London: In Control.

UN (United Nations). (2000). *United Nations Principles for Older Persons*: http://www.un.org/esa/socdev/ageing/un_principles. html#Principles.

Vansteenkiste, M., & Sheldon, K.M. (2006). 'There's Nothing More Practical than a Good Theory: Integrating Motivational Interviewing and Self-determination Theory'. *British Journal of Clinical Psychology*, *45*, 63–82.

Vickers, R., & Lucas, A. (2004). *Case Review: In respect of MP. Died 6 July 2001*. Sheffield: Sheffield City Council.

Vinton, L. (1991). 'Abused Older Women: Battered Women or Abused Elders?' *Journal of Women & Aging*, *3*(3), 5–19.

WAG (Welsh Assembly Government). (2011). *Sustainable Social Services for Wales: A Framework for Action*. Cardiff: WAG, 10-11086.

*Wales Interim Policy & Procedures for the Protection of Vulnerable Adults from Abuse*. (2010). November. http://www.ssiacymru.org.uk.

Walker, A. (1981). 'Towards a Political Economy of Old Age'. *Ageing & Society*, *1*(1), 73–94.

Walker, A. (1982). 'Dependency and Old Age'. *Social Policy & Administration*, *16*, 115–35.

Walsh, C., Ploeg, J., Lohfeld, L., Horne, J., MacMillan, H., & Lai, D. (2007). 'Violence Across the Lifespan: Interconnections Among Forms of Abuse as Described by Marginalized Canadian Elders and Their Care-givers'. *British Journal of Social Work*, *33*, 901–19.

Wastell, D., White, S., Broadhurst, K., Peckover, S., & Pithouse, A. (2010). 'Children's Services in the Iron Cage of Performance Management: Street-level Bureaucracy and the Spectre of Švejkism'. *International Journal of Social Welfare*, *19*, 310–20.

WG (Welsh Government). (2011). *Safeguarding and Protection of Older People from Abuse*. Written statement by the Welsh Government, made by Gwenda Thomas, Deputy Minister for Children and Social Services, 18 October.

WHO (World Health Organization). (2002). *The Toronto Declaration on the Global Prevention of Elder Abuse*. Geneva: WHO.

WHO (World Health Organization). (2011). *European Report on Preventing Elder Mistreatment*. Copenhagen: WHO.

Wilkinson, R., & Pickett, K. (2010). *The Spirit Level: Why Equality Is Better for Everyone*. London: Penguin.

Williams, C. (1993). 'Vulnerable Victims? Current Awareness of the Victimisation of People with Learning Disabilities'. *Disability, Handicap and Society*, *8*(2), 161–72.

Williams, F. (2001). 'In and Beyond New Labour: Towards a New Political Ethics of Care'. *Critical Social Policy*, *21*(4), 467–93.

Wilson, G. (2002). 'Dilemmas and Ethics: Social Work Practice in the Detection and Management of Abused Older Women and Men'. *Journal of Elder Abuse & Neglect*, *14*(1), 79–94.

Wilson, G. (2004). 'Review of Bonnie, R.L. and Wallace, R.B. (Eds) (2003). *Elder Mistreatment Abuse: Neglect and Exploitation in an Aging America*. Washington, DC: The National Academies Press. *Sociology of Health and Illness*, *26*(2), 262–3.

Winter, S., Dinesen, P., & May, P. (2007).' Implementation Regimes and Street-level Bureaucrats: Employment Service Delivery'. Paper presented to the Public Management Research Conference. Tucson, Arizona, October 25–27. Cited in P. Hupe, 2011, p 68.

Wolf, R.S., & Pillemer, K. (1988). 'Intervention, Outcome and Elder Abuse'. In D. Finkelhor & G.T. Hotaling (Eds), *Coping with Family Violence. Research and Policy Perspectives* (pp 257–74). Thousand Oaks, CA: Sage Publications.

Wolf, R.S., & Pillemer, K. (1989). *Helping Elderly Victims: The Reality of Elder Abuse*. New York: Columbia University Press.

Yan, E., & Chan, K.-L. (2012). 'Prevalence and Correlates of Intimate Partner Violence Among Older Chinese Couples in Hong Kong'. *International Psychogeriatrics*, *24*, 1437–46.

Zanetti, L.A., & Adams, G.B. (2000). 'In Service of the Leviathan: Democracy, Ethics and the Potential for Administrative Evil in New Public Management'. *Administrative Theory & Practice*, *22*(3), 534–54.

Zimbardo, P. (2007). *The Lucifer Effect: Understanding How Good People Turn Evil*. New York: Random House.

# Index